V. S. Naipaul of Trinidad

Nivedita Misra

ANTHEM PRESS

Anthem Press
An imprint of Wimbledon Publishing Company
www.anthempress.com

This edition first published in UK and USA 2024
by ANTHEM PRESS
75–76 Blackfriars Road, London SE1 8HA, UK
or PO Box 9779, London SW19 7ZG, UK
and
244 Madison Ave #116, New York, NY 10016, USA

© Nivedita Misra 2024

The author asserts the moral right to be identified as the author of this work.

All rights reserved. Without limiting the rights under copyright reserved above,
no part of this publication may be reproduced, stored or introduced into
a retrieval system, or transmitted, in any form or by any means
(electronic, mechanical, photocopying, recording or otherwise),
without the prior written permission of both the copyright
owner and the above publisher of this book.

British Library Cataloguing-in-Publication Data
A catalogue record for this book is available from the British Library.

Library of Congress Cataloging-in-Publication Data
A catalog record for this book has been requested.
2023943800

ISBN-13: 978-1-83998-919-3 (Hbk)
ISBN-10: 1-83998-919-X (Hbk)

Cover Credit: Mallika Tripathi and Nivedita Misra

This title is also available as an e-book.

To Shashi and Umesh

CONTENTS

Foreword	vii
Introduction	1
Naipaul's Personality	4
Naipaul's Theatrics	7
Naipaul as a Journalist	10
The Context of Decolonisation	12
The Trinidadian Context	14
Scope of this Book	20
1. Early Fiction of the 1950s: The Trinidad Years	25
Gurudeva and Other Indian Tales (1943)	27
The Mystic Masseur (1957)	28
The Suffrage of Elvira (1958)	32
Miguel Street (1959)	34
A House for Mr Biswas (1961)	36
'A Dancing Dwarf on the Tarmac'	39
Critical Response in Trinidad	44
2. The Interloper in Travel Writing	47
The Middle Passage (1962)	49
An Area of Darkness (1964)	57
Critical Reception in Trinidad	62
3. Mimicry and Experiments of the 1960s	65
Mr Stone and the Knights Companion (1963)	66
A Flag on the Island (1967)	70
The Mimic Men (1967)	74
The Loss of El Dorado (1969)	78
Mimicry and Representation	80
4. Displacement Across Borders in the 1970s	83
The Overcrowded Barracoon and Other Articles (1972)	85
(i) The Booker Prize and the Black Power Movement	85
In a Free State (1971)	85

	Black Power Movement in Trinidad	89
	'Michael X and the Black Power Killings in Trinidad' (1980)	95
	Guerrillas (1975)	97
	(ii) The Impact of the Black Power Movement	103
	The Return of Eva Perón (1980)	103
	The first conference on East Indians in the Caribbean (1975)	105
	India: A Wounded Civilization (1977)	106
	A Bend in the River (1979)	110
	Challenges and Misrepresentation	113
5.	The Imperial Vision of the 1980s	117
	Among the Believers: An Islamic Journey (1981)	121
	Finding the Centre (1984)	127
	The Enigma of Arrival (1987)	131
	A Turn in the South (1989)	135
	Naipaul's Turn towards Conservatism	139
6.	Redemptive Journeys in the 1990s	143
	India: A Million Mutinies Now (1990)	146
	'Our Universal Civilization' (1990)	148
	'Argentina and the Ghost of Eva Perón, 1972–1991' (1991)	151
	'A Handful of Dust: Cheddi Jagan and the Revolution in Guyana' (1991)	152
	A Way in the World (1994)	153
	Beyond Belief: Islamic Excursions among the Converted Peoples (1998)	155
	Letters Between a Father and Son (1999)	158
	An Assessment	159
7.	Composing again in the 2000s	161
	Reading and Writing: A Personal Account (2000)	162
	'Two Worlds' (2001)	164
	Half A Life (2001)	167
	Magic Seeds (2004)	170
	A Writer's People (2007)	173
	The 2007 Conference at UWI	175
	The Masque of Africa: Glimpses of African Belief (2010)	177
Conclusions		183
Appendix A: A Note on Trinidad		191
Appendix B: A Note on V. S. Naipaul's Terminology and Use of Spellings		193
Works Cited		195
Index		209

FOREWORD

The idea for this book is an old one. I first read V. S. Naipaul's *A House for Mr Biswas* in the third year of my undergraduate course at Delhi University in India. I did not particularly enjoy the book then. Later, when I came to Trinidad and read it again, I found in it a reflection of my interest in Indian writing in English. The book laid emphasis on documenting the everyday lives of Indo-Trinidadians in a joint family set-up. Its use of English and the familiarity of the subject matter helped me re-discover a deep-rooted Indian culture within Trinidad.

I am a recent migrant from India to Trinidad, a non-resident Indian (NRI), who shares strong ties with my motherland through internet access and social media platforms. As such, I am part of a huge NRI population overseas, but Trinidad is not a typical sought-after destination. A majority of the NRI population resides in the Middle East, the United Kingdom and the United States of America. My distance from these 'diasporic metropolitan centres' provides me with a unique standpoint from where I can negotiate postcolonial and postmodern discourse away from the typified Indian diaspora critic working in the US or UK academy. However, this book is neither ostensibly about me nor my diasporic point of view.

The book references an older diaspora that came to Trinidad over 178 years ago. That diaspora is no longer a diaspora but a strong community that is deeply enmeshed in the political, economic, social and cultural life of Trinidad. Stories abound about how the Indians were tricked into coming so far from home to Trinidad, or 'Chini-dad' as they called it. Vijay Mishra qualifies the differences between the older and the newer diaspora as between those who could not return and for whom India became a land in their imagination, distant and pure, and those who frequently return to the homeland, replenishing their connections to an actual India. My book, in a way, seeks new ways of bridging the gaps between the older and the newer diaspora.

I contend that reading Naipaul in Trinidad has made a difference because location, in spite of recent scholarship on globalisation, has to be lived to be felt. The East Indians were late arrivals in the West Indies, which had earlier seen the near extinction of the Amerindians from the islands through its colonisation first by the Spanish and later by the British. The Spanish had encouraged the French planters and their African slaves to develop plantation estates. After the abolition of slavery, the planters in search of cheap labour imported indentured workers from India, China and Portugal:

> During the period from 1838 to 1917, an estimated 543,596 *girmityas* (agreement signers) were transplanted to the British, French, Dutch and Danish Caribbean to labour primarily on the sugar plantations. These bonded labourers were part of a larger contingent of 1.3 million Indians who were sent to the plantation colonies in Natal, Fiji, Mauritius, La Réunion, the Seychelles, and of course, the European colonies of the Caribbean. (Samaroo 2016, p. 127)

Brinsley Samaroo further adds that only about 25 per cent of these Indians chose to go back to India, with the last group leaving British Guiana as late as 1955 on the *M.V. Resurgent* (Dabydeen et al., 2007, p. xlvii). The rest of the Indians decided to stay in the Caribbean. At present, within the Caribbean, the East Indians constitute the largest ethnic group in Trinidad, Guyana and Suriname.

During colonial rule, the Indo-Trinidadians were often referred to as 'coolies,' a term used pejoratively. In politically and racially charged speeches, they are still sometimes called so, and because of their love of building houses, their houses are commonly referred to as 'coolie houses.' Though the large East Indian population in Trinidad does not share any desire to go back to India, a certain Indianness, primarily ethnic in nature, has survived. Many Trinidadians have visited India in search of their roots, found them and returned thinking better of their grandparents' decision to have stayed on in Trinidad beyond their time of indenture. My interactions with them over the years confirm the fact that they consider themselves economically and educationally better than Indians in India and do not show any sense of loss, disintegration, fragmentation or trauma at having lost contact with their ancestral homes. The nostalgia is restricted to Hindi films, songs and music. The new generation is secure in their place of birth, though racially charged speeches form a part of the election rigmarole that is unleashed every five years. I have also sensed that the Hindu Indo-Trinidadians, in their upbringing and education, are increasingly getting creolised on the one hand and *sanskritised* on the other. Naipaul had highlighted the creolisation of the Indian population in his early books based in Trinidad. However, the counter move towards Sanskritisation has been supported by the import of Hindu literature, bhajans and investment in *satsangs* (community discussions) that have instilled in the population a strong religious and cultural centre-point that other writers such as Derek Walcott have recognised (see the Nobel Acceptance Speech by Derek Walcott).

As a traveller and a recent migrant, I have taken up the challenge of assessing the society where I have arrived. Both the privileges and the limitations offered to the outsider or the traveller are my own. On the one hand, I assess the society by its distance from the physical India that is my home country, but on the other hand, I realise that I may not be as open to the subliminal currents within Trinidadian society. My dual viewpoint springs from the fact that I first read Naipaul in India and now read him in Trinidad.

No book is complete without acknowledging the support provided by family, friends, colleagues and students. My initial years of training at Gargi College and later Delhi University laid the strong foundations for all my future endeavours. I acknowledge all my teachers at Gargi College, especially Prof Radha Chakravarty, who encouraged me to find myself in literature. I also thank my professors at Delhi University for introducing me to the then-current critical scene. Foremost among these is Prof Harish Trivedi, with whom a chance meeting after many years in Trinidad brought home a different understanding of human relationships. I would also like to express my gratitude to my colleagues and students at Maharaja Agrasen College, where I first began teaching in earnest and at Satyawati College (Evening), where I settled for a while. I would also like to thank all the researchers and teaching colleagues who participated in the first International Conference on Travel Literature at Satyawati College in 2007. The papers and the whole experience of organising such a big event have stayed with me. I would like to express my sincerest gratitude to my professors, students and the library staff at The University of the West Indies, where I did my doctoral degree. Prof Brinsley Samaroo and Prof Kenneth Ramchand deserve a special mention because they made me feel at home when I was so far away. I am saddened that Prof Samaroo is not here to see the publication of this book. Last but not the least, I would like to acknowledge the support that my family has provided me, and I thank them profusely for their patience in seeing this project through. My daughter Mallika and my husband Vrijesh have been involved at every stage in the writing of this book. Though this is not the style of book that Mallika reads, she has kept up my spirits by remaining excited throughout the process and helping me design the cover. I dedicate this book to my parents, Shashi and Umesh Chandra Misra, who made extreme sacrifices such that my brother and I never felt a need that was not fulfilled.

INTRODUCTION

The aim of this book is two-fold: one, to show how Trinidad was central to understanding Naipaul's evolving literary, racial and religious politics over the years; and two, how Trinidadians have acknowledged and owned him in spite of Naipaul distancing himself from Trinidad on numerous occasions. His writings endeared him to Trinidadians because they held a 'truth' value, a liveliness of environment and vividness of character that went beyond his slanted attacks at their ineptness in handling the newly independent nation. Being born in Trinidad during colonial times, Naipaul grew up under the colonial system of education learning and studying English language and literature. He realised only later how the English education system had not only coloured but tainted his vision of Trinidad, England and the world. Everything appeared faded and jaded in contrast: 'There was, for instance, Wordsworth's notorious poem about the daffodils. A pretty little flower, no doubt; but we had never seen it… Dickens's rain and drizzle I turned into tropical downpours; the snow and fog I accepted as conventions of books' ('Jasmine' 1964b: 1972, 23) This essential difference between what he saw and felt and what he learnt in school led him to trust his instincts rather than his scholarship. He devised new ways of learning about his environment using his experiences in Trinidad as a touchstone to know the world. This book serves to complement established Naipaulian criticism by presenting a case for viewing Naipaul as 'typically Trinidadian.' This premise is not based upon personal whim or any desperate attempt to claim Naipaul for Trinidad, but it is based upon a commonly held opinion in Trinidadian circles regarding Naipaul and his repeated antics in disclosing yet distancing himself from his humble beginnings. This endeavour finds support amongst numerous commentators such as Llyod Best who reiterate Naipaul's Trinidadian-ness. Yet, Naipaul escaped any stereotyping because he inculcated within himself a sense of contradictoriness that made him challenge commonly held opinions. An example of this is that by staying on in Britain, Naipaul challenged the boundaries of the British literary canon, more so by hardly writing about the British. Similarly, Naipaul challenged the boundaries of Caribbean literature by not staying in the Caribbean but writing about it most often.

The book brings into sharp focus Naipaul's background and how the first eighteen years of his life in Trinidad shaped and defined his writing in the following six decades. It also highlights how Naipaul and his writings were received in Trinidad, how connected he felt to Trinidad, and how anything written about him in Trinidad affected him more deeply than any criticism abroad. For an author whose writing life spanned over six decades, his society (the one he was born in and where he spent his formative years, the one to which he often returned, the one where he felt his books were best understood) is important because Naipaul may have criticised Trinidad, but he also criticised other societies, including the high-society London literary circle that supported him, without having about them the positive feelings he had about Trinidad. Naipaul's unique position stems from his refusal to be associated with any society, individual, ideology or philosophy.

For most people, Sir Vidiadhar Surajprasad Naipaul (1932–2018) was a British writer of East Indian descent born on the West Indian island of Trinidad. In his writing career, Naipaul published over 30 books, including novels, travel writings, autobiographical pieces, essays and mixed-mode prose. He published his first book, *The Mystic Masseur* in 1957 and his last book, *The Masque of Africa*, in 2010. He had written four books by the age of thirty and fifteen books by the age of 45. Along the way, Naipaul collected a number of international honours and awards. He won the John Llewellyn Rhys Prize for *The Mystic Masseur* (1958), Somerset Maugham Award for *Miguel Street* (1961), the Hawthornden Prize for *Mr Stone and the Knights Companion* (1964), W. H. Smith Literary Award for *The Mimic Men* (1968), the Booker Prize for Fiction for *In a Free State* (1971), the Bennett Award (1980), the Jerusalem Prize (1983) and the T. S. Eliot Award (1986). He received a knighthood in 1990 and the David Cohen Prize for Literature from the Arts Council of England in 1993. He was awarded at the Neemrana Festival by the Indian Council for Cultural Relations in 2002 and received a Lifetime Achievement Award by the Mumbai Literature Festival in 2013. Besides these, there are many other honours that were conferred on him by universities across the world, chief among them being an Honorary Doctorate from Columbia University in New York (1981), and Universities of Cambridge (1983), London (1988) and Oxford (1992). The crowning glory of his life's achievements, coming very late in life, was the Nobel Prize for Literature awarded to him in 2001 'for having united perceptive narrative and incorruptible scrutiny in works that compel us to see the presence of suppressed histories' (Press Release of the Swedish Academy 2001).

In his last days, his wife, Lady Nadira Naipaul, arranged for a violinist to play Mozart, and his friends were invited to pay their last visits. It was reported that Naipaul's friend and *The Mail on Sunday* editor Geordie

INTRODUCTION

Greig read Alfred Tennyson's poem 'Crossing the Bar' to him. He died on August 11, 2018 in London. Naipaul was cremated on the morning of August 22, 2018 at the West Chapel of the West London crematorium in Kensal Green cemetery, attended by approximately 100 people who were close friends and relatives. The funeral service, by invitation only, was non-religious, as Naipaul, who was born a Hindu, never professed any religion publicly. Geordie Greig read a few lines from the *Bhagvad Gita* (Azard Ali 2018). Amit Roy, a reporter with *The Telegraph* (online edition), commented: 'The author would have been relieved the majority of mourners were white.' Roy also speculated that his ashes would not be dispersed in Trinidad since Naipaul had once said that being born in Trinidad was a 'mistake' (2018). His surviving sisters, Savi in Trinidad and Mira and Nella elsewhere, were not personally informed of his death or invited to his funeral. The extended family got to know about Naipaul's death only through the media, much like the news of his knighthood and the Nobel Prize. This was not the first time that they had been 'passed up.' In short, Naipaul's apathy towards his family and Trinidad was both publicly known and acknowledged even though his writings, especially *Letters between a Father and Son* and *The Enigma of Arrival*, reveal his deep ties with his family in Trinidad.

A lesser known fact about Naipaul is that Naipaul loved visiting Trinidad—the land of his birth. V. S. Naipaul was recognised and felicitated by the Trinidadian government and the local institutions on several occasions. He was given the Hummingbird Award in 1970, an honorary doctorate from The University of the West Indies in 1975, the Trinity Cross in 1989, an honorary symposium was held by The University of the West Indies in 2007, and NALIS (Trinidad and Tobago National Library and Information System Authority) awarded him the Lifetime Achievement Award in 2012. Though he felt that Trinidad could never be a home for him, he never felt at home anywhere else, neither in India, England, America or Canada. Savi Naipaul Akal, his younger sister, says that Naipaul always 'found it difficult to write when he was in Trinidad [...] Trinidad itself distracted him. The light, the colours, the sounds, the people, the events, the racism, the politics, the hopelessness, the stagnation: all distracted him. It was as if Trinidad was a quagmire that stultified, a land of quicksand that swallowed him. Trinidad always made him restless' (2018, p. 165). I think this is a rather harsh judgement on her part because if Trinidad so stultified him, why did he come here so often? I contend that Trinidad showed him the way to break away from the hold of colonial institutions and value and protect those skills beyond the shores of Trinidad.

Naipaul left Trinidad at the age of eighteen and never returned to live here for any substantial length of time. However, his happiness at leaving Trinidad was short-lived. His disappointments with London and Oxford, his writing career, his social circle—all left him craving for 'home.' In his writings, he played with this distance from Trinidad because each visit back home progressively showed him how distant he had become from his own society. But returning was not really an option because he felt that his talent would suffer.

Naipaul's Personality

V. S. Naipaul had a reputation, and he guarded it zealously, much like his writing. Like Conrad, he believed that a writer's myth sustains his writing, and therefore, he often went to great lengths to maintain his reputation as a genial host but a brusque guest. According to his biographer, Patrick French, 'Using his literary prestige, the mad strength of his new personality and a rare ability to project himself as if in mortal need of assistance, he was superb at persuading people to help him [...]. He milked his hosts for information, often causing a scene when he set off an argument, and was happy to dismiss many of his helpers afterwards as fools and idlers' (French 2008, p. 370). This trait alienated many of his friends and acquaintances, but he continued to use this technique to seek knowledge. In local terms, it is called 'liming' and 'ole talk' which Naipaul used as his cornerstones of knowing the world but, in true Trinidadian style, distanced himself from the same. Clem Seecharan quotes a Belgian journalist who accompanied Naipaul on one of the trips to Trinidad in the early 1990s. Looking at men sitting and talking animatedly at rum shops, the journalist remarked, 'the men are always discussing things.' Naipaul remarked, 'Talking! They have nothing on their minds' (2018, p. 45). Naipaul felt superior to Trinidadians but was also always alert regarding any patronising attitude towards his fellow countrymen.

Strangers meeting Naipaul for the first time often found him to be a difficult person to please. David Dabydeen narrates his troubles when he invited Sir V. S. Naipaul to the University of Warwick in 1992 to celebrate the 150th anniversary of the arrival of Indian indentured labourers to British Guiana. When asked why he had stopped writing about Trinidad, Naipaul drily answered, 'Because it is not important' (2018, p. 52). Dabydeen points out that such banter and mockery are ingrained in Trinidadians, who use them to keep themselves 'interested by being provocative, so as to get a response' (2018, p. 51). Lloyd Best couldn't have agreed more: 'Theroux's book [*Sir Vidia's Shadow*] exposes Naipaul as a real Trinidadian in every sense—including the way he would not pay for the wine. All these little Trinidadian smart-man things: the way he would sing calypso and whistle, the way he would take the mickey out of people, provoking them' (French 2008, p. 359). Orlando Patterson, in the provocatively titled obituary, 'How

INTRODUCTION

he out-trumped Trump on Africans and West Indians,' writes: 'Naipaul's greatest gift, his incomparable irony and cunning wit, is thoroughly Trinidadian […] especially when they [Trinidadians] mercilessly tease each other in the practice known as "picong" or pretend to flatter others by the wicked verbal play known as "mamaguy"' (2018, pp. 111–2). On a more serious note, French argues that Naipaul was ever willing to 'shift between profundity and picong' (2008, p. 395). On the issue of not mentioning Trinidad in his initial response to winning the Nobel Prize for Literature in 2001, according to George Lamming, Naipaul was 'playing ole mas' (French 2008 'Introduction,' p. xiii). Edward Baugh (2011, p. 6) and Derek Walcott (1962, pp. 18–9) have each commented upon Naipaul's use of *picong* but have not provided any detailed reading. According to Sir Hilary Beckles, Naipaul's 'persistent melancholy was as West Indian as cricket, carnival and picong' (2018, p. 55). Kirk Meighoo is convinced that 'there is no person who has written more on Trinidad, for a longer period of time, to a wider audience than V. S. Naipaul' (2018, p. 81). He argues that he would title his own analyses of Naipaul's works as '"Sans Humanité: The Perverse, Trinidadian Worldview of V. S. Naipaul" (Sans Humanité is a phrase associated with extempore Trinidadian calypso duels, in which opponents trade insults in entertaining, clever, often merciless ways) […]. Naipaul shares the wicked, contrarian humour of so many classic calypsos which he loved, or the everyday, absurdist, politically incorrect hilarity of Trinidad' (2018, p. 84). For the uninitiated, in the *Dictionary of the English/ Creole of Trinidad and Tobago, picong* is defined as: 'the teasing, ridicule or insult, especially in semi-formal or ritualized exchanges, e.g. between calypsonians […] an exchange of invective' (Winer 2009, p. 692). Louis Regis working on the developments within the calypso notes that 'the careless—albeit abrasive—Trinidadian *picong* […] is reputed to be the mechanism by which the society transforms potentially violent hostility into cleansing laughter' (1998, pp. 32–3). My guess is that the critics within the Caribbean recognise the harsh invective of picong as part of Naipaul's vision rather than mere vocabulary, and they give it back to him in words that are equally strong. John Maxwell, having taken Naipaul around Kingston (Jamaica), pronounced Naipaul 'a lifeless robot with a second hand soul' (2002, p. 13).

Though Naipaul in *The Middle Passage* said that he hated the sound of the steel pan, he still acknowledged and appreciated the calypso as the voice of the people—not the calypso popularised by the American radios, but the real calypsos that were developed, sustained and dominated by the Afro-Trinidadians. Traditionally, the calypso is a folk medium for the working-class: 'The calypso is a type of song, originating in Trinidad. The music has a 2/2, 4/4, or combination rhythm, usually with the second beat emphasized, with

6 V. S. NAIPAUL OF TRINIDAD

syncopation or off-beat phrasing' (Winer 2009, 157). With the end of slavery, the calypsos emerged from the shadows to the foreground as representative culture of the Caribbean with the celebration of the carnival. With the end of indentureship in 1917 and the strengthening of the labour movement in the 1930s, calypsos began to bridge the gap between the working and middle classes.[1] V. S. Naipaul was exposed to this calypso culture when his family moved to Port of Spain when he was about five or six years old. According to Gordon Rohlehr: 'The calypso [...is] a flexible medium capable of accommodating narrative, social and political protest, scatological humour and celebration' (1992b, p. 4) that 'helped preserve and formalize a certain twist of mind, which I believe helped in the emergence of Selvon, Naipaul and Lovelace' (1992b, p. 29). There is much credence in Rohlehr's assessment because it bears witness to Naipaul's praise for the calypso, as it represents the West Indian life and its ethnic and racial hostilities more effectively than the form of the English novel. Naipaul also recognised the calypso for its ability to poke fun at 'the only convention the West Indian knows [which] is his involvement with the white world' (*The Middle Passage* 1962, p. 66). However, elsewhere Rohlehr moderates his statement: 'In *Miguel Street*, the spirit and gaiety of the calypso are not considered with hope as a new and strange positive which the masses of Trinidad have constructed out of the debris of their lives, but with a sense of pathos as a sign of the pathological insensitivity of the Trinidad people' (Rohlehr, quoted in Thieme 1987, p. 21). John Thieme highlights how Naipaul alludes to calypsos in *Miguel Street* (p. 15),

---

1 Beth Driscoll (2016) enumerates eight conditions/ aspects of a 'middle-brow' culture, namely, the presence of 'middle-class, [who are] reverential towards elite culture, entrepreneurial, mediated, feminized, emotional, recreational, and earnest.' Belinda Edmondson, supports this definition, and defines the middle-brow in Jamaica and the Caribbean as 'a cosmopolitan black professional' who 'strive[s] to reconcile their origins in black-identified culture with its aspirations for social ascendance and international recognition' (2009, p. 2) while 'Authentic Caribbean culture is assumed to be the preserve of the working class' (2009, p. 2). She quotes Peter Koningsbruggen who argues that 'the working-class carnival tradition has now been largely appropriated as a middle-class event.' In the 1960s and 1970s, defining the Caribbean middle classes was difficult because of the emergence of a new political elite who ruled over their brethren in the newly independent states. Also, there is difficulty in describing a distinctly middle-class culture of the times because the society was in a flux with no clear distinction between the upper/middle classes and the lower/ working classes. Often, the difference was generational. The sons and daughters of the working classes became the new aspirational middle class. The East Indian community in Trinidad was part of this transition moving away from agriculture to trades and professions.

INTRODUCTION

presents a picaro trickster figure in *The Mystic Masseur* (p. 34), depicts society as the victim in *The Suffrage of Elvira* (p. 35), and composes the picture of a picaroon amoral society in *A House for Mr Biswas* (p. 52). Thieme argues that Naipaul's gradual development from the use of invective to satire helps him portray Mr Biswas in the mock-heroic mode because the hero fails to live up to his idealised image of himself (1987, p. 52). But Thieme does not carry this image of Naipaul as a calypsonian beyond Naipaul's first four novels based in Trinidad. Patrick French quotes unnamed Trinidadians as calling Naipaul a 'failed calypsonian' (2008, p. xvi) but offers no further analysis. The calypso typifies the Trinidadian attitudes to authority and a certain playfulness and flouting of rules that Trinidadians understand instinctively. When Rohlehr makes his statement he is understood. He does not need to explain it. It is interesting to note that Naipaul praised and enjoyed the calypsos, often singing them himself, but never did write one because his colonial education and training had predisposed him towards writing English novels.

Lloyd Best was by far the most courteous and forgiving, masking his hurt through nostalgia: 'My recollection of him [Naipaul at Queen's Royal College] is as a celebrity, even then [1945 …] I'd glimpsed him on the balcony, in khakhi shorts, Cambridge blue shirt, standing and holding court. It is the image that lasts' (2018, p. 86). Some Trinidadians admire Naipaul more for firmly establishing himself as a *British* writer rather than his more worldly success as a writer. Equally, there are Trinidadians who berate him for having become an Englishman so completely as to be ashamed of his origins. From a strictly academic point of view, Naipaul and Trinidad cannot be delinked but judging from the reactions of Trinidadians upon his death, not many people felt that a great Trinidadian writer had been lost. Many said they had lost him in 1962 when he had written the controversial *The Middle Passage*. Nobody in Trinidad denies Naipaul his right to call himself a success. They are perhaps resentful that his success had not rubbed itself off on them.

Naipaul's Theatrics

Akin to his personality was his brazen image because Naipaul often courted controversies, especially around the time of the publication of a new title, so that media interest remained high and his books sold well. Andre Deutsch would later state that his books were never bestsellers. V. S. Naipaul countered to state that they never marketed him well. In order to generate interest in his writings, Naipaul gave interviews in which he severely criticised the places he had visited and written about, often commenting on the local politics and the local public response or the lack of public response. He made incredible efforts to provoke his interviewers into revealing their own biases while they questioned him on his prejudices. He also ensured that the interviewers were well-read and not standing-in for people behind the scenes. In an interview with Bharati Mukherjee and Robert Boyle, Naipaul discussed his writings on India provoking his interviewers into giving a response to his assertions that 'Asiatics do not read, of course' and 'It takes a long time in India to come to the simple conclusion that, by God, these people are just extraordinarily stupid!' (Bharati Mukherjee and Robert Boyers 1981, pp. 75–92). It is said that *An Area of Darkness* had been almost immediately banned in India upon its publication. According to French, Deutsch's distributor in India refused to handle the book, and copies had to be smuggled in. The de facto ban was lifted in 1968 by Morarji Desai (French 2008, p. 236). Nissim Ezekiel's critical essay, 'Naipaul's India and Mine' (1976), captured the Indian sense of outrage at Naipaul's book. The misperception had been so great that even Naipaul's mother told him to leave India for Indians.

Most critics disavow Naipaul's race-baiting because 'race talk' is uncomfortable, but Naipaul was never shy talking about it. When he pronounced that 'Africa has no future' (Naipaul in an interview with Elizabeth Hardwick 1979, p. 49) and 'Africa is a land of bush' (Naipaul in an interview with Bharati Mukherjee and Robert Boyers 1981, p. 77), he was once again provoking interest in his novel, *A Bend in the River*, and creating a controversy bringing race-talk centre-stage. On his first journey to Africa, Naipaul befriended Paul Theroux, an American expatriate and a budding writer who courted Naipaul for guidance. This was the start of their long friendship and regular correspondence that culminated in an angry tiff at the Hay Literary Festival in 1996. Naipaul put up for sale some signed first-edition books given to him by Theroux as gifts. Theroux was upset and confronted him, but was brushed off. Angry, Theroux wrote about his relationship with Naipaul in *Sir Vidia's Shadow: A Friendship Across Five Continents* (1998: 1999). In Theroux's tale, V. S. Naipaul is presented as U. V. Pradesh, for whom 'Life was torture, writing was hell, and he said he hated Africa' (Theroux 1998: 1999, p. 3). Theroux portrayed himself as Julian Lavalle who was easy-going, loved Africa and Africans, was more comfortable in Africa, greater read, sexually satisfied and physically stronger. In his account, Naipaul was also masochistic who was 'unused to discussing his work with such a tall, self-assured black woman' (Theroux 1998: 1999, p. 18). In a 1999 reassuring afterword, Theroux said, 'I belatedly recalled Vidia's ritually pronouncing, "I am going to open an account with him," meaning he would settle someone's hash; and "Women of sixty think of

INTRODUCTION

nothing but sex," and "how, as I was driving with him in Kampala, he once said, 'They call these [speed bumps] 'sleeping policemen' in Trinidad''' (Theroux 1998: 1999, p. 360). Theroux blamed Naipaul's second wife, Nadira, for the blunder, but Naipaul never apologised. There was a very public reconciliation between the two writers at the Hay Festival in 2011 and later at the Jaipur Literary Festival in 2015. Interestingly, reviewers in Trinidad felt more sympathy for Naipaul than for Theroux (Smith 1999).

His travel book, *Among the Believers*, opened a Pandora's box because it refused to toe the line of the politically correct liberals who spoke in favour of a moderate view of Islam. By stating, 'Muslim fundamentalism has no intellectual substance to it, therefore, it must collapse' (Naipaul in an interview with Edward Behr 1980, p. 38), Naipaul created another controversy just in time for the release of his book. Edward Said led his attack on Naipaul's *Among the Believers*, stating that Naipaul had turned into a 'witness for the Western prosecution' (1998: 2018, p. 118), especially in his portrayal of Muslims: 'it's funny moments are at the expense of Muslims, who are "wogs" after all as seen by Naipaul's British and American readers, potential fanatics and terrorists, who cannot spell, be coherent or sound right to a worldly-wise, somewhat jaded judge from the West' (1998: 2018, p. 119).

The image stuck, as did his professed love for England. The Nobel award ceremony speech cited *The Enigma of Arrival* as Naipaul's ode to the Empire: 'The core of his devotion to European civilisation is that it was the only one of the alternative cultures that made it possible for him to become a writer' (Engdahl 2001). Many in Trinidad read *The Enigma of Arrival* as a confessional book about his desire to be born an Englishman. Strangely, his later works have not received as much academic focus as his earlier works. Many typecast Naipaul as somebody who begins with a thesis and then proves it by quoting the most flimsy testimonials and evidence.

Patrick French wrote *The World is what it is: The Authorised Biography of V. S. Naipaul* (2008) based upon Naipaul's papers housed at the McFarlin Library at the University of Tulsa. The biography is noteworthy for its biographical details highlighting Naipaul's relationship with his first wife, Patricia 'Pat' Hale, and his long-time mistress, Margaret Gooding. The autobiography ends with Patricia's death and Naipaul's marriage to Nadira Alvi in 1996. Almost all the reviewers of French's biography highlighted Naipaul's confessions of visiting prostitutes and his sadistic relations with Margaret Gooding. Coupled with Theroux's portrayal of Pat Naipaul as the long-suffering wife, these reviews took to bashing Naipaul for his sadism. In my view, the myth around his writing personality shielded him from attacks about emotional dysfunctionality in his social relationships. Naipaul the writer covered up for the shortcomings of Naipaul the man. After all, it was the writer in him

10 V. S. NAIPAUL OF TRINIDAD

that allowed French's biography to be published in its wholeness. V. S. Naipaul, by all standards, lived a long fulfilling life, cherishing controversies as essential elements of making himself newsworthy.

Naipaul as a Journalist

Naipaul always complained and convinced himself that he remained unappreciated. It is important to remember that Naipaul began writing on the cusp of decolonisation, when the world order was shifting away from Britain and its colonies to America and its satellite nations. This was also the era when publishers did not offer hefty sums for the first or even the tenth novel as advances. Finances were limited, and in post-war British society, writing became increasingly restricted to those upper-class aristocrats who could live off their estates. Naipaul found living off his writing an extremely difficult task. Barring a few literary awards, writing books was never a profitable business for him. He achieved financial security only in the 1980s.

Often, he fell back on his skills as a journalist to sustain himself until he found a way to join his journalistic concerns with his creative writing skills. Prior to his launch as a writer, Naipaul was the editor of *Isis* magazine at the University of Oxford and later wrote for the *Oxford Tory*. He wrote a number of critical pieces and reviews for newspapers and magazines. He started his career as a freelance contributor and later edited the British Broadcasting Corporation (BBC) programme *Caribbean Voices* from 1954 to 1956. The programme provided a forum for the reading and publishing of Naipaul's first short story, 'The Mourners.' 'This is Home' was the first story that was aired (Cudjoe 1988, p. 21), and 'Two Thirty A.M.' was his first and only poem that was aired (French 2008, p. 77). The programme *Caribbean Voices*, then hosted by Henry Swanzy, not only provided Naipaul financial and literary subsistence during his days of struggle, but also to Seepersad Naipaul, his father, whose short stories Swanzy liked, encouraged and published. Glyne Griffith argues that while other broadcasters on the *BBC Caribbean Voices* programme wished to unabashedly provide Caribbean writers a platform for their works, Naipaul wished to be critical and selective in his presentations. He felt time had come for Caribbean writing to consolidate its base and move forward. With the passing of his father in 1953, Naipaul had a deep sense of the passing of a generation. He also worked as a journalist for the *New Statesman* from 1957 to 1961 (French 2008, p. 192). And from 1963 to 1964, he also wrote a monthly 'Letter from London' in the *Illustrated Weekly of India* (French 2008, p. 238).

In the late 1960s, Naipaul began writing for *The Times Literary Supplement* and the *New York Review of Books*. Some of these were later collected and published

INTRODUCTION 11

under the title *The Return of Eva Perón, with the Killings in Trinidad*. 'The Killings in Trinidad' was written against the backdrop of the spread of the Black Power Movement from the United States and Britain to the Caribbean and Africa. Naipaul's reputation rose in America, primarily through his writings in the *New York Review of Books* based upon his travels through the decolonised world. This search for new markets (in America and India) was accompanied by his experiments with various genres of writing. Beyond the first four novels, Naipaul searched for the right medium that was both profitable and could carry the weight of his thoughts.

Remembering how he used to visit the theatres in Port of Spain and the influence of American movies, especially Humphrey Bogart, on him and the general audience in Trinidad, he was enthusiastic when Peter Brook approached him to produce *A House for Mr Biswas* for the British theatre (French 2008, p. 295). The project was ultimately abandoned because the book had an all-East Indian cast and there were not enough actors available to do the job. Interestingly, Monte Norman composed the music score for the theatrical version that he later used as the signature tune for the 007 James Bond movies. A simple Google search will let you hear the hilarious song that was to be the signature tune for the production. Much later, Tariq Ali tried to convince Naipaul to allow him to make *A House for Mr Biswas* as a television series, as did Jonathan Miller to make it into a film. The projects were shelved because, yet again, they could not find Indian actors to play the roles. 'A Flag on the Island' was written to be made into a film. It was to star Frank Sinatra and be directed by Lionel Rogosin (French 2008, p. 253). But it was never made. Vidia refused to sell the rights of *In a Free State*. The playwright Julian Mitchell failed to produce a stage version of *The Loss of El Dorado*. *Guerrillas* proved an unexpected success in America, and Francis Ford Coppola wanted to turn it into a film (French 2008, p. 390). Naipaul later met Coppola to discuss filming *A Bend in the River*, but nothing much came of it. The only book that was ever made into a film was *The Mystic Masseur* by Merchant Ivory Productions, with Caryl Phillips writing the screenplay in 2003.

Each of these disappointments marks Naipaul's keen interest in reaching out to a newer and different audience. It is also a sign of his love for writing and how he guarded his books for all their worth. He saw them not only as abstract, precious material but as money spinners because he chose to have no career other than to be a writer. Thus, there is a close emotional, aesthetic and financial bond between Naipaul and his works. This is an aspect that is often underplayed in mainstream criticism of Naipaul because it goes against the widely accepted notion that it was England that sustained his writing. In fact, from the mid-1970s, it was America that sustained his writing rather than England in terms of signing him up for projects, funding his travels, offering him a university position and asking him to speak at its universities and think tanks.

Naipaul recognised that other modes of art, apart from writing books, were perhaps more effective mediums for engaging with the world. Being the centre of interest came to Naipaul naturally due to his genius, his early success, his inheritance and his racial difference from the white colonial writer. From radio to television to films and the literary festival circuits, Naipaul tried to adapt to all mediums of media communications. He was known to speak his mind, take interviewers to task over their knowledge of his works and sell his books. Yet in all fairness, in his last public interview, Naipaul stated that he went to the Dhaka Literary Festival in Bangladesh in 2016 only because he wanted to see the birds that migrate to escape the harsh Siberian winter (Akbar 2018, p. 127).

The Context of Decolonisation

There have been many book-length studies on Naipaul, such as those by William Walsh, Anthony Boxill, Peggy Nightingale, John Thieme, Harveen Mann, Selwyn Cudjoe, Shashi Kamra, Timothy Weiss, Rob Nixon, Fawzia Mustafa, Suman Gupta, Lilian Feder, Yashoda Bhat, Dagmar Barrow, Helen Hayward, Suman Bala, Gillian Dooley, Imran Coovadia and most recently, William Ghosh. Even though Naipaul was part of the Caribbean avant-garde brigade in the 1950s and early 1960s, a range of critics since then have spoken about his ideological neutrality. After the publication of *The Enigma of Arrival* and later the winning of the Nobel Prize, Naipaul's conservatism gained credence. This large spectrum indicates the complexity of his writing positions.

In the 1950s, Naipaul was one of the many budding Caribbean writers who arrived in England to get themselves published. They were part of a movement of people from the West Indies, more popularly called the Windrush generation, who went to England after the end of the Second World War due to labour shortages there. However, the writers and creative artists were distinct from their countrymen because they were skilled, educated and creative. Many of this generation would take to activism and return to their countries bound by the spirit of nationalism. Naipaul's decision to stay on in England after completing his studies at Oxford and the publication of his first four novels in quick succession placed him at odds with many of his contemporaries who came back to the Caribbean. Critics often cite this decision to stay on as Naipaul's uncritical acceptance of England as the repository of Enlightenment values.

INTRODUCTION 13

Many critics view him as a figure of universal exile, or as an enigmatic citizen of the world. Such critics invest in the trope of displacement and migrancy in the age of decolonisation. From such analyses emerges a Naipaul who is seen not only as a critic of the chaos and violence that accompanies revolutions but also as a critic of the status quo. It underscores the movement of a few talented *men* from the margins to the centre while maintaining the centrality of the defused centre. Some of these critics have also defined Naipaul as investing in the centre only to highlight his own marginality. Such criticism invests in the 'universal civilization' and discourses on globalisation by declaring their own allegiance to Western Enlightenment values. They forget that though Naipaul never wrote a book that ostensibly criticised Western Enlightenment values, he never unconditionally endorsed them. He viewed the present as a 'universal civilisation' dependent upon the scientific discoveries of the West in the fields of technology, medicine and warfare. He candidly also accepted the fact that such universalism was a direct product of colonialism. An in-depth study of his books reveals that his reference to universal civilisation is a fluid concept that refers to the Islamic civilisation from the seventh century to the thirteenth century A.D., and to the age of European colonialism from the fourteenth century to the twentieth century.

Many times, the critics, or rather the benign interviewers (often writers in their own right), highlight Naipaul's ideological neutrality, though Naipaul's reputation was based upon his highly opinionated political views on countries that he visited during his long career. Farrukh Dhondy writes:

> Indians don't want to be told that they defecate without inhibition in the open [...]. Countries such as Iran don't want to be told that the political ideology they espoused in their support for a republican 'revolution' is a cruel, medieval imposition on a contemporary society [...]. And I have not yet met a Pakistani who does applaud the phrase that Vidia used to declare his or her country: "Pakistan, a criminal enterprise!" (2018, p. 19)

It is clear that Dhondy reads Naipaul as a sociological writer who understands more than the common people. Such critics assess Naipaul as a prophetic writer whose writings have provided postcolonial literature with many of its tropes, such as mimicry and hybridity. Naipaul defined mimicry as a state of colonial schizophrenia where men distrusted everything they knew because there was no connection between men and their environment. Naipaul found hybridity to be a false promise because it led to a denial of one's elemental feelings. As far as he was concerned, such hybridity fostered a numbness towards 'life' because it allowed people to live their lives unexamined; it lulled them into silence and inaction.

A few of these critics view him as saddling the twin cultures of the East and the West. Such critics analyse him as a negotiator between the conflicting worlds of his Hindu upbringing on the small island of Trinidad and his worldly ambitions to be a writer in England. These critics highlight and applaud Naipaul's choice of living in England rather than Trinidad and underscore his cultural conservatism (Tariq Ali 2018, p. 57). Naipaul recognised certain traits in himself as remnants of his Brahmanical caste identity, such as his incapacity to enjoy meat or to eat food prepared by strangers, but he was also sure that he was not a man of faith. His supposed conservatism was further strengthened by his criticism of the ultra-left guerrilla warfare in Trinidad, India, Iran, and Argentina; his view of Islam as an imperialistic religion; his appearance on the platform of the Bharatiya Janta Party in India; his advocacy of a 'universal civilisation;' and his criticism of Tony Blair. Yet such views ignore the fact that Trinidad was not a conservative society with any long history of a civilisational base. It was a *society of arrival*—with people brought there by certain whimsical accidents of history and institutionalised colonial mechanisms.

The Trinidadian Context

A text should always be read in its context, and my book contextualises Naipaul's books within Trinidad. The book considers Naipaul's negotiation of Trinidad in each of his books as a sign of his emotional development. It also considers how perceptions of Naipaul have changed in Trinidad over the years. The book is also an interesting read for someone who wants to see how locals have 'used' Naipaul to strengthen their own arguments on issues ranging from nationalisation of industries to justifying a change in governments. It shows how Trinidadians react at an elemental level to Naipaul while the world sees him as an impartial purveyor of truth about third-world societies.

Naipaul was born in central Trinidad, in the small country town of Chaguanas, where his maternal family had a shop and business holdings. Most people in town still derived their subsistence from agriculture. The East Indian community was close-knit because they shared a sense of insecurity that stemmed from their parents or grandparents finding themselves in the unknown and uncertain terrain of Trinidad once they had signed the indenture contracts. When the indentured reached Trinidad, they were forced down into a social hierarchy with the whites, creole and Africans above them. The indentured Indians were pejoratively called 'coolies' on

INTRODUCTION

the plantations by the managers and the overseers, 'a reminder of lowliness in the hierarchy of a sugar estate, a hierarchy based on race [...] an apparently inheritable marker of ethnicity more than a job description' (Preface, Gaiutra Bahadur 2013, pp. xx–xxi). The East Indians, as the indentured were commonly called, brought their own civilisational values with them, and referred to the Africans as uncivilised (Brereton 1979, p. 188). This inversion at the bottom of the social scale led to bitterness in their limited interaction on the sugar estates, because post-Emancipation most Africans had moved either to the city of Port of Spain or the outback. The African-Indian rivalries were exploited by the colonial masters to justify their rule. It obviously had repercussions in the post-colonial era when Trinidad became independent and a new elite local bourgeois came to rule.

The succeeding generations of Indians felt insecure because they knew of no other place being born in Trinidad. Indeed, growing up in the 1940s, Naipaul would have felt these insecurities as a descendant of indentured Indians. When he was about five or six years old, the family moved to Port of Spain, where Naipaul entered a multi-racial society that looked down upon the East Indians. The older generation still talks about how they were bullied in school because they brought roti for lunch. 'Coolie culture' was generally regarded as low, with Indians being misers who invested their money into business, educating their children and building houses. According to Bahadur, it became an ethnic slur as tensions simmered between Africans and Indians in the 1960s and 1970s. Socially, the Indo-Trinidadians instead invested in the communities, developing the concept of 'jahaji bhai' or brothers from the ship, a symbolic reference to that initial journey that had brought their ancestors to Trinidad. However, Naipaul never used the 'coolie' or the 'jahaji bhai' references to describe either himself or other East Indians, though in his books he explored his community's perceived marginality to the national culture of Trinidad and Tobago.

Naipaul elided not only his community's history but his family's history as well. Savi Naipaul Akal, Naipaul's younger sister, has written *The Naipauls of Nepaul Street* (2018) about the family's life at their St. James house, which the family continued to occupy till the death of their mother, Droapatie Naipaul, in 1991. Her book is a personal account of how life went on for the Naipaul siblings after Naipaul's departure to England. While Naipaul achieved his success in London, all of Droapatie and Seepersad's children went on to get university degrees, against the established norms of the then Trinidadian society. The book speaks about the close relations shared by the siblings with Naipaul visiting them frequently in Trinidad, especially between 1968 and 1973. She also speaks about the close but estranged relationships between the two brothers, Vidia and Shiva Naipaul. Family relations also became strained after Naipaul's open confession about his relationship with Margaret Gooding. It further deteriorated after Naipaul chided his mother for giving an interview to an Indian journalist on her visit to India. However, Droapatie Naipaul and the Naipaul clan remained indebted to Vidia and Kamla, the eldest siblings, for the love and support they provided during the difficult years after the death of their father in 1953. Naipaul highlighted his humble background, being born on an island in the Caribbean to descendants of Indian indentured labourers, but he rarely emphasised his close and not too close relations with his siblings. Naipaul only documented his relationship with his father as a source of inspiration for his international success.

Nicholas Laughlin, for his 2006 revised edition of *Letters Between a Father and Son*, had been granted permission to rework some letters (with obvious mistakes in transliteration) and went on to include 79 more letters by Kamla, Naipaul's elder sister and Droapatie Naipaul, Naipaul's mother. However, for no apparent reason, the publisher informed him that there would be no further editions of his work and that the publisher would revert back to the edition done by Gillon Aitken in future. Laughlin argues that Naipaul did not wish to dilute his special relationship with his father or destroy the myth of a direct link between the limitations of his father and his own (supposedly unsupported) success (2016, p. 10).

When Naipaul left Trinidad at the age of eighteen, he thought he had made it in the world because he had devoted all his school life to gaining the scholarship that would take him away from Trinidad. Naipaul visited Trinidad in 1956 only after he had secured his contract with Andre Deutsch and his books were soon to be published. He felt distanced from everybody and everything because, in the interim, his father had died and the family had re-adjusted to his absence. He felt both connected and disconnected with Trinidad. The experience led him to write *A House for Mr Biswas*, his masterpiece, that helped him pay a lengthy tribute to his father's struggle to become a writer in a society that was only then recovering its own identity.

Naipaul's first four novels, with their Indo-Trinidadian protagonists, were received very enthusiastically both in Britain and the Caribbean. But many critics point out that though a book such as *A House for Mr Biswas* is a representative text, true to its time and context, not many Indians in the Caribbean felt that it told their story. The book generated controversy locally because the Capildeos in Trinidad were angry at the way they had been portrayed as selfish, pompous fools in the novel. Naipaul's mother's family were politically active members of the Indo-Trinidadian community and felt that they had not received their due in the book. Clem Seecharan, an Indo-Guyanese-British historian, appreciates Naipaul's descriptive acumen

INTRODUCTION 17

but disputes Naipaul's cynical portrayal of the joint Hindu family and its support systems. He writes:

> We are both descendants of Indian indentured labourers from eastern Uttar Pradesh, taken to sugar plantations in the Caribbean in the late nineteenth century. Naipaul's people went to Trinidad in the 1880s, mine to Demerara (British Guiana) from the 1870s. They were Brahmins, mine Ahirs (contemporary Yadavs), the traditional cattle-herders of Uttar Pradesh and Bihar [...]. (2018, p. 41)

Seecharan goes on to narrate the happy childhood memories that he cherishes to this day. He had a relatively easy childhood of plenitude where provision food was supplemented with fresh produce from their own fields; the get-together functions of his extended family were happy occasions where he met with hundreds of his cousins. None of his experiences find an echo in Naipaul's numerous accounts of his childhood, which Naipaul remembered as one of shame, hunger and embarrassment (2015).

Naipaul's early novels got the praise that they richly deserved. However, while the other Caribbean writers were well-received within the George Padmore-led Afro-Caribbean pan-Africanist movement in Britain, Naipaul felt left out. He also rejected any idea of him being West Indian or a West Indian writer: 'I don't know what the word means, I have nothing in common with the people from Jamaica, or the other islands for that matter' (Rouse 1968, p. 10). This was also the time when the Caribbean Artists Movement (CAM) was being initiated in Britain by a group of Afro-Caribbean writers and artists, namely the pioneers John La Rose, Edward Kamau Brathwaite and Andrew Salkey. Naipaul resisted his co-optation into any political group or alignment at a time when the spirit of nationalism and regionalism was running high. He repeatedly avoided declaring his political allegiance. Edward Kamau Brathwaite and George Lamming saw success in Britain, went on to live for brief periods of time in Africa, and later returned to the West Indies as committed members of its new literati. Even though Naipaul went to India on a supposedly similar mission to seek his roots, his writing about India was far more critical and he returned to England far more convinced than before that India could never be a home to him. His travels in Africa also made him feel alienated by the air of animosity against Indians in the then turbulent Uganda.

Naipaul continued to maintain that the Caribbean islands lacked the literary paraphernalia and an audience to sustain his writing. Derek Walcott, George Lamming, Michael Anthony, Wilson Harris and Kamau Brathwaite dismissed his claims as spurious, emphasising their connectedness to the land, the islands and the sea. They argued that it was the connection between the writer and his land that sustained good writing, suffusing it with an organic quality, nationalism and a quest for identity. Lamming characterised Naipaul's writing as incapable of moving beyond 'castrated satire' because he wrote as if he was superior to his countrymen. Kamau Brathwaite praised Naipaul for fully representing the plight of the Indo-Trinidadians, if not the Afro-Trinidadians, in his novels. Edward Baugh, Selwyn Cudjoe and Jamaica Kincaid argued that Naipaul had a derogatory view of the West Indies. Generally, Naipaul was severely criticised by those who invested heavily in an Afro-centric revival of creole culture in Trinidad. But, for Naipaul any vision/discourse that did not firmly invest in the socio-economic-political-literary growth of the nation was suspect of its racial and class affiliations. Naipaul's later criticism of the Black Power Movement, furthermore, saw him being marginalised from the 'mainstream' Caribbean discourse.

Naipaul enjoys the unique honour of being canonised in the Caribbean on the one hand and marginalised and hated on the other. Notwithstanding this criticism, Naipaul shared many of the concerns of his contemporaries regarding the future of the Caribbean states. In an early essay, 'London' written in 1958, Naipaul wrote that he was an oddity in the English literary world because he was 'an Indian writer writing in English for an English audience about non-English characters who talk their own sort of English' (1958b: 1972, p. 12). He gave primacy to his Indian heritage in Trinidad and went on to enumerate the reasons why he could not be a typical writer from the colonies because he did not write about sex, did not use the Caribbean settings as only background material with a British or American protagonist in the foreground or talk race (1958b: 1972, p. 13). He excused himself from writing about all three because his 'mother would be shocked' if he wrote about the first, he would be untrue to his art if he created characters with whom he did not identify, and in Trinidad, race talk, instead of being only about the white rulers and the black enslaved, was also about relations between people of the East Indian descent and African descent in the politically charged atmosphere of the formation of the West Indian federation. Written on the cusp of Trinidad declaring its political independence from British colonial rule, *The Middle Passage* focuses on the confusions surrounding a 'national' culture in Trinidad. Many locals criticised Naipaul for portraying Trinidadians as fools and tricksters. They said that he had sold his soul to the devil, the colonial master, just when the country had chosen to become independent. But Naipaul's early exposure to issues of race and racial violence made him uncomfortable about denying their existence. He was not politically correct because nobody in Trinidad is. Trinidadian literature abounds in implied and obvious references to race, inter-racial mixing, and racial conflict. Race is only absent in the rather sanitised versions of the 'sun and sand' literature that are also noteworthy for the absence of overcrowded beaches, loud music and crying children. No election rally is complete without acknowledging the racial divide between the Afro-Trinidadians and the Indo-Trinidadians, and equally, promises of racial unity. Neither is any musical event complete without the blending of the sounds of the steel band and tassa. Nor is any meal complete without the shadow beni and pepper sauces. Yet Naipaul rejected any vision for any developing society that celebrated its mixed culture at the expense of hiding its fault lines.

Naipaul's resolve that he would not return to the country of his birth for a living remained a rather shaky promise. It is possible that Naipaul desired to be rootless, delinking himself from Trinidad, England and India. But even this rather expansive view of the world was rooted in Trinidad because rootlessness in the Caribbean has no relation to the western notion of the exile who becomes a global citizen. Rootlessness is celebratory only because it commemorates a forced amnesia, an amnesia about their roots in Africa, India and elsewhere. Unlike many of his British contemporaries who celebrated rootlessness, Naipaul blamed colonialism for his anchorless life. He analysed colonialism as an imposition of language, culture and civilisation on those who had been forcefully brought to Trinidad. His early novels analyse the psychologically devastating effects of English education on the colonials. In an early essay, 'Jasmine,' Naipaul, who said that he knew no other language than English, found that he could not connect the smell of the jasmine flower with its name because he had never made the connection before (1964b: 1972, p. 29). Naipaul hinted at the deep impact English education had on the colonials who not only lost their language but, by extension, a sense of themselves, their history and their identity.

Naipaul's problem is as great as that of all the other anglophone Caribbean writers: they must use the language of the coloniser to tell their stories. And they must transcend the victim-perpetrator binary to engage with the ex-colonisers on their own terms. Naipaul never denied the fruits of colonial rule, but he was very clear that he placed his own faith in individual intelligence, endeavour and enterprise, things that were mistaken for his support of Enlightenment principles. Naipaul fiercely protected his own individuality and promoted individual endeavours, but these need to be understood in the context of Trinidad, with its history of the extermination of the natives, the violence of slavery and the impoverishment of the indentured. When one speaks about language as

20   V. S. NAIPAUL OF TRINIDAD

acquired, culture as a memory and myth as history, one must contextualise these with the incumbent losses of native languages, culture as a living artefact and history that cannot be retrieved.

Naipaul's continued travels to and from Trinidad and his need to touch base were as much a reality as the fact that he never did return to live in Trinidad. He was not a nationalist because he could not overlook the real problems of underdevelopment and a continued dependence upon the ex-colonial powers. At the core of his writing lies the conviction that cultures and individuals must find the courage to break away from the cycle of destruction and destitution that engulfs humanity in general. Readers who are caught in his web of writing sense a pessimism because he makes them see their own 'semi-derelict communities.' Naipaul is a unique writer in many ways, mixing the personal with the political, the self with a larger community and the larger community with nullity. He appreciates human endeavour but refuses to give credence to any action or movement that cloaks itself in the language of a higher vision. He criticises his own middle class for failing to address the challenges in their societies. Here I am defining his audience in terms of Trinidad, not a British audience.

Naipaul invested in a traveller's perspective, one who would not settle down and, hence, could not invest in the development of his society. From this perspective, the writer is not a leader but leads society towards making the world a better place to live. This is also the reason why Naipaul disagreed with writers who combined their activism with their writing in the Caribbean and elsewhere. Years later, when Naipaul was to claim that his success as a writer from the Caribbean was a singular success, this was as much a jibe at his listeners and their limited knowledge of Caribbean literature than an accurate portrayal of his achievements. Naipaul's anti-Trinidadian posturing can be read as a manifestation of a very Caribbean behaviour, a role-playing mode that is distinctly, if not uniquely Trinidadian. After all, 'he was never more Trinidadian than when he was bad-talking Trinidad' (Laughlin 2018, p. 97).

Scope of this Book

It is true that Naipaul never wrote a book while in Trinidad. I have organised my book decade by decade, with the 1950s beginning in 1950 to 1959, the 1960s beginning in 1960 to 1969, etc. There are possibly two exceptions: *A House for Mr Biswas* (1961) is treated as a 1950s novel because it is thematically linked to his writings in the 1950s; and *The Return of Eva Perón, with The Killings in Trinidad* (1980a: 1981) are about the happenings in the 1970s and were published in 1980 only due to legal issues. The one drawback of analysing

INTRODUCTION

Naipaul's books decade-by-decade is that such an analysis does not yield itself to a thematic analysis. Though Naipaul has never been ignored in any stated Caribbean canon, Naipaul represents an element in Caribbean literature that refused to be reined in. Alternatively, he represents one of the many loose strings that are frequently seen as ideologically weakening a forceful representation of an Afro-centric Caribbean vision. Within the flourishing Anglophone Caribbean critical scene, there is Afro-Trinidadian literature, Indo-Trinidadian and Indo-Guyanese literature, Chinese, Syrian and Portuguese diasporic literature, white creole literature, and literature of the First Nation People. All these strands (oral and written) are part of a cross-cultural creolised/ douglarised literary space. At a micro level, political differences between these groups often define the ever-evolving Caribbean literature. This book elucidates Naipaul's position in this ever-evolving Caribbean canon, untangling the web of Naipaul's vision that is indeed multiracial and cross-cultural, though he is not sanguine about it but recognises it for its own set of prejudices. He steers clear of nationalist agendas and invests in a global vision that was born in Trinidad. Each following chapter emphasises how Trinidad played a role in defining his responses to the world and how his relationship to Trinidad changed over the years.

In Chapter 1, I deal with Naipaul's early novels, *The Mystic Masseur, The Suffrage of Elvira, Miguel Street* and *A House for Mr Biswas*. These early novels reveal the deep influence of his father, Seepersad Naipaul, on his writings. His writings in the 1950s are tempered by his awareness of two audiences: one in the West Indies (those who hail or criticise) and one in Britain (those who see him as an exotic or representative of the Third World or underdevelopment). These books are also exceptional for their presentation of East Indians in Trinidad and the use of Trinidad locutions. It is a carefully composed world—not static, but composed in such a way that no outside forces trouble it. The books offer an honest vision of 'one side' of Trinidadian life—the East Indian one. And they are noteworthy for the elaborate nature of their narrative structures.

Chapter 2 explores Naipaul's early travels across the Caribbean and India in search of his distinctive position. He develops a narrative voice that speaks like and unlike that of an English traveller of the nineteenth century. While most critics view his use of first-person voice for his travel writings uncritically, I read it as a deliberate and elaborate frame to protect his real feelings while attempting to record the truth. The discussion offers a view on the place of Indo-Trinidadians within multicultural Trinidad. Though his displacement from Trinidad was an aspirational move, Naipaul was surprised by his inability to settle elsewhere. Three themes emerge from his shift from novels to travel writing: his criticism of British models of travel writing, his interrogation of traditional religions and cultures and, disapproval of welfare state politics. This is also the first time that Naipaul presents a multiracial and multicultural Caribbean. On these two trips, Naipaul brushed against the sentiments of Indians and Trinidadians, who expected him to be grateful to them for his existence. Naipaul fell into a pattern. He had found his oeuvre. He knew he could attack through his writing, and he was happy when people reacted at this elemental level to his writing. Naipaul let his writing take over his social relationships because people began to see him through the sole prism of his writing.

Chapter 3 explores the debates about the folk versus the educated middle-class aspirants in the Caribbean. While the early novels represented the East Indians in Trinidad, Naipaul built a multi-racial landscape of a fictional Caribbean island in *A Flag on the Island* and *The Mimic Men. The Mimic Men* is a significant book because it showcases race relations in Trinidad beyond petty island politics. Equally, he wrote a history of the island of Trinidad in *The Loss of El Dorado.* The trial of Luisa Calderon was a spectacle that was used to enhance British self-esteem as the great protector of humanity. Nobody knows what happened to her later. The book explores historical reasons for racial enmity between the four primary groups in the Caribbean and more specifically, Trinidad: the white creoles who were descendants of the planter class, the nearly extinct Amerindians, the descendants of the African slaves and the descendants of the Indian indentured labourers. The chapter offers a discussion on Naipaul's break with his own past as he addresses issues within contemporary Trinidad. A contrast to the dynamism of these books was Naipaul's own monotone novel, *Mr Stone and the Knights Companion.*

Chapter 4 is divided into two sections: Section 1 offers another discussion on race relations in *In a Free State,* 'Michael X and the Black Power Killings in Trinidad,' and *Guerrillas.* Section 2 deals with *The Return of Eva Perón, India: A Wounded Civilization,* various essays published in the *New York Review of Books* and *The Overcrowded Barracoon,* and *A Bend in the River.* The 1970 Black Power Movement/the February Uprising was a major development in Trinidadian politics that affected the political, social and cultural life in Trinidad. Naipaul's position was far more nuanced than he has ever been given credit for because he realised that the movement had different meanings for his disparate audiences, the one in Trinidad, the one in England and the one elsewhere. He knew that the movement was a grassroots movement that had ironically gained support and funding from the British bourgeois class, who felt engaged with the newly redefined 'white man's burden.' Naipaul's understanding of the Black Power Movement coloured his understanding of race relations forever. For Naipaul, the 1970s were life-defining years, as he

INTRODUCTION

felt disillusioned with the politics in Trinidad and England. His travels to South America brought a storm to his personal life, and he wrote his last fictional venture for a long time to come, *A Bend in the River*.

Chapter 5 deals with his varied writings in the 1980s, which include *Among the Believers: An Islamic Journey*, in which Naipaul travelled to Iran, Pakistan, Malaysia and Indonesia. In *Finding the Centre*, he returned to the theme of his autobiography (after the Foreword to *The Loss of El Dorado*). This phase culminated in two tributes to the developed world: *The Enigma of Arrival* and *A Turn in the South*. The former, a veiled autobiography, is said to recapitulate his growth as a writer by colonising English literature and landscape through his presence. The latter, a journey through the American southern cities of Atlanta, Charleston, Tallahassee, Tuskegee, Jackson, Nashville, Durham, and Charlottesville, summarises his poor understanding of the race relations in America. As Naipaul attempted to move away from Trinidad in his writings, his vision receded in its depth and scope. On the personal front, as he settled down in his Dairy Cottage in Wiltshire, Trinidad pulled him back to seek solace with his family as he lost his beloved younger sister Sati and his much younger brother Shiva Naipaul. He then began to increasingly rely upon his Trinidadian Hindu roots for advocating a different perception of the world.

Chapter 6 expounds on his return journeys to all the places he had visited in the 1960s and 1970s: India, Africa, Argentina, Trinidad and Guyana. His essays and the three travel books, *India: A Million Mutinies Now*, *A Way in the World* and *Beyond Belief: Islamic Excursions Among the Converted Peoples* are about his changing perceptions about these countries and regions. All the journeys are reconciliatory in nature, and Naipaul re-invents himself as a much-travelled, wise man who is no longer the nervous wreck that he was in his younger days. He seems to be at ease with his Trinidadian self and feels he has defined himself adequately enough (in his previous visits) to focus on the places and people out there.

Chapter 7 is about his writings since the year 2000. These include the long essay 'Reading and Writing,' *Half a Life*, its sequel *Magic Seeds*, *A Writer's People* and *The Masque of Africa*. Naipaul returned to writing fiction after a gap of two decades. Naipaul received the Nobel Prize in 2001. Many associated the timing of his winning the Nobel Prize with growing Islamophobia in America and elsewhere. It seemed to have come at the end of a long writing career. The locals were angry at being ignored in his initial reaction but were happy that one of their own had received it. Naipaul chose to highlight the suppressed history of Trinidad in his Nobel acceptance lecture. Though Trinidad did not feature in his fictional writings in the 2000s, he remained loyal to Trinidad. His book on Africa reignited the critics who felt that Naipaul had merely repeated his insults, but Naipaul appears at ease with his references to Trinidad in his last published book, *The Masque of Africa*. The writings have a staid quality to them, where he is nostalgic about his career both as a traveller and a writer.

The 'Conclusions' chapter re-assesses Naipaul's legacy as a writer of East Indian descent and his perceived marginality to the national creole culture of Trinidad and Afro-centric Caribbean literature. The book concludes that Naipaul's concept of a writer as a responsible citizen writing for his society was achieved in spite of his scepticism and cynicism. He explored the dark areas of his background and visited countries that had connections to his own Trinidad, the Trinidad where he had spent the first eighteen years of his life.

Chapter 1

EARLY FICTION OF THE 1950s: THE TRINIDAD YEARS

I think it was in '58 that I ceased to be destitute, really (Naipaul in conversation with Walcott 1965, p. 9).

V. S. Naipaul was the eldest son in a family of five daughters and two sons. Naipaul's mother, Droapatie Naipaul was one of the nine daughters and two sons of Kapildeo Maharaj and Soogie Rosaline Capildeo. This large household was a well-established family settled in Chaguanas, in central Trinidad, in a house with an impressive facade, with its concrete balustrades, elephants and lions with a shop on the ground floor. It was originally called *Anand Bhavan* (House of Happiness), but due to the decorative lion heads, it came to be known locally as the Lion House. Droapatie had had a basic education and had been married informally but was not sent away with the man due to the emergence of some last-minute questionable details (Akal 2018, p. 26). Even though she was very young when she was married to Seepersad Naipaul, it was a late marriage according to the customs of the time. She did odd jobs in her family's establishments and, after the death of her husband, became the breadwinner for her family.

Naipaul's father, Seepersad Naipaul, was a second generation East Indian whose parents had not thrived in Trinidad. Seepersad's grandmother had come as an indentured labourer, carrying her little son, who was a free Indian. Seepersad's father died early, leaving behind two sons and a daughter. Seepersad's mother married again and had another son from the second husband. At a certain time in the family, it was decided that they would all go back to India. However, Seepersad developed cold feet at the thought and hid in a toilet to avoid the journey back to India. The family stayed on in Trinidad. Since Seepersad's father died early, the family was left at the mercy of richer relatives. His life, recapitulated in *A House for Mr Biswas*, typifies the tale of the common man working in a hostile environment. He did odd jobs, learnt English, painted signboards and finally got employed at the *Trinidad Guardian* newspaper. However, unlike

Mohun Biswas, Seepersad began work as a freelance reporter on the *Trinidad Guardian* in 1929 before his marriage with Droapatie. Seepersad's marriage had also been fixed early but his bride had run away on the day of the marriage (Akal 2018, p. 27). Hence his later marriage to Droapatie in 1929 was also late by the customs of those times. He nurtured dreams of becoming a writer and self-published his stories in Trinidad in 1943, which were later compiled and re-published by V. S. Naipaul in 1976 under the title *The Adventures of Gurudeva and Other Stories*. More recently, Aaron Eastley and his team have been working on digitalising Seepersad's articles in the *Trinidad Guardian* with the ultimate aim of producing a library of his writings. Seepersad Naipaul was the first Indo-Trinidadian writer-journalist who documented life within the East Indian rural community in Trinidad in the 1920s and 1930s.

In 1938–9, the family moved from Chaguanas in central Trinidad to the capital city of Port of Spain, where Naipaul completed his schooling, first at Tranquillity Boys' School and later at the Queen's Royal College, where he won a scholarship to Oxford—one of the very few scholarships to be won at that time. Seepersad bought a house in the St. James area of Port of Spain in 1946 and resided there till his untimely death in 1953. Droapatie Naipaul continued to reside there until her death in 1991. Seepersad's St. James's house has since been bought by the Government of Trinidad and Tobago and leased to a non-governmental organisation, *Friends of Mr Biswas*, which has been set-up to promote literary tourism akin to the Shakespeare circuit in England and promote scholarship on V. S. Naipaul and his family. This is a singular honour given to any writer in the Caribbean.

From an early age, Naipaul nurtured dreams of becoming a writer. He decided early that he would leave the island at the age of 17. Naipaul knew that he did not have the privileges enjoyed by his uncles but that he could prove himself different from them by beating them at their own game. His uncle, Rudranath Capildeo, had been one of the first few Indo-Trinidadians to have studied at the prestigious Queen's Royal College and to have received a colonial scholarship to England. Naipaul had to follow a similar path because opportunities were very few on the island. He eventually did leave Trinidad at the age of 18, winning a scholarship to Oxford to study English and Spanish. However, all was not smooth sailing. Naipaul was not on the list of original scholarship winners in spite of achieving distinctions in French and Spanish. He had been denied a seat due to a change in rules. The Trinidad government made a special plea on his behalf, which was granted in his favour. The local newspapers reported this widely (French 2008, p. 57). He was a local celebrity and already a newsworthy personality by the time he left the island.

EARLY FICTION OF THE 1950s

This chapter deals with the struggles of a young writer from Trinidad who laboured, toiled and found literary success in England. He knew that he had to write about Trinidad because that was the only world he knew about. His father was an early influence because he often read books to his children. This, coupled with V. S. Naipaul's school education and the lively reporting of happenings in Trinidad in the daily newspapers, provided the foundation. V. S. Naipaul had both the example and advice from his father to write about Trinidad since his father had published a book of stories called *Gurudeva and Other Indian Tales*. A comparison between V. S. Naipaul's four early novels, namely *The Mystic Masseur, The Suffrage of Elvira, Miguel Street* and *A House for Mr Biswas* and his father's *Gurudeva and Other Indian Tales* highlights the overlap in themes and content alongside differences in tone, narrative structures and an overall vision of and for the society that they grew up in. Naipaul resisted any attempt to position his writing within a regional context, yet the impact of the then developing Caribbean literature on his writings and his impact on them cannot be undermined. Naipaul's use of the ironic voice was new because he seemingly mocked yet sympathised with the efforts of the colonised to fit into the straitjackets prepared for them by the colonisers who had 'gifted' the colonies the school system, the institution of democracy and the concept of individual freedom.

Gurudeva and Other Indian Tales (1943); later published as *The Adventures of Gurudeva and Other Stories,* with a foreword by V. S. Naipaul (1976)

Seepersad Naipaul was a self-educated man who learned to write on his own. In the longest story titled 'Gurudeva,' Seepersad presents a young Hindu East Indian man named Gurudeva who is born to parents of indentured Indians but is not compelled to follow the path of his father. Gurudeva learns stick-fighting and gains fame as a strongman of the family. During the Hosay march, Gurudeva fights with Sookhwa and a police constable and ends up in jail for 12 months. He emerges from the prison as a hero and a devout pundit, renouncing meat and alcohol. He builds himself a separate *Kuti*, or thatched hut, to live in, takes to wearing a *dhoti*, a traditional Hindu garment, and speaks in Hindi. Soon after, he falls in love with Daisy, a bob-haired Presbyterian convert who entices him and brings him into disrepute. Ratni, his childless wife, leaves him but makes him answerable to the *panchayat* (a body of village elders). Gurudeva presents his case well, citing the *Ramayana*, where King Dasaratha, Ram's father, had three wives. He further pleads that since Ratni did not have children and since she had left him of her own will, he was free to marry another. The *Panchayat* rules in his favour but asks him to convert

Daisy back to the Hindu ways of wearing an *odhni* or veil, and growing long hair. Gurudeva promises, but Daisy refuses to become Hindu, and in the end, Gurudeva is left alone as a 'bachelor' (Seepersad Naipaul 1943, p. 123).

Simbhoonath Capildeo paid for the 1943 edition (French 2008, p. 43) brought out by the Trinidad Printery that carried a dedication from Robert Burns: 'Oh, wad some pow'r the gift die us, / To see ourselves as others see us!' Naipaul refers back to this thought in *A Way in the World* (1994) when he writes about the necessity of the external witness to know that their lives could be written about. The introduction to the writer comes with a photograph of Seepersad Naipaul and a foreword humbly stating that the stories were a 'succession of pictures.' Further, he states upfront that he had a problem with regards to the use of language by his characters since 'people like the Gurudeva household express themselves as often in English as in Hindi— but mutilate both tongues. It is easy enough to leave broken English as it stands, but I could hit upon no English equivalent for broken Hindi' (Seepersad Naipaul 1943, pp. 6–7). Seepersad anticipated criticism from local critics because he knew he had created a new lingo for his characters. The use of Hindi words within the book, sometimes with English translations, is a way of putting in mongrel Hindi and creole English since the Indian population spoke a mixture of the two. V. S. Naipaul resolved the issue by rendering Hindi and broken Hindi into Standard English in his early novels.

The senior Naipaul set an example for the son to write about the social and cultural life of the East Indians in Trinidad. The younger Naipaul admitted that without that early guidance, he would have felt lost in the larger world. Seepersad Naipaul's articles in the *Trinidad Guardian* newspaper as well as his stories provided the young Naipaul with an archival perspective on the society of his birth. Yet, in strange ways, the young Naipaul also felt a critical distance from this material that had been passed on to him. This shows up in his writing in his struggle to find a medium through whom to write about a society which he knew intimately but felt distant from because he had spent the first 18 years of his life distinguishing himself from his fellow countrymen. Seepersad's writing, on the other hand, is direct and straightforward.

The Mystic Masseur (1957)

The Mystic Masseur is the story of Ganesh Ramsumair, who receives a colonial education and gets a temporary teaching job but subsequently chooses to become a mystic masseur in the backwaters of Trinidad. He becomes so popular and powerful that he is elected as a Member of the Legislative Council (MLC) and is later awarded a Member of the Most Excellent Order of the British Empire (MBE). The book is woven around the events of the 1946

EARLY FICTION OF THE 1950s 29

General Elections, when adult franchise was extended for the first time to all Trinidadians without strict income and property qualifications. Unlike his father's narrative voice, Naipaul creates a distinctive narrator who places the story in his past, assuring the reader that the protagonist, like himself, would later be a success, both in the Caribbean and in Britain.

The events in the book occur between 1939, which was the beginning of the Second World War, and end around 1953, the year Seepersad died. The book follows Ganesh's fortunes from being the son of a wealthy country man to a schoolteacher to a penniless bachelor to a mystic masseur to an island politician to receiving an MBE. His fame spreads far and wide as he is able to deal with clouds, balls-of-fire, soucouyants, loups-garoux, a woman who couldn't eat, lover-boy, thaumaturges, charlatans and obeah. He gets invited to *panchayats* and prayer meetings where he speaks in Hindi and puts up displays of books written in English. His new career gives impetus to his writing career as well, composing no less than eight books: *The Guide to Trinidad, The Road to Happiness, Re-incarnation, The Soul as I see it, The Necessity of Faith, What God told Me, Profitable Evacuation* (*The Mystic Masseur* 1957: 1978, p. 159) and *Out of the Red* (*The Mystic Masseur* 1957: 1978, p. 213). And it is his ability with words that makes him a successful politician and an MBE. It is Ganesh's ability to constantly reinvent himself that becomes the cornerstone of his success. In spite of Ganesh anglicising his name to G. Ramsay Muir later, his identity remains wedded to his race, his culture and his island.

According to Lizabeth Paravisini-Gebert, Ganesh was based upon the figure of Bhadase Sagan Maraj, a union leader and leader of the Sanatan Dharma Maha Sabha, who manipulated his social and religious influence 'into the foundations of a successful political career' (2008, pp. 162–3). Paravisini-Gebert also quotes Louis Simpson, who argues that Ganesh was based upon 'a Camar from Jangli-Tola—that is, an East Indian of lower caste, who set himself up as a Brahmin pundit' (qtd. in Paravisini-Gebert 2008, p. 162). According to Brinsley Samaroo, Ganesh Ramsumair could be based on Doon Pundit, a popular pundit in the areas of Las Lomas and Arouca who was regularly consulted by people of all races. Doon Pundit even cured the Governor's wife (as Ganesh does in the book) and was awarded the MBE, which honour is reflected in the book as Ganesh moves from being an MLC to an MBE. The man with a monocle is perhaps Uriah Butler, and the brash Port of Spain politician is Albert Gomes. It was Gomes who initiated the practice of lying down in the parliament to be forcibly lifted away by the police (Personal Communication with Samaroo, October 16, 2016). In the book, the politician Ganesh Ramsumair initiates the walk out in the manner of Gomes. According to Patrick French, V. S. Naipaul satirised the self-published leaflets brought out by Simbhoonath Capildeo in the depiction of Ganesh the politician (2008, p. 38). The fact that so many critics have found prototypes of Ganesh in Trinidadian society points to the success of Naipaul in portraying a character that is both individualistic and representative. Aaron Eastley argues for the similarities with particular personalities that dominated the Trinidadian national conscience in 1946. According to Eastley: 'In the novel the genesis of party politics in 1946 is belittled, the very notion of serious agitation in Trinidad is belied, and the lived complexities and the larger nationalistic and imperial significance of island politics are severely elided' (2009, p. 28). Eastley views Naipaul as being critical of his countrymen observing 'all things from an urbane, cosmopolitan, Oxford-educated distance' (2009, p. 4). Rob Nixon argues on similar lines, but I think that comparisons to real-life politicians are self-defeating because the politicians are reduced to poor caricatures of themselves and as fraudsters who have no mass appeal.

In fact, this has been the cornerstone of most criticism that views Naipaul as a turncoat who never wrote sympathetically about his countrymen. They overlook the complicated narrative design mounted by Naipaul to write about his fellow countrymen. According to Barbara Lalla, the 'use of the "false document" technique [in *The Mystic Masseur*], that is, the explicit projection of the narrative as a record of fact, backed up by repeated reference to other records [...] undermines the normal authenticating function of records and discredits the value of written discourse that is valorised throughout the action of the novel' (2011, p. 100). Lalla sees this as leading to 'the failure of identity construction (ethnic, intellectual and so forth) at an individual level' that mirrors 'a failure of national construction' (2011, p. 103). I would rather argue that throughout his career Naipaul exploited constant self-fashioning as a lived reality and resisted any attempt at defining a unified singular identity. Ganesh reinvents himself in school (calling himself Gareth) in his brief stint as a school teacher, as a mystic masseur, as a pundit, as a MLC and as an MBE. The journey is a long one and needs to be told, even if nobody can say that what was told was the truth.

Besides developing a complex narrative structure to overcome his creative challenges, Naipaul had decided to place his primary audience in England. This shows that Naipaul was aware that his books were going to be read by readers across geographical regions (England and the Caribbean), racial lines (Whites, Blacks, Indians and everyone in-between), and class affinities (upper- and middle-classes). This is evident from the disclaimer that appears at the beginning of the book:

All characters, organisations and incidents in this novel are fictitious. This is a necessary assurance because, though its politicians have taken

EARLY FICTION OF THE 1950s

to calling it a country, Trinidad is a small island, no bigger than Lancashire, with a population somewhat smaller than Nottingham's. In this novel the geography of the island is distorted. Dates are, unavoidably, mentioned; but no actual holder of any office is portrayed. The strike mentioned in Chapter 12 has no basis in fact. (1957: 1978, p. vi)

While the first three lines are directed at the British audience, the next three are directed at his own countrymen. In the preface to *The Adventures of Gurudeva and other stories*, Naipaul recalls how the locals were angry with Seepersad Naipaul for having portrayed the East Indians in this manner. While Seepersad's art had its own moral fulcrum, for V. S. Naipaul, the lesson was that the locals wanted their lives to be sugar-coated. While the British audience expected his fiction to reflect West Indian realities, the locals expected a romantic treatment. Thus, for the British audiences, the older narrator is the native informant, while for the local audiences, he is the insider-outsider who knows his society but is equally aware of how to reproduce the difference for the British audiences.

The West Indies had been written about earlier, but not necessarily from a 'native' point of view. *Robinson Crusoe* is an early example even though Daniel Defoe never visited the island of Tobago. Defoe's island was not populated, and certainly not populated with politically conscious electorates. From within Trinidad, C. L. R. James's *Minty Alley*, Alfred Mendes's *Pitch Lake* and *Black Fauns*, Albert Gomes's *All Papa's Children*, Ralph de Boissiere's *Crown Jewel* and *Rum and Coca Cola* and Seepersad Naipaul's *Gurudeva and other Indian Tales* had previously been published. Naipaul must have been aware of these literary works and many more due to his personal exposure and his stint as the editor of the *Caribbean Voices* programme (from 1954 to 1956), but he chose an attitude of feigned ignorance merely to confirm to his British readers his ostensible orientalist outlook towards his place of birth.

A middle-class reader from the Caribbean had as many expectations from the book as a middle-class reader in England. But their responses were vastly different. While middle-class readers within the Caribbean saw the book as reflective of their surroundings, British readers saw 'exotic little' 'frauds' struggling with their daily lives as the world moved on. This is where a kind of rhetorical ambivalence came into play, and Naipaul began to play the fool, seemingly making fun of people. Naipaul knew that the book was truly appreciated only by his fellow Trinidadians. The early politicians recognised that the colonial authority was not interested in giving them power but wanted them represented on the boards to serve their own petty interests. The Caribbean audiences saw through the narrative design and enjoyed how the 'hero' of the novel outplayed the British school system and the British electoral system to make significant financial and worldly gains. This was the starting point for Naipaul's building up a persona for himself, inculcating an attitude of nonchalance, a particular 'bent of mind'—a perspective—on the lives of those within his own community. This persona could be reviled and criticised, but the truth of his writing could not be questioned.

Naipaul followed up this book with an equally breezy narrative of the 1950 election in his next published book, *The Suffrage of Elvira*.

The Suffrage of Elvira (1958a)

The Suffrage of Elvira uses a third-person omniscient narrator, but unlike *The Mystic Masseur*, Naipaul does not follow the fortunes of a single protagonist. The key event in the book is the General Elections of 1950, which tests the fortunes of many people in an off-the-map village of Elvira. The opening line sets the tone of the book: 'That afternoon Mr Surujpat Harbans nearly killed the two white women and the black bitch' (*The Suffrage of Elvira* 1958a, p. 7). The protagonist, Surujpat Harbans, is a candidate in the general elections from the fictional Naparoni constituency, which has a total of 8000 eligible voters. Harbans negotiates with the prominent members of each community: Hindus, Afro-Christians, Spanish cocoa-panyols and Muslims. There are 4000 Hindu votes 'controlled' by Chittaranjan, who wants to marry his daughter Nalini or Nelly to Harbans' son, 2000 African votes 'controlled' by Preacher, who is standing as a contender in the election, 1000 Spanish cocoa-panyols' votes who are undecided due to their belief that the world would soon come to an end; and a 1000 Muslim votes led by Baksh who negotiates a van, a loudspeaker and 75 dollars a month to lend his son for the campaign. What starts out as a moderate campaign turns into a huge fair with a free-for-all, with each person contributing to the chaos. Harbans wins the election with 5336 votes.

The book reiterates the mixed culture of Trinidad: 'Things were crazily mixed up in Elvira. Everybody, Hindus, Muslims and Christians owned a Bible, [...] Hindus and Muslims celebrated Christmas and Easter. The Spaniards and some of the Negroes celebrated the Hindu festival of lights [...] Everybody celebrated the Muslim festival of Hosein' (*The Suffrage of Elvira* 1958a, p. 69). When a puppy is discovered in the house, Mrs Baksh, a devout Muslim, devises the Bible and key method to know who got the puppy inside the house. Seepersad Naipaul had referred to this method in the short story 'My Uncle Dalloo,' where Dalloo, a Hindu pundit, used the same method to answer the villagers' questions. Naipaul later referred to the method in *A House for Mr Biswas* when Chinta discovers the theft of 80 dollars at Shorthills (*A House for Mr Biswas* 1961, p. 422).

Yet this intermixed culture is at odds with the ethnically divided election campaigns run by the two main candidates. The islanders fashion their own meaning out of the democratic process: Rampiari's husband connives to get free medicines for himself by prodding Chittaranjan that he would go to the Preacher otherwise; Sebastian takes money from Mahadeo 'as though it was money from the government' (*The Suffrage of Elvira* 1958a, p. 130); and Mahadeo convinces Harbans to sponsor an African's funeral in order to appease the community. Hindus, Muslims, Afro-Christians and Spaniards all make little profits for themselves in the elections, not to mention the printer and the taxi-drivers. Meanwhile, Chittaranjan and Ramlogan speak dismissively in culturally loaded language when they say, 'Negro and Muslim. They is two people who never like to make anything for theyself, and the moment *you* make something, they start begging. And if you ain't give them, they vex [...] As the saying goes, however much you wash a pig, you can't make it a cow' (*The Suffrage of Elvira* 1958a, p. 148). Such attitudes are commonplace in Trinidad. The Hindus and Muslims in Trinidad distrusted each other yet also supported each other to gain ethnic political leverage. They came together to ask for the teaching of Hindi and Urdu and the impartation of religious teachings of Hinduism and Islam in ward schools because they felt threatened by the Christian missionaries who were seeking to convert their children by offering school education. Seepersad Naipaul's writings have plentiful details regarding these issues, and V. S. Naipaul would have had early exposure to such issues while growing up. Hence, it is important to recognise these early influences on Naipaul and how his sociological understanding of racial and religious differences played a large role in developing his perceptions as a writer. The partition of India into India and Pakistan in 1947 made Hindus and Muslims see each other as betrayers of trust. The contemporary generation is more socially conscious, yet the slippages from the rhetoric of ethnically and religiously divisive politics push the younger generation into keeping up the pretence of differences amongst themselves, harming a vision of a unified Trinidad.

Harbans is made to feel that democracy is a monster that has opened up everybody's appetite for money: 'This democracy not going to get up and run away' (*The Suffrage of Elvira* 1958a, p. 151). While Harbans declares, 'Elvira! You is a bitch!' the omniscient narrator declares, 'And so democracy took root in Elvira' (*The Suffrage of Elvira* 1958a, p. 204). The narrator recapitulates in the conclusion: 'So, Harbans won the election and the insurance company lost a jaguar [car]. Chittaranjan lost a son-in-law and Dhaniram lost a daughter-in-law. Elvira lost Lorkhoor and Lorkhoor won a reputation.

34 V. S. NAIPAUL OF TRINIDAD

Elvira lost Mr Cuffy. And Preacher lost his deposit' (*The Suffrage of Elvira* 1958a, p. 240). The pitter-patter rhyme summarises the mood of the book, which is breezy in tone and woven around the single episode of the election. The best part of the democratic process is that there are no expectations from Harbans of having to work in the constituency or for him to even visit Elvira post his election. It is a scathing comment on the alienated colonial authority that may have brought the process of democracy to the backwaters of Trinidad but had not made any adjustments to its dispensation. It is also a highly critical analysis of so-called 'democracy' and the system of 'participatory representation.'

International critics have not really read the book for its true worth. They see it as another condemnation of Trinidadians as fraudsters. They overlook the oblique criticism of the British 'gift' of democracy to its colonies. They also overlook the presentation of race relations within Trinidad between its major races. The omniscient narrator is rather more indulgent than critical about the events. Kenneth Ramchand notes the truth element of the book and the fact that race rivalries have dominated each election ever since independence. Brinsley Samaroo suggests that the fictional constituency of Naparoni may be in central Couva or further down south. It is not known how or when the young Naipaul may have been exposed to this landscape, but it definitely exists in Trinidad with its varied populations.

Miguel Street (1959)

Miguel Street was the third book to be published, though, by Naipaul's own admission, the first to be written (*Finding the Centre*, 1984, p. 25). There are signs that the novella was revised before its final publication. Unlike the child narrator of *The Mystic Masseur*, who was a city boy who went down to Fuente Grove to meet Ganesh, this child narrator is a recent migrant into the city. The child narrator's perceptions in this book are particularly sharpened because of his move from the village of Chaguanas to the city of Port of Spain. The mother had got him from Chaguanas after the death of his father. The story, 'The Enemy' published later in the collection *A Flag on the Island* is a prequel to the character. In that story, the boy considers his mother to be his enemy because she leaves the father and son in the bush in constant fear of the possibility of one of the labourers turning wild and killing them. Upon the death of the father, the mother brings the boy to the city.

Miguel Street is a series of character sketches that depict the lively street life of a young city. The boys are all aspiring to be big adults. The adults are waiting for old age. The old are waiting to die. Many get into trouble with the authorities: Bogart for bigamy, Hat for beating his woman, Popo for

EARLY FICTION OF THE 1950s

stealing furniture, Man-man for harming himself and threatening others and Morgan for arson. Hat is the narrator's much older friend and guide, taking him to watch cricket at the Oval stadium, introducing and commenting upon everybody and running the informal Miguel Club. As the narrator continues to draw portraits, he reveals himself: his mother, his beatings, his studies, his school, his experiences with George, who lets his Alsatian dogs bark menacingly at him, and the poet B. Wordsworth, who invites him to eat mangoes in his yard. The family lives are often disruptive, with the women dominating either too much or too little. George kills his wife with cruelty and violence, while Morgan is unable to fool his wife, who has borne him ten children. The narrator finally leaves Miguel Street because he fears losing himself in alcohol and women.

According to V. S. Naipaul, the sketches were based on the time he spent at 17, Luis Street in Port of Spain. Rhonda Cobham-Sander endorses the truth content of the sketches, identifying: 'Man Man really must have been Mr Asse, whose endless chalked sentences on the pavement of Damien Road we were careful to circumvent when we took the short cut from the Avenue to Roxy Roundabout' (2011, p. 53). Naipaul said that he had written the short story, 'The Raffle' (published later in *A Flag on the Island*) as part of the *Miguel Street* but had taken it out because it was too strong for the book. In that story, the boy was given a goat as part of a raffle drawn by the teacher. The goat is useless because it gives no milk but eats a lot of fodder. The teacher then buys back the goat for double the raffle amount. The next time the teacher does this, the boy's mother sells the goat to a butcher. The teacher gets angry and beats the boy with a soaked leather belt. The book, *Miguel Street*, has no narration of such incidents of personal violence. The book also has a reference to Ganesh Pundit, who arranges for the boy to finally leave the island on a scholarship. Ganesh Pundit is now an MLC and lives in St. Clair and wears a three piece suit, instead of a dhoti and *koortah*. The first three books are thus a trilogy about life in Trinidad and are bound up closely in the mind of the writer as stemming from the same time frame of 1938–53. Cross-references work out very well, though there is no indication that they were written by the same narrator.

The book lends itself to analyses of Naipaul's deep-seated ties with Trinidad of a certain era. The Trinidad in the story is the city of Port of Spain, with its multi-ethnic and multiracial cultures. It also deals with Trinidadians' and Naipaul's fascination with schooling, cricket and calypsos, as expounded in the critical essays by John Thieme (1981), Paula Morgan (2005) and Claire Westall (2005). It depicts a society in transition from being a colonial city to becoming an American base. The life of the urban poor alongside the absurdities of a colonial education (the scripts were sent to Britain to be checked) are highlights of the story. The criticism of colonialism per se is very subtle, almost non-existent, because the boy decides to leave the island armed with this same education, even if his future is uncertain.

A House for Mr Biswas (1961)

A House for Mr Biswas can truly be called Naipaul's magnum opus on Trinidad. It is a veiled story about Naipaul's father's struggles through life. It is the story of a man who is unable to leave the island. Though the book was published in 1961, it is very much a book about Trinidad in the 1930s and 1940s. The narrator, omniscient, factual, precise, yet sympathetic to his protagonist, presents Trinidad through the eyes of Mr Mohun Biswas, who dies when he is only forty-six years old and a father of four children. The book's opening sentence is quite arresting: 'Ten weeks before he died, Mr Mohun Biswas, a journalist of Sikkim Street, St. James, Port of Spain, was sacked' (*A House for Mr Biswas* 1961, p. 7). It tells the reader that the story is about a character who is already dead, that he was a journalist who lived on a street in Port of Spain, that he had been ill for some time, and that he had been sacked from his job before he died.

V. S. Naipaul had tried to inspire his father into writing his autobiography. *A House for Mr Biswas* is a fictional biography of his father, with details taken from Seepersad's writings. The Hanuman House where the Tulsis lived was the Lion House in Chaguanas. Chase village and Sans Souci are real places, while Pagotes, Arwacas, Green Vale and Shorthills are Tunapuna, Chaguanas, Couva and the Northern Range thinly disguised. So are the Luis Street house in Port of Spain and the St. James house that Seepersad bought in 1946. The Shorthills house in Petit Valley Estate was earlier owned by Margaret Mallard, Derek Walcott's wife's family (Akal 2018, p. 110). Besides the houses, Mrs Tulsi, her numerous daughters and two sons, Shekhar and Owad, are based on his maternal grandmother Soogee Capildeo and her family including her two influential and politically powerful sons, Simbhoonath Capildeo and Rudranath Capildeo. While most critics view Naipaul's early novels as non-controversial, these caused enormous storms locally. The book angered the Capildeos of Trinidad who were not happy about how they had been portrayed in the book. The Capildeos were public figures in Trinidad and held important portfolios in the chief East Indian political party and the Sanatan Dharma Maha Sabha, setting up Hindu schools across Trinidad to educate the children of the East Indians. They also fought elections and Simbhoonath Capildeo (Shekhar in *A House for Mr Biswas*) was an elected member of Parliament from 1956 to 1966, while Rudranath Capildeo (Owad in *A House for Mr Biswas*) was the leader of the opposition in Parliament from 1961 to 1963 and the leader of the Democratic Labour Party from

EARLY FICTION OF THE 1950s

1960 to 1969. Rudranath Capildeo telephoned André Deutsch in a fury over the publication of *A House for Mr Biswas* to demand the book's suppression (French 2008, p. 200). The contribution of the Capildeos to Trinidadian politics is well-documented. Their path-breaking vision of establishing Hindu schools for the children of previously indentured labourers in order to cull religious conversion has had a social impact that is visible in the now thriving Hindu community in Trinidad. Whatever their political shortcomings, Seepersad Naipaul relied on them for money in times of crisis and for finding suitable teaching assignments for his educated daughters, Kamla and Sati. They were also relied upon to provide social security for the sons, Vidia and Shiva, in London (*Letters Between a Father and Son* 1999). V. S. Naipaul's mother, Droapatie Naipaul, after the death of her husband, went to work at her brother's quarry in 1959. The emotional dependence of the parents on the Capildeo family was an important aspect of the children's lives, though the girls went on to find better employment in Christian missionary schools and the boys never really stayed at their uncle's house in London. The relations remained tense, with the Naipauls feeling the pinch of being poor relations to a wealthy and influential family.

The book begins with Mr Biswas's birth, when he is pronounced unfortunate and troublesome for his parents. He is inadvertently responsible for his father's death and the dispersion of his poor family among his richer relatives. He is initially trained to become a pundit, but his misadventures in the night lead him to become a sign painter. He gets married and becomes a part of the Tulsi household. Here, he loses his personality as he is coached into compliance, quite unsuccessfully, by Seth and others. However, Biswas hits upon his own revenge when he starts assigning names to members of the largely compliant Tulsi household. He calls Mrs Tulsi 'she-fox' and 'old hen' (*A House for Mr Biswas* 1961, p. 129), but he gets few appreciative listeners. Mr Biswas then moves to Chase Village, where he sets up a shop. Soon he is in a debt and has to 'insuranburn' to get out of it. He then becomes a driver (supervisor) at Green Vale, where he tries to build his first house. The second attempt at building a house is during their Shorthills stay, and the third time, he buys a built house in the St. James area. We are given a glimpse of the relationship between Naipaul's father and mother in the relationship between Shama and Mohun Biswas.

Often, Naipaul has been accused of presenting women as weak sex objects, especially in his later books, *Guerrillas* and *In a Free State*. Unlike those later portrayals, women in these early books are not physically but mentally strong and prepared for the worst. They show steadfastness and adaptability, whether it be Leela in *The Mystic Masseur*, Nelly or Dhaniram's *dulahin* who runs away with Lorkhoor in *The Suffrage of Elvira*, Laura, who has eight children from seven husbands or the boy narrator's mother in *Miguel Street*, Mrs Tulsi or Shama in *A House for Mr Biswas*. In this book, Mrs Tulsi and Shama are both strong women who keep their families together, rising to occasions to keep the family and children cared for. Because this book is written from the perspective of Mr Biswas, Mrs Tulsi is presented as a despotic queen and Shama as a village bumpkin. It surprises Mr Biswas that Shama can run the shop at Chase Village and that she reads his unfinished stories. She conducts herself well with Miss Logie of the Community Welfare Department and makes an impression with her general knowledge of contemporary issues such as 'the new constitution, federation, immigration, India, the future of Hinduism, the education of women' (*A House for Mr Biswas* 1961, p. 504). Much like Ratni in *Gurudeva*, Shama is no feminist fighter, asking for women's rights but does not take blows lying down. She emerges as an anchor in the largely destabilised world of Mohun Biswas.

In a letter dated September 21, 1949, to his sister Kamla, then studying in India, Naipaul wrote, 'Jane Austen appears to be essentially a writer for women; if she had lived in our age she would undoubtedly have been a leading contributor to the women's papers. Her work really bored me [...] The diction is fine, of course. But the work [*Emma*], besides being mere gossip, is slick and professional' (*Letters Between a Father and Son* 1999, p. 4). It is an opinion that he does not change or modify, even as late as 2011, when he publicly voiced the same criticism of Jane Austen. After the publication of Patrick French's biography, Naipaul's public image received a huge bashing because he had confessed to cheating on his wife. The criticism of Austen's sentimentalism triggered a fresh attack on Naipaul for being a misogynist. But this criticism was not new. According to Consuelo Lopez de Villegas, 'Of Naipaul's creative characters none are women; of the women characters none write. Because they lack the power of imagination, none of them recognise individual change as something related to them' (1977–78, p. 605). In *A House for Mr Biswas*, the portrayal of women is balanced, though their lives are projected through a series of negatives: 'not to be unmarried, not to be childless, not to be an undutiful daughter, sister, wife, mother, widow' while the women in his later novels Sandra, Linda and Jane, are treated as 'the greatest evil to man' (1977–78, p. 612). Gillian Dooley examines Naipaul's views as a criticism of the form of the English novel. She notes that while '"Happily ever after" is undercut in Austen,' in Naipaul, 'it is never allowed as a possibility' (2008, p. 15). His bias against women can only be juxtaposed with his portrayal of men, who are rarely physically strong and strong-willed. Moreover, the men lack intellectual depth at an equal, if not worse level. Though these concerns are further written about later in this book, it needs to be clarified that there is a distinct difference between the portrayal of women of East Indian descent in and from Trinidad, and women of other ethnicities as portrayed in his later novels.

The omniscient narrator for the most part of *A House for Mr Biswas* is sympathetically inclined towards Mr Biswas and shifts his sympathies towards Anand in the latter quarter of the book. The character of Mr Biswas is portrayed lovingly and is likeable in spite of all his faults. He is successful in buying a house for his family, declaring a symbolic independence from his mother-in-law's family, but by this time, he has proven himself to be completely dependent upon the same family for his money and health. The scope of this book is restricted to Mr Biswas's limited success in earning an independent livelihood and buying a house. Characters other than the family are few, except for Mr Burnett at the *Trinidad Sentinel* and Miss Logie at the Community Welfare Department. The other characters remain in the background, and the focus is on the individual rather than the social milieu or the race relations that are integral to an understanding of the Caribbean, though the book retains strong doses of plantation culture in the West Indies and of Indian culture as carried on by the indentured in the West Indies.

'A Dancing Dwarf on the Tarmac': How representative is Naipaul's early writing of Trinidad and the Caribbean in general?

Seepersad Naipaul's vision of the 1920s and 1930s Trinidad was complemented by the Trinidad of V. S. Naipaul's growing-up years in the 1930s and 1940s. It is a tribute to his father that many of Naipaul's narrators and protagonists are aspirational writers. The father-son relationship was founded upon literary camaraderie, with each advising the other on their writing. The father and son kept in touch with each other through letters once the young Naipaul had left Trinidad for London. V. S. Naipaul wanted his father to write about his life, while Seepersad encouraged his young son to use his life as an example. Seepersad had also sent several of his stories to Henry Swanzy, who had been editing the BBC *Caribbean Voices* programme. When V. S. Naipaul first met Swanzy in England, Swanzy mistook him for his father. In *Letters between a Father and Son*, we see Seepersad Naipaul imploring his son to look for publishers for his stories. V. S. Naipaul, being the young budding scholar, irresolutely looked for a publisher for his own talent. Seepersad died in 1953, while V. S. Naipaul was at Oxford, with neither fulfilling the dream of being published in England up to that point.

There are a number of continuities between the two writers, as well as some very crucial differences. Both the father and son abhorred Hindu rituals.

However, Seepersad's protagonists complied with the rituals in full faith, as when Gurudeva builds his *kuti* and gives up meat and alcohol to live like a sadhu, while V. S. Naipaul's narrators do not believe but follow the rituals mindlessly. Thus, Mohun may chant 'Rama' during the storm at Greenvale (*A House for Mr Biswas* 1961, p. 289), but the omniscient narrator stands aloof and critical of the superstitious belief in a benign god who will save Mr Biswas. Both Seepersad and V. S. Naipaul refer to people's beliefs in practices such as obeah and idol worship as pure superstitions. Whether it is Uncle Dalloo, Obeah man, Ganesh or other mystics, they are presented as picaroon smart-men using drama and the Hindi language to their advantage. Neither writer presents mysticism as exotic, unknowable, truthful or knowledgeable. It is pure exploitation of simple people's beliefs in spirits.

Seepersad's reformist zeal gave his worldview a Hindu framework within which crises happened and were resolved. The younger Naipaul's early exposure to the overzealous Hindu household of the Capildeos, combined with his father's cynical nose left him with little or no faith. Seepersad's world sets the Hindu world of the East Indians in dynamic tension with an outer persistent Christian one. Though he does not state them fully, he refers to two things obliquely: the ploy of the Presbyterians to convert Hindus through education and the Hindu perception of colonial authority as a hostile force. Hence, Gurudeva stops going to school after his marriage, and Gurudeva's imprisonment does not bring him a bad name. Seepersad spoke about wife-beating with the ostensible purpose of reforming Hindu social systems. V. S. Naipaul, on the other hand, normalised wife beating as a rite of passage in instances such as when Ganesh beats Leela on their wedding night in *The Mystic Masseur* or when Mohun beats Shama in *A House for Mr Biswas*. Also, the colonial authority is never presented as a hostile force in the younger Naipaul's works because his protagonists learn to use colonial institutions for their own good, as when Ganesh becomes an MBE in *The Mystic Masseur* or when the unnamed narrator of *Miguel Street* secures his escape to England. While the Christian missionaries used education as a ploy for conversion, Naipaul's Hindu protagonists use education to escape their destinies on the island. The difference between the older and younger Naipaul is most obvious in the generational divide in *A House for Mr Biswas*: Mohun Biswas self-educates himself in English and becomes a reporter, though he is severely challenged by his talent and his health. Anand has no other option but to win the scholarship and leave the island to make a life for himself.

Gurudeva in Seepersad Naipaul's 'Gurudeva' and Ganesh in V. S. Naipaul's *The Mystic Masseur* follow similar career paths. Initially, they avoid Hindi, preferring to speak Creole and standardised English in their day-to-day lives. However, once they turn towards a Hindu way of life, they acquire proclivity in Hindi to make a more powerful impact upon the Hindus while reciting the religious verses. They also begin to lecture in Hindi and translate their lectures into English for their respective audiences. However, this 'return' to Hindi is compounded by the fact that the primary religious text, the *Ramcharitmanas*, was written in *Awadhi*, a dialect of Hindi written and spoken in Uttar Pradesh and Bihar in India, areas from where the indentured had come. The original *Ramayana* and *Bhagvad Gita* are in Sanskrit, and their recitation involves correct interpretations for the general masses. Thus, the learning of Hindi is interlinked with learning Sanskrit, standardised Hindi of the printed material and *Awadhi* to gain the tag of a pundit. The continuum along which the Caribbean creole developed is inclusive of these other influences in the Caribbean. Naipaul later commented in *An Area of Darkness* that the younger generation had completely lost the Hindustani/ Bhojpuri language, and thus little communication took place between the old and the new generations. The Naipauls were both aware of the trajectory of the disappearance of Hindi (inclusive of *Bhojpuri* and *Brijbasi*) as the predominant language in Indo-Trinidadian homes and its appearance as a 'secret language' to be used only by the elders and/or in the religious sphere.

Kenneth Ramchand, in his 2004 introduction to *The West Indian Novel and its Background*, celebrates the development of a West Indian Standard English in Caribbean writing. He praises Naipaul for using Trinidad creole in his early books but also points out that Naipaul later moved away to standardised universally acceptable English Standard (1970, p. xxiv). Robert Hamner praises Naipaul's use of creole English in these early books: 'The main features of the native language he preserves are the simplified grammar, limited vocabulary [...] and slightly unique but plain syntactical structures with normal spelling. [...] it has the advantage of being readily comprehensible to the metropolitan English reader, and it retains enough of the authentic flavour to convey the lyrical rhythm and effervescent spirit of the vernacular' (1977, p. 215). Contrary to this, Christian Mair argues: 'Sociolinguistically speaking, the distribution of "high" and "low" varieties in *Miguel Street* is the same as in society at large, and the narrator's mastery of the "high" variety, the literary standard, becomes an outward sign of his personal growth—away from the narrow provincial surroundings of his boyhood' (Mair 1989, p. 148). In his final verdict, Mair argues that Naipaul uses creole English only to add 'local colour' and in instances of low comedy, preferring to stay with Standard English in his narrative. Mair's comparative standard was Sam Selvon, who in *A Brighter Sun* used Caribbean Creole in his narrative voice as well. It is another matter that this Caribbean Creole was itself an adaptation of the local Creole dialect and hence creatively employed. Jeremy Poynting, in his doctoral thesis, 'Literature and Cultural

Pluralism,' quotes Dukhedin-Lalla who hypothesises 'the existence of two distinct creoles, one starting from African contact with English, the other from Hindi contact with Afro-creolese and English. Other linguists have, however, rejected the hypothesis' (1985, p. 44). Though many still reject such a hypothesis, there are clear indicators that tonal differences exist between those living in the East-West corridor and those living in central and south Trinidad. As already pointed out, Naipaul used standard English not only for his narrative voice but also to render broken Hindi in these early books.

On the one hand, Naipaul and his father's writings depicted the culture of the Indians as it was evolving in the Caribbean, including a questioning of social practices, such as wife-beating, drinking and empty bravados that were steeped in cultural innuendoes of manhood. On the other hand, the father-son duo presented society as they had found it at a certain time in their lives. Brinsley Samaroo writes that Seepersad Naipaul was a regular contributor to the *East Indian Weekly, The Beacon, The East Indian Advocate, Spectator, Minerva Review* and the *Trinidad Guardian* (2019, p. 61). Seepersad strongly advocated for girl children to be educated, for the government to build a home for destitute Indians, and for the legalisation of cremation for Hindus. Cremation was legalised in the very same year that Seepersad Naipaul died in 1953, and he was cremated rather than buried (2019, p. 67). Hindu marriages were legalised only in 1945. Savi Naipaul Akal recounts, 'They [East Indians] lived in a land where no other ethnic or racial groups spoke their language, where they struggled to master English, where their religions were seen as heathen and where the elite saw schooling as a luxury not to be wasted on "servants"' (2018, p. 15). This may have been true in the 1920s and 1930s but is no longer true in present-day Trinidad.

Critics often underestimate the role played by the Capildeo family in Naipaul's development. When V. S. Naipaul and Kamla were left in the Lion House for long periods of time, they were exposed to Hindu rituals and a Hindu way of life that Seepersad Naipaul, with his reformist bent of mind, would never have been able to provide. *A House for Mr Biswas* depicted, and more importantly, voiced, the social and cultural lives of the Indo-Trinidadians as they lived in the rural backwaters of Trinidad. It also portrayed how families often migrated to Port of Spain and/or converted to Christianity to ensure that their children received a good education. Patrick French's biography gives the following details about Naipaul's maternal grandmother: Soogie Capildeo or Soogie Capildeo Maharaj 'was born and baptized Rosalie Gobin, a Roman Catholic of unspecified caste' (French 2008, p. 23) and maintained a Hindu household very successfully for nearly 50 years after the departure of Naipaul's grandfather to India. The ensuing contradictions show up in the book in instances such as the Tulsis eating salmon on Good Friday and celebrating Christmas. The lives of many Hindus in Trinidad are marked by such contradictions between stated and practiced religion since the Christian missionaries insisted on conversion before or after offering English education. In my opinion, *The Suffrage of Elvira* captures this creolised living space in all its resplendent glamour.

The father-son books are also about the curbed ambitions of a whole generation of Indians who had no means of livelihood besides agriculture. There were few employment opportunities within Trinidad, and young scholarship winners left the island to make careers in the United Kingdom. These four books use material that was available to V. S. Naipaul through his father's writings, though the writing style and the worldview are his own. The Indo-Trinidadians were feeling the pressure of opening up to creolisation, both from within (through conversion to Christianity) and without (inclusion into the creole cultures of other populations). Seepersad Naipaul, in his letters, constantly urged Naipaul to write about the West Indies, the Indians in the West Indies and even about himself because he knew that that was saleable to metropolitan audiences. In *Letters between a Father and Son*, Seepersad told his son to take his life as an example and write about him, especially his habit of seeing people through the lens of their animal-like behaviour. Naipaul not only took his father's advice for *A House for Mr Biswas*, but also reworked Seepersad's short story, 'They named him Mohun' into the narrative. In Seepersad's tale, Bipti gives birth to a child with six fingers on each hand under inauspicious planets at midnight on a Saturday. A pundit is called to read the almanac and foretells that the boy would be a womaniser and a spendthrift. Still, Soomin, Bipti's mother, decides to have a *barahi* (rituals held on the twelfth day from birth) in order to fulfil social obligations, and she invites the whole village except Durga, the father. Durga duly arrives on the day and creates a ruckus about not being invited. Soomin gives him a piece of her mind before the pundit counsels her that a girl is given in marriage and a gift cannot be reclaimed and therefore she must make peace with Durga. A similar scene is re-enacted in *A House for Mr Biswas*, though Naipaul leaves out the terms of the reconciliation between the father and the mother. In his foreword to the 1976 edition of Seepersad's writings, V. S. Naipaul paid a tribute to his father's writing, 'this way of looking, from being my father's, became mine: my father's early stories created my background for me'. Both the father and the son wrote from their hearts, presenting a society that was changing before their very eyes. However, while Seepersad remained a writer connected to his material by his circumstances, by the time the younger Naipaul began writing, he was physically disconnected from this society since he was living in London. This led him to qualify his vision repeatedly.

In *Miguel Street*, he wrote from the point of view of a young man reminiscing about his years spent on the street. In *The Suffrage of Elvira*, the omniscient narrator does not reveal much about himself, but his analysis of democracy is fresh, cynical and optimistic. In *The Mystic Masseur*, the young narrator is in London, reminiscing his earlier meetings with Ganesh Ramsumair. In *A House for Mr Biswas*, the omniscient narrator shifts his commitment from loving Mr Biswas to revealing his deepest fears about himself. In the books, the narrative structures are built as a defence mechanism against revealing the real Naipaul or to reveal only certain aspects of himself. This may have been because he saw too much of his father in his father's writings. It is almost as if Naipaul watched himself write his story. It is similar to the narrators of *The Mystic Masseur* and *Miguel Street*, where the adult narrator (not Naipaul) watches his younger self tell the story of the protagonist in the third person. In *Miguel Street*, as the narrator leaves the island for England, he describes his shadow as a dancing dwarf in the midday heat of the sun. In a rhetorical fashion, Naipaul watches the reader read the narrator's self-portrait. The reader is part of the paraphernalia that Naipaul builds as an aura around his book. This is an important aspect of Naipaul's myth-making ability about himself and his writing. The slippage from his writing to his personality is a deliberate artistic effect of his writing. He projects his personality as aloof and beyond the reach of his readers, while the reader is brought within the ambit of his writing.

Critical Response in Trinidad

Early critics from the Caribbean interpreted Naipaul's portrayal of the East Indian world as a static, decaying world. George Lamming saw Naipaul as unable to 'move beyond a castrated satire.' Gordon Rohlehr interpreted satire as 'a means of running away from the sordid truth, by seeking refuge in laughter, whose basis is an assumption of one's own cultural superiority to the world one ridicules' (1977b, p. 178). He argued that though Naipaul did not vouch for British values, he was 'a Trinidad East Indian' who could not come to terms 'with the Negro-Creole world in Trinidad, or with the East Indian world in Trinidad, or with the greyness of English life, or with life in India itself, where he went in search of his roots' (1977b, p. 179). For Rohlehr, Naipaul's books were 'autobiography set at a distance through irony' (1977b, p. 181). In another essay, 'Character and Rebellion in *A House for Mr Biswas*,' Rohlehr argued that Biswas was allowed to make those jokes which affirmed 'his self- contempt and strengthen[ed] and justif[ied] the stereotype which his masters ha[d] created of him' (1977a, p. 91). A. C. Derrick felt that 'the "sick" and moribund nature of the family's Hindu rites [is] suggested through the portrayal of the religious functionary, Hari, who spends most of his time in the latrine' (Hamner 1977, p. 202). Selwyn Cudjoe read the book as inspired by the classic *Ramayana*, with the protagonist, Mr Biswas, being presented as Ram. Since Cudjoe read the sacred Hindu text of the *Ramayana* as essentially being about displacement (Ram was banished for 14 years by his father), he related the book to Mr Biswas's journey across Trinidad, as 'the author invert[ed] and distort[ed] the *Ramayana* to express his new historical reality' (1988, p. 64). John Thieme read *A House for Mr Biswas* as 'a fable in which the hero is ultimately a qualified success in Hindu terms' (1983, p. 70). Instead, Jeremy Poynting argued that the book portrayed the Biswas family as a 'creole stereotype of the Indian family' that was composed of 'an arranged marriage, authoritarian wife-beating husbands and economic ties rather than mutual affection' (1985, p. 41). The latter two critics lived in the Caribbean for brief spells of their adult lives.

More recent critics in the Caribbean no longer read Mr Biswas's Hindu world as static, stifling and oppressive but as struggling against changing circumstances on the verge of defining a new identity. J. Vijay Maharaj opposes the view that Naipaul conceptualised Mr Biswas as a tragic figure caught within a Hindu joint family household because she demonstrates that Mr Biswas becomes a success in spite of his Hindu background by placing faith in karma, learning and persistent hard work. Further, she writes that Mr Biswas can be read as easily 'within the European tradition of the picaroon hero, or the Caribbean tradition of Anansi, as he can be read within Hindu traditions' (2011, p. 123). Jennifer Rahim confirms Mr Biswas as a proponent of 'intercultural inheritance' of Naipaul's 'colonial education, the influence of a West Indian folk tradition and, of course the myths of his Hindu ancestral affiliation' (2011b, p. 136). Elsewhere, J. Vijay Maharaj links Mr Biswas's use of creole English to imbibing creole virtues. She reads Mr Biswas as a paragon of creole virtues and highlights aspects of Mr Biswas's interaction with the creole world as an enabling discourse, whether it is through his friendship with Alec, sign painting or writing in the newspapers (2013, p. 84). Cameron Fae Bushnell asserts that *A House for Mr Biswas* rejects standardised English, the language outside home, and Hindi, the language of the Tulsi household, in favour of Creole English, which Mohun Biswas uses in his speech and writing. I have elsewhere read *A House for Mr Biswas* as a postcolonial epic (Misra 2023). Setting up these different traditions as exclusive traditions makes Naipaul a fence sitter; setting them up as cross-cultural influences makes Naipaul a proponent of syncretism. In his own mind, Naipaul was neither the first nor the second, though this takes away nothing from the analyses of either critic as they continue to see Mr Biswas as a representative figure of the new emergent middle class's desire to own a home.

At this stage of his career, Naipaul addressed his primary audience in England. He did not view Caribbean writing as coming of age, and in his writing, he only saw his own success in mastering his past shadows. The 'dancing dwarf' at the end of *Miguel Street* was no doubt Naipaul himself happy to leave the island on the plane to London. In reality, he flew to New York and then boarded a ship to England. From the time that he escaped living on the island to using his past life to explicate his characters in the first four books, Naipaul matures from disapproving to accepting his past. Naipaul's urge to define his success as singular in nature began early and soon turned into a lifelong passion. In a letter to Henry Swanzy dated February 19, 1954, Naipaul wrote, 'In England I am not English, In India I am not Indian [though Naipaul had not visited India yet]. I am chained to the 1000 square miles that is Trinidad; but I will evade that fate yet.' His 'affair' with Trinidad in this sense never ends, though Naipaul never returned to live in Trinidad. By the end of the 1950s, Naipaul had made a name for himself. He was an established writer in England and was married, though his family had not yet met Patricia Hale. In the next decade, Naipaul broke through his dependence on his father's experiences to write about his own. And he was seeking a new turn in life.

Chapter 2

THE INTERLOPER IN TRAVEL WRITING

While Naipaul was in Trinidad in 1959, Eric Williams, soon to be the First Prime Minister of Trinidad and Tobago, invited him for lunch and asked him to write a book on the Caribbean (French 2008, p. 207). Naipaul accepted the offer looking for new material for his writings. In retrospect, Naipaul said that his social experiences in Trinidad had lent the material for his first four books. But he had exhausted his memories and imagination. This was an important juncture in his writing because he realised that England had failed to provide him any solace or comfort while he no longer saw Trinidad as home. He was an oddity in British society; though he tried to enter the society, he felt constantly pushed away as an immigrant. Naipaul felt personally betrayed by the Notting Hill riots of 1958 and the 1962 Immigrants Act and the suggested trip around the Caribbean provided a new way forward. It was a challenge because he had never travelled with a view to write about his experience. He had seen his travel to England as a necessity and not fit for any account. His travel back to Trinidad in 1956 was long overdue since he had not returned on his father's death in 1953. In Naipaul's mind, travelling and travelling for writing were two distinct activities.

Further, travel writing had its own history and tradition within which it operated. Race, gender and class affinities were strongly built into the tradition of English travel writing. In the nineteenth-century, English travellers journeyed through British colonies within a certain secure travel circuit and, in general, wrote in favour of the colonial rule. Fawzia Mustafa and Rob Nixon argue that Naipaul unapologetically wrote as a Victorian traveller. I argue that Naipaul did not have the supporting structures of colonialism in place and thus, could not write as a Victorian traveller. Further, he was deeply aware of this. The nineteenth-century English traveller was an authoritative figure. Most colonial texts presented the colonised as people lacking subjectivity. They were subjects to be written about with a focus on their clothes, looks, manners and low professions. They were things to be gazed at but could not be interacted with because of their lack of language (the onus of learning the language of the traveller lay with the travellee/local). With the empire gone, though of the right gender, Naipaul did not have the security—he did not belong to the right race or class to participate in that kind of travel. He realised that he had to carefully distinguish himself from the Victorian, Edwardian and Georgian travellers who had travelled out from London to the colonies in the tropics.

While Naipaul had used multiple distancing points between the writer and the narrator in his fictional works, now he had to create a 'self' since the traveller always wrote in the first person. This was a challenge because the colonial system had systematically denied the colonised any subject-hood in literature and in the socio-cultural sphere. Naipaul had been part of the represented for far too long to be able to make the sudden flip and write in the first person. He also realised that this travelling persona was an invention as the traveller chose to disclose aspects of the self and the land visited only if they worked in his favour. Though Naipaul's narrative self never talks about his family, acquaintances or relationships, he presents a constructed self that was as true to Naipaul as any self-portrait could be. This publicly acknowledged persona of Naipaul, the travel narrator, was aware of his emotions and intellectual engagement with his material and will be referred to as a distinct personality from Naipaul the writer through the rest of this book. This position or perspective was not something that Naipaul begins with in his non-fiction. It was a position that he arrived at only in hindsight.

In the early novels, Naipaul had claimed an authorial distance and a sympathy with his subjects as aspects of his own self and his community, but now through travel writing, he had the task of differentiating himself from the very men who were his brethren. The genre demanded that he wrote about his fellowmen from the perspective of the coloniser since the British audience— the armchair travellers—expected that far-off lands be written about from their perspective. Travel writing was traditionally written about a 'home' and an away, with clear distinctions between the self and the other, the civilised and the barbaric, the cosmopolitan and the country. Naipaul became a new age traveller because he did not begin from 'home.' Naipaul's dislocation allowed him to write critically about travel to 'home' while traditional travel writing was always directed at travel away from home. This reversal of dichotomy went against the tradition of the English Victorian traveller who travelled from what was known to the unknown, from the familiar to the unfamiliar and from the definitive to the undefined. Travel writing was also said to bring the unfamiliar within the folds of the familiar. However, in this case, the space where the writer came from, wrote from and belonged to remained unfamiliar, unknown and undefined. Thus, instead of producing an exotic subject, Naipaul produced both himself and *an-other* within his writing. It is noteworthy that in his later travel books to the Caribbean, Africa and Asia, Naipaul referred to himself as an East Indian from the West Indies building his narrative authority upon his previous travels.

This chapter looks at the development of a narrative 'I' in Naipaul's travel writings as an extension of his experiments of the narrative structures of his earlier fiction. While it was Eric Williams who asked Naipaul to write about the Caribbean, Naipaul knew that for his book to sell, he had to address a British audience. While, in all probability, Williams thought that he was inviting one of his own to write sympathetically and optimistically about the Caribbean at the time of independence, Naipaul could not write free of his concerns about Trinidad gaining political independence without economic stability and political maturity. Naipaul the narrator can be seen laughing at his fellow men emphasising his intellectual superiority, but he also assesses British rule in the West Indies poorly since colonisation failed to produce a nation state.

The Middle Passage (1962: 1981)

The starting point of all Naipaul's travels, here and later, is England. By choosing to travel to the Caribbean from England, Naipaul set in motion a travel self that could claim absolute difference from his fellow travellers and locals belonging to these Caribbean countries as opposed to one who was returning to Trinidad. Naipaul quotes frequently from his British predecessors to mark his difference. The epigraph from Froude's *The English in the West Indies or the Bow of Ulysses* (1888) states: 'They [the Caribbean islands] were valued only for the wealth which they yielded [...]. They are no people there in the true sense of the word, with a character and purpose of their own' (*The Middle Passage* 1962: 1981, p. 1). The epigraph is followed by a quotation from Froude's opening lines from his text: 'In the carriage with me were several gentlemen; [...] The elders talked of sugar and of bounties, and of the financial ruin of the islands' (*The Middle Passage* 1962: 1981, p. 1). Juxtapose this with Naipaul's opening line: 'There was such a crowd of immigrant-type West Indians on the boat-train platform at Waterloo that I was glad I was travelling first class to the West Indies' (*The Middle Passage* 1962: 1981, p. 1). Naipaul achieves three things with this opening: one, he establishes himself in a certain tradition of English travel writing with the similarity in the opening passages; two, in spite of the similarities, he establishes his difference from earlier travellers because of the changed circumstances when he travels amongst the 'immigrant-type' West Indians rather than 'gentlemen'; and, three, he establishes his difference from other travellers *to* the Caribbean by emphasising not only his class (he travels First class) and race (there are only two East Indians on the ship), but also due to his status as a writer.

Thus, in the opening section of *The Middle Passage*, Naipaul constructs a narrator who establishes his distinctiveness by emphasising his first-class ticket, his reading habits, his eating and drinking tastes, his sense of superiority to his fellow travellers, those on the lower deck and the American students. In other words, he constructs himself as superior to all other Trinidadians and Caribbean people on the ship. Fawzia Mustafa, Timothy Weiss, Gillian Dooley and William Ghosh do not make a distinction between the first-person narrator and the writer in Naipaul's travel writings. This leads them to be less critical of Naipaul's art and more critical of Naipaul's persona in his non-fictional works.

There was a reason for the disconnect between Naipaul the writer and Naipaul the narrator. Trinidad and Tobago was to be the capital of the West Indies Federation that comprised the ten territories of Antigua and Barbuda, Barbados, Dominica, Grenada, Jamaica, Montserrat, St Kitts-Nevis-Anguilla, Saint Lucia, St Vincent and Trinidad and Tobago. Eric Williams and the People's National Movement (PNM) were part of the winning coalition of the West Indian Federal Labour Party. But ironically, Williams' party lost to the East Indian dominated Democratic Liberal Party (DLP) within Trinidad (Mahabir 1975, p. 106). Of the ten seats in Trinidad, Eric Williams-led PNM won only four of the seats. The other six seats were won by DLP led by Bhadse Sagan Maharaj. Eric Williams was so angry that he abused the Indian community and called it a 'hostile and recalcitrant minority' (Mahabir 1975, p. 78). With the declaration of independence and transfer of power, optimism ran high in Trinidad and Tobago. But Naipaul was disappointed with the racially-charged election campaigns which he watched with great interest as the Capildeos contested the elections. Savi Naipaul Akal recounts that the political situation was volatile: 'In 1961, during a blistering election campaign, Rudranath witnessed mob behaviour on several occasions. There were PNM-inspired gangs called Morabuntas, tyre-slashings, open fights and snakes let loose at public meetings. PNM supporters not infrequently upset and looted Indian vendors' stalls, and some of the vendors tried, largely in vain, to retaliate. The police seemed indifferent to injustice if the victim was Indian' (2018, pp. 140–1). Further, she writes that Rudranath Capildeo called on the Indians to arm themselves with cutlasses and break-up PNM meetings. Naipaul was already disheartened with the Race riots of 1958 in Notting Hill in England. The campaign for the Commonwealth Immigration Act against the migration of people from South Asia and the Caribbean to Britain, was supported by groups such as the National Front, the British League, the National Socialist Movement, the Newcastle Democratic Movement, the Birmingham Immigration Control Association and the New Liberals (Richmond 1982, p. 130). Personally, Naipaul was looking for a governmental assignment, perhaps a diplomatic post with the newly formed Government of Trinidad and Tobago (French 2008, p. 206). Instead he was offered a scholarship to come and write about the islands. Hence, his mood did not match the optimism of independence since he had already been disheartened by race violence in Trinidad and the race riots in England.

Exploiting the gap between the narrator and the writer to the writer's advantage in *The Middle Passage*, the narrator writes, 'We were in the West Indies. Black had a precise meaning: I was among people who had a nice eye for shades of black' (*The Middle Passage* 1962: 1981, p. 5). The writer allows the reader, whether in England or in the West Indies, to understand the narrator's point of view as judicious and knowledgeable. He, then, begins to expound on the flaws of the West Indians: 'West Indians are English-speaking and when confronted with the foreigner display the language arrogance of all English-speaking people' (*The Middle Passage* 1962: 1981, p. 6); 'Like all good West Indians, he was unwilling to hear anything against England' (*The Middle Passage* 1962: 1981, p. 10); 'This studying in England is one of the strange activities of West Indian youth, of well-to-do Indians in particular. It can last until early middle age' (*The Middle Passage* 1962: 1981, p. 11); 'And the West Indian. Knowing only the values of money and race, is lost as soon as he steps out of his own society into one with more complex criteria' (*The Middle Passage* 1962: 1981, p. 13). Constantly, Naipaul the narrator distances himself from his fellow countrymen. Yet ironically, if we fall for his stratagem, he is no different from his fellow countrymen since he is an arrogant racist apologist for the British. It is the beginning of his definition of the mimic man in the tropics. The four quotations are all about the mimicry of British attitudes, looking at England as a mother country though coming from Africa and Asia, and seeking education as a way of life. However, he is also critical of the British when he uses the simile, 'the language arrogance of all English-speaking people.' Further, he is scathingly ironical when he writes, 'For nothing was created in the British West Indies, no civilization as in Spanish America, no great revolution as in Haiti or the American colonies' (*The Middle Passage* 1962: 1981, p. 19). He speaks about the inability of the British authorities to produce anything of worth in the Caribbean. For the British, the colonies were merely plantations to be managed but not invested into through human efforts. Most critics overlook the change in voice in the last quotation analysing it as an instance of the high-handed comments made earlier by Naipaul the narrator. It is clearly an expression of temporary exasperation which is immediately tempered by the next section, which starts 'In the morning I was calmer.'

Rather than being an apologist for the Trinidadians with its multi-racial communities and inflated sense of selves, Naipaul adopted an ironic tone that critiqued the islanders while carefully distancing himself from them. The true irony was that the British audience never forgot that Naipaul was an islander, and therefore, viewed his writing sympathetically as coming from a true local, while the islanders viewed him as a betrayer who put the faults of his society up for scrutiny by the standards of the erstwhile coloniser.

The narrative on Trinidad (Chapter 2 of *The Middle Passage*) begins with the narrator feeling overwhelmed on returning to his birth place. Yet, by the end of this first paragraph, he re-establishes his distance from the natives, 'the steel band used to be regarded as a high manifestation of West Indian Culture, and it was a sound I detested' (*The Middle Passage* 1962: 1981, p. 34). Being a writer and living in England for the last 12 years, Naipaul the writer felt that he was sufficiently insulated from the everyday realities of the islanders. Naipaul the narrator says that while 'the England of 1914 was the England of yesterday; the Trinidad of 1914 belonged to the dark ages' (*The Middle Passage* 1962: 1981, p. 43). He claims to know Trinidad like a local yet is an outsider claiming non-alliance and non-allegiance to his own country because he is a writer. In a much later review of the book, Robert Chee Moone, quotes Yehudi Menuhin saying that the steel drum was the biggest contribution made to the world of music in the twentieth century. Further, 'It has reached symphonic employability as could be seen in its latest usage by one of the world's greatest percussionist Stomu Yamash'ta who is a tympanist with the Kyoto and Osaka Philharmonic Orchestras of Japan' (1982). Trinidadians continued to love the steel pan using Naipaul's book as a springboard to defend their love for it.

Rob Nixon believes that Naipaul travelled for romance rather than to critique his society and modelled himself after the Victorian travellers [Trollope, Kingsley and Froude] because of his education, insecurities and desire to emulate the authorial voice of the Victorians (1992, pp. 50–1). Further, Naipaul writes against his more immediate predecessors, the Georgian travellers [Waugh, Greene, Lawrence and Huxley] who sought to escape a civilization that seemed mechanistic, soulless and adrift (1992, p. 53). Nixon argues for this distinction because he sees Naipaul's 'gesture of articulating his experiences through a Victorian tradition of travel [as] symptomatic of his need to rid himself of the West Indies by ventriloquizing an English identity' (1992, p. 49). Other critics such as Lilian Feder and Tobias Döring do not share Nixon's assessment because they read Trollope, Kingsley, Froude and Naipaul's writings as critical of the colonial mission.

THE INTERLOPER IN TRAVEL WRITING

My own reading of Trollope, Kingsley and Froude reveals that Naipaul read them critically marking their distinctive British concerns that stretched beyond the British isle to the then contemporary Trinidad.

Anthony Trollope's *The West Indies and the Spanish Main* (1859) is almost nostalgic in tone about the time 'when planters were planters and slaves were slaves' (1859, p. 207). His writing displays the superiority of colonial planning in its depiction of Port of Spain: 'The spaces have been prepared for a much larger population than that now existing, so that it is at present straggling, unfilled, and full of gaps' (1859, p. 208). Quite contrarily, Charles Kingsley's *At Last: A Christmas in the West Indies* (1871) sets up the West Indies against its previous literary presentations: 'From childhood I had studied their Natural History, their charts, their Romances, and alas! their Tragedies; and now, at last, I was about to compare books with facts, and judge for myself of the reported wonders of the Earthly Paradise' (1871, p. 3). If the West Indies was a paradise on Earth established by England, then it meant that all unsavoury things had to be kept under wraps. The book is focused almost entirely on Trinidad with a chapter each on the history of the British travellers to the island, the different ethnic populations, flora, fauna and animal life, visits to smaller islands, the high mountains and La Brea, before turning its attention to the social and political life of Trinidad under the British. J. A. Froude's *The English in the West Indies or the Bow of Ulysses* (1888) acknowledges Kingsley and his descriptions, and delves into the political future of Trinidad, converting 'the West Indies of romance and adventure into the West Indies of sugar and legitimate trade' (1888, p. 52). He decides not to go to the Pitch Lake because it affords no new adventure, conscious of his need to present newer aspects of a colony (1888, p. 64): 'We made several similar small expeditions into the settled parts of the neighbourhood, seeing always (whatever else we saw) the boundless happiness of the black race' (1888, p. 70). While Trollope travels in the security of the empire, Kingsley responds to concerns in England about the future of the colonies due to labour shortages, and Froude is superficially concerned with mismanagement of labour in the colonies.

The racial differences among the imported labour are commented upon by the three Victorians albeit with different emphases. Trollope notes the physical differences and dominance of the Africans over the Indians and Chinese labour: 'The negro will never work unless compelled to do so [...] He is as strong as a bull, hardy as a mule, docile as a dog when conscious of a master – a salamander as regards heat. [... The Coolie or Chinaman] must work in his own defence. If he do not, he will gradually cease to have an existence' (1859, pp. 213–4). Trollope uses racial hostility between the ostensibly 'native' populations as an excuse for the continued need to station white troops over the populations as also the commendation of

54 V. S. NAIPAUL OF TRINIDAD

the colonial policies of importing labour into Trinidad at the expense of free slaves. Kingsley depicts a change in inter-racial rivalry between the Negroes and the Indians as the Indians appear to be fighting back:

> No wonder that the two races do not, and it is to be feared never will, amalgamate, that the Coolie, shocked by the unfortunate awkwardness of gesture, and vulgarity of manners of the average Negro, and still more of the Negress, looks on them as savages; while the Negro, in his turn, hates the Coolie as a hard-working interloper, and despises him as a heathen; or that heavy fights between the two races arise now and then, in which the Coolie, in spite of his slender limbs, has generally the advantage over the burly Negro, by dint of his greater courage, and the terrible quickness with which he wields his beloved weapon, the long hardwood quarterstaff. (1871, p. 124)

The British Empire is justified in the name of disciplining the 'native' populations and the goodwill of the colonial mission. Froude further cements inter-racial rivalry between the Africans and the Indians by highlighting the Indians' unwillingness to mingle (1888, p. 65). Though he advocates self-government, he warns that the blacks must be protected from themselves (1888, p. 79). All three writers are concerned only with the British society.

Naipaul's awareness of his difference from the Victorian writers makes him quote them judiciously. When Nixon says that Naipaul ventriloquizes the Victorians, he collapses the differences to make his own point that Naipaul mimics the English travellers. Nixon also fails to report on Naipaul's quotations from Tacitus and Thomas Mann that deal with the colonisation of England, viewing England as a colonised territory as opposed to it being the coloniser. Further, in contrast to the Victorians, Naipaul's particular interest is to show how the so-called 'natives' have internalised the values of the coloniser. Naipaul tasks himself with providing an alternative view to the British by juxtaposing accounts published in the local newspapers, magazines, calypsos and his numerous anecdotal interactions with the locals. Moreover, instead of quoting local material approvingly, he is critical of the race relations between the Afro-Trinidadians and Indo-Trinidadians:

> The Negro has a deep contempt, as has been said, for all that is not white; his values are the values of white imperialism at its most bigoted. The Indian despises the Negro for not being an Indian; he has, in addition, taken over all the white prejudices against the Negro and with the convert's zeal regards as Negro everyone who has any tincture of Negro blood [...] Few non-Indians know much about the Indians,

THE INTERLOPER IN TRAVEL WRITING 55

except that they live in the country, work on the land, are rich, fond of litigation and violence. (*The Middle Passage* 1962: 1981, p. 80)

Further, some would say he was overly critical of the Indian community in Trinidad describing it as: 'A peasant–minded, money–minded community, spiritually static because cut off from its roots, its religion reduced to rites without philosophy, set in a materialist colonial society' (*The Middle Passage* 1962: 1981, p. 82). In popular legends of 1930s Trinidad, Indians were depicted as poor, mean, rural, heathen, aggressive, ethnically exclusive and illiterate (French 2008, p. 13). French also notes that during the time they were indentured, 'wandering more than two miles from your designated estate was a criminal offence punishable by imprisonment' (French 2008, p. 11). This led the East Indian community to be intensely private maintaining their customs while the African community led an increasingly creole life in the city. And therefore Naipaul is perhaps voicing a popular opinion. On the one hand, Naipaul the writer is judging his own community for its worth. On the other hand, Naipaul the narrator is merely repeating a commonly held opinion he comes across in his travels. In either case, Naipaul the writer enjoys his ability to compose judiciously. After all, 'the "smart man" who manages to deceive others cleverly was much admired in Trinidad, as was the hustler in *The Middle Passage* who sold tickets for a fictitious Sam Cooke concert and disappeared' (French 2008, p. 53).

Naipaul the narrator is also critical of the locals for their love of foreign goods. In spite of having the best bananas, papayas and cocoa, Trinidadians love only imported American goods and chocolates. Their ability to access American goods is rivalled only in their pride in being a preferred island destination for immigrants from other Caribbean islands. Immigration was particularly high in the late 1950s because of the talk of the federation. By placing or layering the presentation of Trinidad as a sought–after land, and setting the immigrants' stories in England against stories that ridiculed the Grenadians and small islanders in Trinidad, Naipaul the narrator effectively undercuts the one-sided perceptions of the Victorians. Further, the personal tone of the narrative offsets the authority of the travel writer's voice effectively creating a gap between Naipaul the writer, who was stung by nostalgia and fear on his return 'home,' and, Naipaul the narrator, who is comfortably travelling through places that he knows.

The difference between Naipaul the writer and Naipaul the narrator becomes less pronounced as he travels through societies that are not his own. As he enters British Guiana (now Guyana) where he goes to see (note, not meet) the Amerindians, he becomes aware that the two African policemen appear to be 'exotic' in the locale that is full of Amerindians. The change in perspective is announced and commented upon though

Naipaul does not turn the gaze upon himself. He knows that he too would be appearing exotic to the Amerindians but there is no self-consciousness. He lets the narrative filter out his presence in the foreign locale. The change in perception is emphasised by pointing out international boundaries that cut across natural vegetation; and in matters of local vocabulary: while the word 'negro' was despised in British Guiana, 'the preferred word is "African", which [would] cause deep offence in Trinidad' (*The Middle Passage* 1962: 1981, p. 99). In contemporary world, Indo-Trinidadians, Afro-Trinidadians, Indo-Guyanese and Afro-Guyanese are the acceptable terms of reference.

As Naipaul moves from British Guiana to Surinam (now Suriname), he realises that the colonial markers of identity are changed from England to that of Holland. The language and rule of the Dutch have a different colonial tenor in Surinam. Naipaul finds further differentiations in his visit to the French colony of Martinique. He writes: 'the Martiniquan, who openly calls himself "coloured" because the whole island knows he is only fifteen-sixteenths white, never has to bear [...] Prejudices have been imported wholesale from the *metropole*' (*The Middle Passage* 1962: 1981, pp. 196–7). He notes how Indians remained unaccommodated even in this wide definition. He also notes that the Indians though converted to Catholicism continued to practice Kali puja: 'the Indian remained an outsider [celebrating...] kali puja, which, though Catholic converts, they still practice' (*The Middle Passage* 1962: 1981, p. 205). This leads Naipaul to question both the norms of a mixed identity and the advantages of religious conversions, if any. After all, Christianity and the dictum of liberty, equality and fraternity were brought to the New World with the European civilisation. The acceptance of the Black brother remained a distant dream well into the late twentieth century. Naipaul stayed with this theme of irreverent religious conversion as he travelled to other places including Africa and the Muslim world later on in his career.

The final stop in this book is Jamaica. Naipaul comments upon the popularity of the Rastafari movement that looks upon Ethiopia as the land of return (*The Middle Passage* 1962: 1981, p. 217). The illusion of a return to the land of one's ancestors is obliquely commented upon since Naipaul was himself soon going to India, the land of his ancestors. He exposes the falsity in harbouring dreams of an unconditional happy return because of social and cultural changes in the two locations. This also becomes an abiding interest as Naipaul travels to India and Africa in the 1960s.

Thus, in spite of the differences in colonial authorities, geographical, linguistic and demographic compositions, Naipaul the writer notes the attitude of disdain for one's culture across the Caribbean. John Thieme criticises Naipaul's *The Middle Passage* pointing out Naipaul's choice of various personae to write about his experience in the Caribbean: 'Victorian traveller, enfeebled explorer, novelistic observer, cultural analyst, and, lastly, as purveyor of second-hand information' (1982, p. 149). Thieme comments that certain personae chosen by Naipaul are recognisable voices from Naipaul's novels, so that Naipaul the travel narrator, and Naipaul the novelist, are part of a common artistic concern. Thieme argues that this important link, the sociological basis of the material a writer was writing about, cannot explain away the final failure of Naipaul's book, *The Middle Passage*, 'to produce a genuine answer to the problem of tone' (1982, p. 149). While Thieme sees this as confusion, I read it as Naipaul's unannounced challenge to English literature. Naipaul refused to write about the Caribbean islands as virgin lands to be explored. He recycled many of the themes from his British predecessors—Trinidad's cosmopolitan self-fashioning, the derision for local produce, the presence of many races and their rivalries, the depiction of island culture and calypsos—but infused them with local voices commenting upon the long-term effects of colonisation on the colonised. Naipaul's use of multiple voices in his book signifies his ability to take on multiple standpoints without imposing a 'wholistic' assessment on the Caribbean. This reading goes against those critics such as Elizabeth Jackson who see a unilinear development in Naipaul's oeuvre from being a Trinidadian to being a cosmopolitan writer based in England. She defines cosmopolitanism as 'a flexible approach to identity which more accurately reflects the lived experience of an increasing number of people in a world characterized by mass migration and mobility' (2022, p. 33). She overlooks the earlier global migration of the enslaved and the indentured to non-metropolitan places during colonial times and therefore is unable to see the significance of Naipaul's repeated returns to Trinidad to resuscitate his writing throughout his career. We see Naipaul define himself as a Trinidadian in his travel to India next.

An Area of Darkness (1964a: 1981)

At almost the same time as writing about the Caribbean in *The Middle Passage*, Naipaul was given an offer to journey down to India and write a book about it. Brinsley Samaroo recounts that he once suggested to Naipaul that his grandparents may have come to Trinidad as indentured labourers to escape the tightening noose on the 1857 rebels (Personal Communication, May 23, 2017). Naipaul did not contest it but never wrote about it except for a brief mention in his lecture in the 1975 conference in Trinidad on the East Indians in the Caribbean (1975b). There he mentions that some Indians had gone to Belize to escape British prosecution following the 1857 revolt. This idea has its roots in the descendants' quest to know the reasons behind their parents or grandparents' decision to enrol themselves as indentured labourers and their coming to Trinidad. Many descendants felt that since their forefathers belonged to upper castes and talked about owning land back in India, they might have come due to reasons other than poverty and famine. The problem with verifying this notion about their possible involvement with the 1857 revolt is hard because there are no official records of the indentured having any history. However, according to Brinsley Samaroo, this idea is entirely feasible because: first, there are records to show that planters in the Caribbean and Australia were willing to take on disbanded soldiers as indentured labourers if the colonial administration paid for their transport. Second, there was an increase in the enrolment of the indentured following the mutiny. And third, that the planters forever feared a possible mutiny among the indentured labourers (2012, pp. 71–93). The 1857 mutiny was a multifarious dissipated event that occurred in different parts of India at different points of time over a year. It was reported as a consolidated event in the colonial records and even then, there seemed to be little agreement— while some referred to it as a mutiny, others called it a revolt. Nonetheless, there was an atmosphere of fear since the British were vengeful and gunned down Indians at the merest mention of dissension in the colonies. Moreover, more contingent to our discussion is the fact that the claim to their forefathers being mutineers and indenturing to escape political persecution instilled a sense of patriotism (as against abandoning one's country) and heroism (as opposed to escape) upon the descendants. This narrative does not usually find mention in history books and it does not suit the more dominant narrative that states that Indians were innocent victims who were duped into coming to Trinidad which the Indians called 'Chini-dad' because of its sugar plantations.

In *An Area of Darkness*, Naipaul the narrator constructs himself as an East Indian Trinidadian who is repulsed by the poverty and dirt in India. As he settles into his new travelling oeuvre, Naipaul the writer begins to play with his constructed narrative self. Travelling to India was a new challenge since India was the land of his ancestors. It was also an ancient civilization but had been under foreign rule for over a thousand years, first by the Muslims for nearly 800 years, and then under the British for 200 years. Unlike Trinidad, which was a 'dot on the map of the world,' India was a known and documented civilisation. The Indians are also racially differentiated from the rest of the world. No matter where he went, Naipaul knew that he was racially identified and socially marginalised as an Indian whether he was in Trinidad, England, Africa or America.

Similar to his predicament in writing about the Caribbean, Naipaul felt particularly handicapped in writing about India. While in *The Middle Passage*, Naipaul the writer had felt disadvantaged by the British colonial fantasies about Trinidad, for his India travelogue, he realised that he had to negotiate not only the fantasies of the British writers, but also the fantasies of the Indo-Trinidadians about India as the land of their ancestors, and the contemporary Indian

THE INTERLOPER IN TRAVEL WRITING 59

writers' fantasies about India. Thus, Naipaul set his narrative against a variety of perceptions and depictions about India: the India of poverty from where the indentured labourers had come, the India re-created by those first travellers to the Caribbean, the imperial India of British writers such as E. M. Forster and Rudyard Kipling writing about India of the 1920s, the India in the personal and political writings of Mahatma Gandhi in the 1940s, and the India of contemporary Indian writers in English such as R. K. Narayan writing about India in the early 1930s and 1940s. This was compounded by the fact that the British contended with an ancient civilisation, India, in a certain way in order to colonise it, unlike the Caribbean which they had simply depopulated to create a 'pristine paradise.' As the loosely autobiographical narrator remarks in the later *The Enigma of Arrival*:

> In travelling to India I was travelling to an un–English fantasy, and a fantasy unknown to Indians of India: I was travelling to the peasant India that my grandfathers had sought to recreate in Trinidad, the "India" I had partly grown up in, the India that was like a loose end in my mind, where our past suddenly stopped. (1987, pp. 153–4)

Naipaul's descriptions of Indians defecating in the open which were most widely criticised by the Indians were, in fact, a way of Naipaul establishing his differences from other colonial travellers who always presented India in romantic light.

Naipaul's narrator suggests that when he thought about India, he was thinking of a mythic India that his ancestors and the Indian community in Trinidad had created for themselves. This India was very different from the portrayal of India in English literature and the actual India. Though popularly held opinion was that India was revered as a land of their ancestors, the Indo-Trinidadians shunned India as a land of their possible return. Indo-Trinidadians generally felt that there was disillusionment awaiting those who went back to India. One of the newspaper headlines of Seepersad Naipaul's numerous articles on East Indians in the *Trinidad Guardian* read:

> Repatriated Indians bitter homecoming in India. Disillusion and dismay in their homeland. Friends and relatives become enemies. All beg to be brought back to Trinidad. (Samaroo 2008, p. 13)

Horrific tales of Indians who begged to come back to Trinidad circulated among the Indo-Trinidadian community. Samaroo records how the repatriates wanted to come back to Trinidad even as late as 1955 when the last ship went to deposit the last returnees from Guyana.

60 V. S. NAIPAUL OF TRINIDAD

Even though Naipaul does not remember details, he records that his maternal grandfather had travelled not once but twice to India. Yet, in general, the Indians felt that they were better off in Trinidad than in India. This feeling continues to this day since most people looking for their ancestral families find them living in poor conditions in India. Their Trinidadian sense of achievement is bolstered by such trips. In a letter Naipaul wrote to his sister, Kamla, then studying in India in 1950, he advised her to keep her eyes open because 'the Indians are a thieving lot.' He speculated whether Beverly Nichols was right in characterising India as 'a wretched country, full of pompous mediocrity' or Huxley was right when he said that India was full of 'half-diets that produced ascetics and people who spend all their time in meditation' (*Letters Between a Father and Son* 1999, p. 5). In another letter, Naipaul told Kamla, 'This is the picture I want you to look for– a dead country still running with the momentum of its heyday' (*Letters Between a Father and Son* 1999, p. 9). Naipaul's overriding feeling in this correspondence between Kamla and himself, aged 19 and 18, was that India had lost its prior prestige in the hands of its foreign rulers. Though India should have functioned as a metropole for the Trinidadians, it was not so because both India and Trinidad were colonised by the British. Now actually travelling to India for the first time, at the age of 30, Naipaul was a bundle of nerves since he knew not what to expect.

Unlike *The Middle Passage*, where Naipaul begins from home turf before embarking on journeys to other islands, Naipaul visits his relatives last, almost as an after-thought, because he knows that 'visiting home' adds to the problem of finding the right voice. The travel book on India is divided into three parts: part one dedicated to defining his relationship with India; part two about his holiday in Srinagar, Kashmir; and part three on dismembering his fantasy about India. Most of part one is dedicated to the differences between Trinidad and India, with an emphasis on India not being a home for him. Comparing India with Trinidad, he sees a difference in how the two nations suffered under British rule and how they responded and managed their legacies differently:

> The British empire in the West Indies was old. It was an empire of the sea and apart from a square here and a harbour there it had left few monuments; and because we were in the New World—Trinidad was virtually without a population in 1800—these monuments appeared to belong to our prehistory. By its very age the Empire had ceased to be incongruous. It required some detachment to see that our institutions and our language were the results of empire. (*An Area of Darkness* 1964a: 1981, pp. 201–2)

With the almost complete loss of original language and inherited institutions, cultural and religious conversions, the West Indians came to believe that they

THE INTERLOPER IN TRAVEL WRITING 61

were the true inheritors of the British language and culture. The Indians coming as indentured labourers to the West Indies were allowed to practice their faith. However, disassociated from their land, the Indians reified their rituals. Naipaul shunned Hindu rituals yet maintained that his understanding of Brahmanism gave him a sense of his elitism within the community in Trinidad without understanding the implications of the workings of caste: 'Examining myself, I found only that sense of the difference of people, which I have tried to explain, a vaguer sense of caste, and a horror of the unclean' (*An Area of Darkness* 1964a: 1981, p. 33). Naipaul refers to his superior caste as a marker of his identity both within the Hindu community because caste had no meaning in day-to-day life where all Indians were treated the same, looked the same and did the same work; and in multi-racial Trinidad because it functioned as a way of preserving distinctness in foreign terrain, since within caste hierarchy, the East Indians looked upon the blacks as uncivilised, thus reversing the class hierarchies (Brereton 1979, p. 188). The largely insular East Indian world was never far from the mixed life all around them. Naipaul recognises that he shared more with the 'mixed' culture in Trinidad than with Indians from India:

> The confrontation of different communities, he [Lamming] said, was the fundamental West Indian experience. [...] To me the worlds were juxtaposed and mutually exclusive. [...] It [the exclusive Indo-Trinidadian world] was yielding to not to attack but to a kind of seepage from the other. (*An Area of Darkness* 1964a: 1981, p. 30)

The three part-sentences quoted here define in a single paragraph the movement from a Hindu world to an understanding of a multiracial Trinidad. Naipaul contends that though he writes exclusively about the Indo-Trinidadians, the society is ever changing and the intermixing of food, culture and lifestyles was a process that was inevitably happening though slowly acknowledged.

Naipaul recognises Trinidad, a very particular Trinidad of a certain time and place, as the repository of his origins. He also shows an awareness that his Trinidad had already changed. He builds a distinct persona, a narrating self, that does not mention his reliance and support on companions, friends, acquaintances, interpreters or the state. Naipaul the writer shares with Naipaul the narrator his common ancestry, social and cultural values, his anxieties at the end of colonial empire, his aspirations for success but hides his anxieties about his nation, about his home, his relationship with his wife and his lack of children. Built in this way, he is able to recognise and critique the fact that he was as colonised, and as much a mimic man, as his fellow countrymen.

62 V. S. NAIPAUL OF TRINIDAD

Just as Naipaul analyses English travel writing in *The Middle Passage*, he analyses the form of the nineteenth century English novel in *An Area of Darkness*, but it is a concern that outlasts his own objections. He argues that Indian writers merely imported the form and filtered Indian life through that form. It was ineffective and unrealistic because in Hindu philosophy 'human existence is a dream' (Wheeler 1977, p. 43). The detachment with the here and now implied in such an attitude comes under further scrutiny in his second book on India, *India: A Wounded Civilization*. Later, he analyses his own early novels through this very strict lens and finds them to be flights of fantasy in *A Way in the World*.

While the immediate reaction in India with regards to Naipaul's book was anger, amply exemplified in Nissim Ezekiel's "Naipaul's India and Mine," more contemporary writers are far more forgiving. Farrukh Dhondy concedes that growing up in the recently decolonised India of the 1950s and 1960s, he had unassumingly accepted the rhetoric of nationalism and Naipaul's *An Area of Darkness* woke him from that stupor of the nationalist dream marketed by the party in power. Most critics from the Indian subcontinent read *An Area of Darkness* before they read *A House for Mr Biswas*. Fakrul Alam claimed that this skewed his assessment of Naipaul's writings. He agrees with the criticism offered by Ezekiel (on Naipaul's portrayal of India), Said (on the portrayal of Islam), Walcott (on the portrayal of the Caribbean), and Achebe (on the portrayal of Africa). Alam chooses to like Naipaul's fiction and autobiographical writings rather than his travel writings where he insists that Naipaul presents himself as a 'conservative, fastidious, and truth-telling traveller' which he was not (Alam 2003, p. 195).

Critical Reception in Trinidad

Naipaul is accused of using an ineptly masked racist self in *The Middle Passage*. Rohlehr argues: 'Naipaul's hatred of the steel band and all it indicates is no mere rejection of West Indian culture, but a rejection of the single common ground where Trinidadians of all races meet on a basis of equality' (1977b, p. 187). Rohlehr's nationalist vision where Trinidad is seen as a melting pot of all cultures colours his interpretation. He recognises Naipaul's distinctiveness but laments Naipaul's refusal to integrate into the Afro-creole culture of Trinidad. The steel pan is a unique musical instrument that was created in Trinidad by beating old steel drums. It represents the creative spirit that refused to die in spite of the historical and physical violence of slavery. But Naipaul counters its projection as a national instrument through his personal dislike for its sound.

Gordon Rohlehr in another article, "Intersecting QRC lives" (2007) traces how Eric Williams and C. L. R. James patronised and subsequently distanced

THE INTERLOPER IN TRAVEL WRITING   63

themselves from Naipaul's writing. In 1963, C. L. R. James reviewed *The Mystic Masseur* for the *New Statesman*, praising the book for its "subversive" qualities. Naipaul returned the favour by positively reviewing C. L. R. James's *Beyond a Boundary* for *Encounter* in the same year. James viewed literature as a 'form of social activism' and perhaps was instrumental in asking Williams to offer Naipaul to write a book on the Caribbean. Rohlehr conjectures that perhaps it was Williams who discussed the project with Naipaul familiarising him with the works of Trollope, Kingsley and Froude. Fitzroy Fraser reported that Naipaul got a stipend of $600 a month for his first three months of fellowship (1960, p. 3). The ensuing book, *The Middle Passage*, was a far cry from what James and Williams had expected though there were no public repudiations. Williams applauded Naipaul's scathing criticism of the middle class in his own *History of the People of Trinidad and Tobago* (1964). Even though he also argued that Indian immigration was unnecessary if only the colonial government had chosen to import free (black) West Indian labour instead. He used Naipaul's critique to further his view that the political parties, trade unions and the professionals were a threat to the newly found nation. Further, Williams wrote *British Historians and the West Indies* (1966) in which he discussed the trio of Trollope, Kingsley and Froude. He severely castigated the British travellers for their portrayal of the Afro-Trinidadians. In spite of Charles Kingsley being the Regius Professor of Modern History at Cambridge, he wrote that the Afro-Trinidadians aka 'Negroes' were 'Lucky dogs, who had probably never known, possibly a single animal want which they could not satisfy.' Trollope thought that the abolition of slavery was deplorable, and Froude advocated 'the preservation of the old order of racial inequality' (1966, p. 140). Quoting long passages from their travelogues, Williams reiterated the racial prejudices that prevented the British from seeing the West Indians as real people.

    C. L. R. James vented his anger on Naipaul in his later review of *An Area of Darkness* and *The Middle Passage* titled "The Disorder of Vidia Naipaul" for the *Trinidad Guardian*: 'What Vidia said about the West Indies in *The Middle Passage* was very true. But what he left out was twice as true and four times as important' (qtd. in Rohlehr 2007, p. 216). He viewed *An Area of Darkness* as a failure because it failed to 'knit us in the West Indies to India, knit the West Indian of African descent to the West Indians of East Indian descent, and knit the conflicting elements of his own personality into a more comprehensive and effective whole' (qtd. in Rohlehr 2007, p. 217). James failed to realise that Naipaul's mission was to emphasise the disparateness and separation of East Indians from India rather than rejuvenate old alliances. According to Rohlehr, it was Williams who brought back James to edit the official newspaper of his newly formed party, the PNM, but later there was a fall-out between Williams and James as well because Williams 'viewed himself as a West Indian nationalist and saw James as having forsaken the parochial but tangible issues of the West Indies for what he termed "the absurdities" of world revolution' (Rohlehr 2007, p. 219).

An important aspect of Naipaul's early travel writings was his criticism of the new elite in the ex-colonies who came to dominate the political scene. But instead of attacking them upfront, since in most cases, he was a state guest or relied on state paraphernalia for assistance in his travelling arrangements, he attacked them obliquely through a criticism of investment in national icons, symbols and a false pride in the past. In Trinidad, he was critical of Eric Williams' investment in the steel pan. In India, he was critical of Mahatma Gandhi, the 'Father of the nation,' and his deification. Naipaul highlighted the symbolism of the beggar in the Mahatma's renouncement of clothing. In spite of being educated in the Enlightenment principles of equality, fraternity and freedom, Gandhi's nationalist vision for India was based on the concept of *Ram-Rajya* (the Rule of Ram) with a tokenism for reforming caste divisions. Naipaul found Gandhi's investment in a Hindu India for uniting it against the British troublesome because he saw no merit in investing in a long forgotten past that delinked the present from its more recent past of Muslim domination.

Another significant aspect that has not received much attention in critical circles but is important to understand Naipaul's oeuvre was the dominance of a socialist ideal at the time of the independence in Trinidad and India. Socialism, or parties advocating a strong socialist inclination came to power in Trinidad and India, and in Guyana as incumbent in our discussion here. Naipaul had been the state guest of Cheddi Jagan in his travel to Guyana. The socialists invested a great deal in the development of a welfare state. The top down approach visualised the poor looking up to the state for sustenance, instead of investing in any individual efforts to defeat poverty. Naipaul was ruthless in his criticism of such an approach and/or attitude. This often led critics to label him a right-wing conservative. However, Naipaul was always interested in individual endeavours and came to define himself as a self-made man, to the exclusion of almost everybody else. This almost excessive emphasis on individuality is important because it excludes a reference to his wife, Patricia, as a companion on his travels. In his construct, his confidante is the reader and not his wife and companion. Pat is missing in *The Middle Passage*, and is mentioned only once in *An Area of Darkness* when she faints in an office. The incident is used to highlight the apathy of the clerk who did not offer water himself because it was not his job. The wife was dispensable. However, soon Naipaul was to realise that Pat was not indispensable to his writing.

Chapter 3

MIMICRY AND EXPERIMENTS OF THE 1960s

V. S. Naipaul's travels to Trinidad and India led him to create a narrative 'I' for his race-class-ethnic-gender-time specific experience of travel writing. Due to his travel writing experiments, Naipaul got interested in the point of view technique and the resultant fiction of the 1960s produced a narrative emphasis on the protagonists' limitations in knowing the world. Naipaul had protected his writer self from public scrutiny through the use of boy-*ish* narrators (adults writing from the point of view of their younger selves) in his social comedies of the 1950s. His travel writing of the early 1960s created a narrator who voiced his insecurities and anxieties with reference to an issue or geographical area but also hid his constant need for social and financial support. Naipaul the narrator could be under the critical eye while Naipaul the person retreated from the public space. Naipaul's writings of the 1960s, more generally, are dominated by a schizoid personality as he watches himself construct various narrators who are sometimes only observers, sometimes participants and most times participants and observers to their own drama of life.

Though it is often thought that Naipaul did not write about Trinidad after the first four books, Naipaul, in fact, began to write about Trinidad from his own experiences in the 1960s and the 1970s. The differences are manifold: while the fiction of his 1950s books was based upon his father's transference of material and techniques, he now came to write directly from his own experience. This is not to say that the material used by him for his 1950s writings were not his experience, but to emphasise that those experiences were his while ensconced in his father's care. A second difference is that just as he produced a difference between his narrator and writer personae, he now created the landscape of a fictional Caribbean island, that was like Trinidad yet not exactly so, whether it was as an unnamed island in the short story 'The Nightwatchman's Occurrence Book,' the island in the novella 'A Flag on the Island' or the island of Isabella in *The Mimic Men*. This marks a growth in Naipaul's oeuvre as he felt distanced enough from his raw experiences to write about Trinidad as a fictional landscape (Poynting 1985, p. 775). He was no longer transforming reality into art but artfully crafting a distance between his experience and his writing. Third, while in the first four books of fiction, the protagonists did not have a past or were ashamed of their past, constantly inventing themselves to move ahead in life; in the books of the 1960s, Naipaul's heroes began to live in their own idyllic pasts invented by themselves. For them, the possession of a past became more important than the value of experience in the present while tackling the failure and despondency that accompanies the achievement of simple goals such as 'going to England,' 'getting a degree' and 'marrying a white woman, possibly to produce white children.' While Naipaul wrote about England as a land of opportunity and settlement in the fiction of the 1950s, the 1960s are about his disillusionment with England. Repeatedly, through his short fiction and novels, he presents an England where migrants are not welcome.

Mr Stone and the Knights Companion (1963)

In 'London' (1958b), Naipaul outlines the difficulties in writing about London, or England in general: 'I have met many people but I know them only in official attitudes—the drink, the interview, the meal. I have a few friends. But this gives me only a superficial knowledge of the country and in order to write fiction it is necessary to know so much: we are not all brothers under the skin' (*The Overcrowded Barracoon and Other Articles* 1972, p. 14). Since he was an East Indian from the West Indies and was positively and racially recognised on the streets as an Indian, he remained a fringe element in the elitist literary groups in England. His association with Arthur Calder-Marshall and Hugh and Antonia Fraser began late in his career and their social circles left him feeling like an outsider. Naipaul turned this to his advantage by making himself believe in the ingenuity of his position of being an East Indian from the West Indies and a Britisher without being born British. However, this was not the only difficulty. At the university, he confesses that studying English literature was a mistake because he felt that it took away the magic of reading due to an over-emphasis on available scholarship and structured readings: 'But while knowledge of England has made English writing more truly accessible, it has made participation more difficult' ('Jasmine' 1964b: 1972, p. 28). His hesitancy is evident in a number of short stories that he wrote before writing *Mr Stone and the Knights Companion*. In two short stories, written in 1957 but published later in *A Flag on the Island*, titled 'Greenie and Yellow,' and 'The Perfect Tenants,' the narrator is a young boarder who has recently arrived in England. The short stories are innocuous tales about the narrator's landlady Mrs Cooksey's pet birds and pet boarders. The narrator focuses upon his limited vision because his interaction with his landlady and other boarders is restricted. In both the stories, the narrator is merely watching the changing nature of relationships. The narrator could be of any race or colour since he is needed only as a witness to the surrounding drama. These two short stories can be read as practice writing by Naipaul. He knew that he was a witness to the British life and hardly a participant in their affairs. The short stories highlight his discomfort in writing about the British because he has no access to their minds and he was yet to find the setting that would inspire him to write about them. Yet, having lived in England for over ten years, he experimented with his material in *Mr Stone and the Knights Companion.*

The book focuses on the life of an Englishman who, near his retirement, designs the Knights companion programme to look after the old pensioners in a bid to extend emotional and physical support to the old. It is an England of old people with the heydays of colonial rule behind them. Naipaul wrote this book while on a holiday in Kashmir in India, in a way, putting a physical distance between himself, his location, his emotions and his story's location. The opening lines of the book set its sombre tone: 'It was Thursday, Miss Mellington's afternoon off, and Mr Stone had to let himself in' (1963, p. 5). As opposed to the young hero of the nineteenth-century English novels, Mr Stone is lonely, unexceptional and old. As opposed to Naipaul's own early novels, the protagonist is well-established with a regular job and a house. Yet, none of these aspects make him feel secure about his future.

Naipaul's presentation of England is interesting because he no longer presents England as the epitome of civilisation. England is not the land one aspires to escape to, but rather a morose land of old people which offers no escape. In the book, England is a rather insulated country and the colonies are mentioned only thrice. In the first instance, Margaret brings to Mr Stone's house a tiger skin and a sepia photograph with a man sitting with a rifle over his knees and his boot over a dead tiger while three Indian bearers stand behind in attendance (1963, p. 42). The second reference is when Margaret burns a piece of cake sent by Mr Stone's sister, Grace, mentioning that Indians often make such offerings to the fire (1963, p. 54). The third reference is when Mr Stone notices black men on the streets of London while going out for lunch with Whymper (1963, p. 114). The blink and miss references are in contrast to the elaborate traditions of serving teas (ostensibly from China) and wearing shawls (ostensibly from India). However, the characters never even once refer to the colonies directly. Is this vision of England any different from that of Jane Austen albeit in a different time era (and the pun is intended)? In nineteenth-century fiction, the colonies were presented as places from where money czars suddenly arrived or where undesirable elements of society were sent. Here, the novel symbolically plays out the resistance of contemporary British society to a social and cultural integration of colonial people. On the one hand, Naipaul found himself grateful for his literary success in England. On the other hand, he suspected that he was included in their social circles only as an ingenuity and a curiosity. Perhaps the society lacked an equanimity of approach in accepting people from varied colonial lands.

Like Mohun Biswas, Mr Stone, always Mr Stone, rather than Richard or 'Doggie,' strives for a crowning moment in his life. Unlike Mr Biswas, he is truly rewarded yet remains lonely and cynical of his own success. Hena Maes-Jelinek views Mr Stone as an extension of Mr Biswas with his 'East Indian attitude towards life. Their constant fear in life was chiefly due to their awareness of the insecurity of their position in society' (1968, p. 510). There are many other critics who support this view. For example, Anthony Boxill argues: 'All three men desire escape; Ganesh and Biswas from chaos, Mr Stone from the weight of his ossified order' (1974, p. 22). Harveen Mann writes that *Mr Stone and the Knights Companion* examines 'the middle-class English who, despite aristocratic leadership and an established cultural and historical tradition, are equally adrift as they indulge in their peculiar brand of mimicry—a performance of ritual empty of content' (1986, p. 6). Thieme argues that though the book 'may be read as an allegory about the little man's alienation in the modern world [...] But [...] it has distinctively English ramifications' (1984, p. 503). He is part of a league of critics who see Mr Stone as an extension of Mr Biswas albeit in a more stable environment (Lee 1967; Derrick 1977, Weiss 1992). However, given the different social circumstances of Ganesh and Mr Biswas on the one hand, and Mr Stone on the other, any attempt to see them through a common lens is suspect. It is to universalise at the expense of the local. While Mr Biswas died at the age of 46 when he was the father of four children, we meet the unmarried Mr Stone at the mature age of 57 when he is nearing retirement. Mr Stone's life is given to role-playing with his daily rituals and set patterns, and perhaps, the wild cat creates more drama than any other character in the novel. As soon as Mr Stone and Margaret stop playing the prospective groom and the expectant witty socialite bride, they begin playing husband and wife. The British life or a version of life in England, so infinitely desirable in the colonies, is revealed as a series of unambitious role-playing postures. The easy success of Mr Stone contrasts sharply with the failures of Mr Biswas. The creative genius of Mr Biswas remains unexplored with most of his attempts at writing trailing off after a promising beginning with 'Amazing scenes were witnessed yesterday when [...]' (*A House for Mr Biswas* 1961, p. 211) or 'At the age of thirty-three, when he was already the father of four children [...]' (*A House for Mr Biswas* 1961, p. 344). No such restrictions hamper Mr Stone who marries late in life, is unencumbered by social

MIMICRY AND EXPERIMENTS OF THE 1960s

responsibilities and achieves almost instant success. The British are revealed as too self-conscious and class-conscious to mix with the new mixed society in London. Kenneth Ramchand sums it up in a footnote:

> [The book] is a unique performance; here, a colonial using the language of the colonising country has the confidence in his art to discover and express a universal theme in purely English raw material. (I think *Mr Stone and the Knights Companion* has not been well received in England as *Miguel Street* or *A House for Mr Biswas* because it has gone beyond what is expected of a colonial). (1965, p. 49)

Ramchand hints at the class and racial biases that prevent the British from considering writers from the colonies on an equal footing as their very own. Similarly, consider Naipaul's short story titled 'A Christmas Story' written in 1962, the same year as *Mr Stone and the Knights Companion*, but published later in the collection, *A Flag on the Island*. The story is written in the first-person and the narrator-protagonist is a retired school principal and currently a School Manager of three schools in Trinidad. He is a convert to Christianity from the Hindu fold. At the age of 18, Choonilal became Randolph and took up the job of a teacher in a Presbyterian school. He was happy with his conversion because it allowed him to rise to the ranks of a Principal. However, he realises rather late in his life that he is lonely and just before retirement, he marries the daughter of a school inspector, becomes a father to a son and prolongs his career by becoming a school manager. Since his responsibilities lie heavy on him, he begins to swindle money to the extent that he knows that the new school building will not pass an independent inspection. He is told by many including his wife to go and burn the building before the inspection, a reminder of the 'insuranburn' from *A House for Mr Biswas*. He refuses. A mysterious fire burns the building down on Christmas day, and his reputation and name are saved. Irony operates at many levels since the story is titled 'A Christmas Story.' It is unclear if the writer is being sarcastic about the goodwill and spirit of forgiveness that is to be found in any Christmas story or if he is using the ploy of the Christmas story to hide the guilt of the narrator and his wife.

Compared to Mr Stone, Randolph's life is colourful, palpable and vibrant, not because he is any less morose than Mr Stone but because Randolph's environment makes us see him as a trickster figure. Rather than devising the rather nostalgic scheme of looking after old pensioners, Randolph's greed and desire for a good life knows no bounds. Naipaul's unwillingness to draw on the British setting in *Mr Stone and the Knights Companion* is in sharp contrast to his precise and accurate account of the environment that produces and sustains Randolph. Randolph is a picture of gluttony when his friend Hari passes by.

He writes proudly: 'I was in my Sunday suit of white drill, my prayer book was on the table, my white solar topee on the wall, and I was eating beef with knife and fork' (*A Flag on the Island* 1967a, p. 28). Yet, his smugness takes a backseat when he is invited to a Hindu wedding where he feels left out of the food and festivities. Naipaul draws on the vibrancy of a multicultural and multiracial Trinidad to get his protagonist off the moral hook. In contrast to the dreary uninviting England, Trinidad appears as a meeting ground of many different ethnicities and races.

Naipaul won the Hawthornden Prize for the book, though in hindsight, he acknowledged that the book was rather unsatisfactory. Yet, when an interviewer suggested that the book was unsatisfactory he walked out of the interview. In another interview, this time with Aamer Hussein, Naipaul confessed that the book could have been written better if he had not suppressed the narrator and used the point of view rather than pretending to be an unseen creator (1994, p. 156). The book is important because it documents Naipaul's early view of England as a cold-hearted place. It reflects his own emotions at this time when he was actively looking for a stable employment *anywhere* in the world. The book is also important because critics who thought that the colonial had finally made the transition to mother country were to discover that Naipaul did not make England his home turf though it remained a point of departure for his travels.

A Flag on the Island (1967a)

Naipaul's interest in the point-of-view technique is exemplified in the ten short stories that accompany the long story, 'A Flag on the Island.' The short story, 'The Nightwatchman's Occurrence Book', is a first-person account of writing reports by a newly appointed night watchman at a tourist resort, possibly somewhere in the Caribbean. C. E. Hillyard, the nightwatchman is told by the manager to file a report on the activities taking place in the resort while he is on duty. What begins as a short report regarding 'nothing unusual' turns into a harrowing task. Each night the scope of his duties increases as guests become more and more rowdy. He is at the receiving end cleaning up the vomit of overdrunk guests while being suspected of stealing food and tampering with hotel property. Added to this is the charge of failing to wake up a guest on time. Hillyard provides a detailed description absolving himself of all charges. Towards the end, the reader realises that the manager is using him to pry on his guests. It is only when the manager is beaten up by Mrs Roscoe's husband that the manager is replaced. The following night report is brief to the relief of the manager, the security guard and the reader. The tourist centre is presented as a centre for drinking, thieving, gluttony and debauchery with the guests and the police constantly in and out of the 'closed' bar.

MIMICRY AND EXPERIMENTS OF THE 1960s

Using short sentences, Naipaul displays both his artistry and technique in using two distinct voices clearly marking out their differences. The interchange between the manager and the night watchman carries the weight of their backgrounds, social class, educational attainments and bullying. The significance of this piece of writing for Naipaul can be surmised from the fact that Naipaul chose the label, *The Nightwatchman's Occurrence Book and Other Comic Inventions* (2002a), for a combination book containing the three novellas, *The Suffrage of Elvira, Mr Stone and the Knight's Companion* and *A Flag on the Island*. The comic touches are light-hearted even as the reader perceives the growing anxiety and exasperation of the night watchman. The comic, however, soon turns to sardonic as Naipaul constructs the following narrative through a male American's point of view in 'A Flag on the Island'.

Frank, an American soldier, had once been posted on the American base during the Second World War and now returns for a holiday to the same island in the Caribbean. The then and now double perspective colours the whole narrative. During his earlier stay, Frank had clandestinely sold off items such as uniforms, steel drums, cigarettes, chewing gum, typewriters and even a truck from the American base. On his return, he finds Henry, earlier the whore-house keeper, making plans to run for the city council. Mrs Henry now runs a bar-cum-restaurant, 'The Coconut Grove,' which hosts American visitors from charitable foundations (such as Tippy, Chippy or Bippy) looking for poor beneficiaries (such as Pablo, Sandro or Pedro) ('A Flag on the Island' 1967a, pp. 196–7). When all the old friends, Frank, Selma, Henry and Mr Blackwhite meet, they wish that the expected hurricane would end the world. But the hurricane shifts its course and their hopes for an end or a new beginning are ruined.

The American soldier and the whorehouse keeper both became established characters in the Trinidad carnival after the Second World War. Besides the incorporation of these two characters, the book also explores the fate of a writer, Mr Blackwhite, who is a clear development from B. Wordsworth in *Miguel Street*. Mr Blackwhite had once written a book about lords and ladies in the style of Jane Austen but the manuscript had been rejected by his publisher who had expected him to write about island life. Mr Blackwhite had found it difficult to write about the island and the islanders' lives because it had never been written before in literature. He had then written in patois defending his culture. And that had failed because the publishers found it unreadable. He then went to Cambridge on a scholarship but returned because the university was a 'tedious place' ('A Flag on the Island' 1967a, pp. 188–9). Mr. Black-white or H. J. B. White had finally found success by writing popular books with inter-racial romances. He had found that a romance between a black man and a black woman

72   V. S. NAIPAUL OF TRINIDAD

or about a bad black man as a hero were still not considered publishable. While Mr Blackwhite would like to write about the islanders as real people, the sponsors/ publishers want to see the islanders as poor people requiring not subject hood but financial assistance. Though Naipaul does not make Mr Blackwhite his doppelgänger in this story, Mr Blackwhite's struggles are real. From subject matter to the use of English to the publisher's expectations, Mr Blackwhite faces the same challenges as Naipaul or any other Caribbean writer of that era.

Rhonda Cobham-Sander reflects back on these touristy expectations from Caribbean writing when she writes that even the islanders expected the Caribbean novels to deal with sexual content. She argues that, in spite of the sexual content, the books did break through the usual stereotypes:

> Indians did not just skulk around in exotic, Kiplingesque settings, charming snakes and sleeping on nails. Blacks did not merely cower and croon. Chinamen were not sages whose pigtails always hung behind them. They were teachers, bakers, shoemakers, school-children, cane farmers, laundresses, insurance salesmen and saga boys. Some were enterprising, others lackadaisical, still others downright evil but, at least in Mittelholzer, in a savvy, complex fashion. The whites were not all missionaries or Governor General doing time in the tropics either. Many were bored housewives or struggling clerks, who had never been to the Mother country, and who lived in backwaters like Berbice, British Guiana, or on sugar estates [...]. (2011, p. 52)

Cobham-Sander catalogues the various racial stereotypes in the Caribbean. The books did not disappoint because their appeal lay in the fact that they dramatised racial transgressions. She notes the contributions of writers such as Naipaul to the mix of literature written in and about the Caribbean.

The failure of Mr Blackwhite's manuscripts reflects the failure of Naipaul's manuscript since the manuscript was never made into a film. Naipaul was required to cater to the tastes of an American public who wished to see their American hero having a breezy romance with an island beauty while he was on a mission to save the world. Instead, Naipaul offered a world where Selma set the tone of her relationship with Frank, Henry manipulated Frank into selling items from the American base, and Mr Blackwhite involved him into his struggles as a writer. Naipaul positions Frank as a medium to know the islanders. But those who had commissioned the script, perhaps, found it too weak since the American hero failed to play himself saving the lives of the poor islanders. The stereotypical island life of sea, sand and surfing is totally missing from the storyline. Instead we have an island on the brink of destruction by a hurricane and a hero who has no expertise or desire to save the world (read island).

Naipaul had briefly mentioned the role of the American Base in Trinidad earlier in *Miguel Street, The Mystic Masseur* and *A House for Mr Biswas*. However, he now presents the more lasting effects of that base upon Trinidadian lives. Both in 'A Flag on the Island' and *The Mimic Men*, he explores the base as a centre of activity during the war years. In *Miguel Street*, Hat had taken the boys for a picnic beyond the Base. The yankee dollar had made an entry on *Miguel Street* when George let his house open to the Americans. Edward began to work on the base and acquired American clothes and the habit of chewing gum. Many of the characters found employment on the base itself. In *The Mystic Masseur*, the American Base was mentioned in reference to Ganesh's contemplation of a possible attack by the Nazis. In *A House for Mr Biswas*, the American Base provided the transport when the family lived in Shorthills and needed to transport children to Port of Spain. In *The Middle Passage*, Naipaul attacked the American radio, jingles and the marketing of the calypso as the voice of the Caribbean people. In *An Area of Darkness*, Naipaul's narrator spoke of the time that the American soldiers behaved irresponsibly in Trinidad. In *The Mimic Men* (written around this same time), the American Base provides easy employment to Browne during the war years. Hence, Naipaul assessed the presence of the Americans both in positive and negative terms.

There had been a controversy regarding the continuation of the American Base in Chaguaramas in Trinidad post-Second World War amid talks surrounding the federation and independence of Trinidad. In 1957, the then Chief Minister of Trinidad, Eric Williams, began a campaign to get the Americans out since the British had provided the Americans this land on a 100 years lease without consultations with the locals. The Americans valued the base for its strategic position during the ensuing cold war years, especially because of its proximity to Cuba and the near communist win of Cheddi Jagan in Guyana. The Americans were allowed to stay in return for American economic aid (Mawby 2012). This was a positional shift in the politics of Trinidad as Eric Williams moved away from the communist driven Workers' struggles to establishing a more socialist Trinidad with a fair amount of capitalist ventures. This was one of the reasons of the heartburn between C. L. R. James and Eric Williams. Many of these political and literary issues reappear in Naipaul's much later *A Way in the World*. His novel, *The Mimic Men*, highlights the issues at stake, and it truly reflects the political situation in Trinidad in the 1960s with the talk about nationalisation of natural resources on the one hand and industrial action on the other.

74 V. S. NAIPAUL OF TRINIDAD

The Mimic Men (1967b)

Jeremy Poynting in his doctoral dissertation argues that the book, *The Mimic Men*, is a veiled account of politics in Trinidad:

> The Tamango of the novel is clearly based upon the Daaga of history; Isabella Imperial is closely based on Queen's Royal College and there are looser connections between the Gurudeva episode and such social movements as the Butlerites in Trinidad or the Bedwardite sect in Jamaica; between the fictional Browne and Singh and the real Dr Eric Williams and members of the Mahabir family, between Singh's political exile and those of real Trinidadian politicians such as Albert Gomes or R. R. Capildeo. The race riots which occur in Isabella echo those in British Guiana between 1962-64. (Poynting 1985, pp. 767–77)

Though Poynting lists these parallels, he clarifies that the book is not a 'roman a clef.' He argues that the book is ultimately more important for its commentary on the colonial neurosis than its historicity. It is also important to showcase Naipaul's vision of Trinidad as a multi-cultural and multi-racial society.

As opposed to the previous books narrated by boy narrators, the first-person narration by a middle-aged narrator gives *The Mimic Men* a nostalgic flair: 'When I first came to London [...]' (1967b, p. 7). The protagonist-narrator, Ralph Singh, appears disorientated and dislocated because of events in his recent past. Soon the narrator reveals a lot more details about himself: he was from the tropical Caribbean island of Isabella; he had been a colonial politician; Isabella was a newly independent state; he is now 40 years old; he feels his life is over. The narrative shifts between his life in Isabella and his life in London in two time frames, that is, his past and his present. Slowly a cohesive picture begins to emerge out of the general chaos of his emotions. The book is divided into three parts: when the narrator first came to London, fell in love, married and returned to Isabella; his early childhood and growing up in Isabella; and his political life after Sandra, his wife, leaves him on the island.

Through a series of reflections, the narrator introduces the multi-ethnic diversity of the island through three families: the Deschampsneufs, who were a French creole family traditionally owning the estates, the Brownes, who were descendants of the African slave population, and his own Indian family who had been in indenture previously. The Deschampsneufs were the unannounced white nobility on the island who owned race horses with African names such as Tamango. The Brownes felt that they were the natural inheritors of the island because they had lost their original moorings in the travel across the Atlantic. The narrator's position in the political hierarchy is a little tricky because the Indians had the money but did not have

MIMICRY AND EXPERIMENTS OF THE 1960s

the numbers to win elections. Ralph's inter-racial friendships are limited in scope because there is little family contact between them. Though all the representative figures are 'natives' of the island, they behave differently because they differ in how they claim the island. The image of 'shipwreck' is used repeatedly to emphasise the isolation of one's world within worlds. At the time of independence, the races unite in leadership under Browne, the leader of the folk. Browne becomes the Chief Minister of the dominion while Ralph becomes the voice of inner opposition. The inclusion of the white creoles in government formation is also an important aspect because of their declaration of being locals. However, the self-government turns out to be a disaster with Ralph advocating the nationalisation of sugar estates to protect his own political future. Upon failure, he accepts a free passage to London with 66 pounds of luggage and 50,000 dollars, a fraction of his island fortune but a decent amount, nonetheless. Eighteen months have passed since his arrival in London. The book ends with Ralph finding solace in the idea that he has fulfilled his householder's role and is now a recluse: 'I have been student, householder and man of affairs, recluse' (1967b, p. 300).

The book is an important landmark in the development of Naipaul's oeuvre because it marks his growing up, shedding past influences, and striking out on his own. The book provides a generationally different version of his father's favourite character named Gurudeva. While Seepersad had portrayed Gurudeva as growing up in the countryside and becoming a pundit after his stint in jail, Naipaul portrays Gurudeva as a mature *sanyasi* and leader who sets up his own commune. The trickster happy-go-lucky figure is now a figure who challenges colonial authorities by leading a folk movement.

The book is also a landmark because the book displays Naipaul's conception of writing away from the dominant literary view in the Caribbean. In his review of the first Association for Commonwealth Literature and Language Studies (ACLALS) conference proceedings of 1964, Naipaul insisted that a writer should not be nationalistic or political (Hamner 1977, p. 28). Here we have a novel whose main protagonist is a politician and the novel reflects the contemporary political situation of Trinidad. Yet, Naipaul distances Ralph Singh from his country's political crisis and concentrates upon his personal crisis. The 1960s saw George Lamming, Kamau Brathwaite and Derek Walcott advocating the artists to participate in nation building by writing about their countries. Naipaul refused to toe this line. Gordon Rohlehr analyses this difference in terms of how cricket was presented by C. L. R. James and Naipaul in *Beyond a Boundary* and *The Mimic Men*. According to Rohlehr, James wrote about 'how the rituals and codes of cricket had transformed Britain's Victorian ruling, lower and middle classes, and how they had been part of the moral growth of a new, responsible class in the

West Indies' (2007, p. 217). In an essay, 'Cricket,' first published in *Encounter* in September 1963, Naipaul had analysed the place of cricket in the West Indian imagination and sought a literary camaraderie with C. L. R. James. He had praised the efforts of the West Indian cricket team since the team signified the triumph of the spirit: 'In islands that had known only brutality and proclaimed greed, cricket and its code [gentlemanliness, fair play and teamwork] provided an area of rest, a release for much that was denied by the society: skill, courage, style: the graces, the very things that in a changed world are making the world archaic' (1972, pp. 18–9). He had praised C. L. R. James's *Beyond a Boundary* as 'one of the finest and most finished books to come out of the West Indies' (1972, p. 22). He recognised that both of them spoke the same language and were part of the 'cultural boomeranging from the colonies' (1972, p. 19). Yet, he insisted that the two of them came from different backgrounds: 'He was Negro, Puritan, fearful of lower-class contamination; mine was Hindu, restricted, enclosed' (1972, p. 21). And this provided them two different points of view. As opposed to James's view, Naipaul in *The Mimic Men* presents cricket as 'an "absurd" induction of the sons of the colonised and brainwashed, into the rituals of the imperial ruling class' (Rohlehr 2007, p. 217). Naipaul clearly made a break from the dominant thought of the time. Cricket is criticised as an aspect of the same colonial project to produce mimic men. In a related instance from 1965, Naipaul had brusquely elided a question on the similarities between writers and cricketers in his interview with Derek Walcott (1965, p. 7). Jesse Noel recollects: 'As one who knew him well,—we [Naipaul and Noel] were joint scorers for the QRC First Eleven in 1950, during the Cricket season; he taught me English too, in substitution for an indisposed master—I do respond instinctively to most of his literary touches.' Further, he stated: 'The implications of being a Hindu at a college where the British way of life was stressed, and which was predominantly creole and Christian in flavour, form a subtle ingredient in his work' (1967). Naipaul played cricket for the Queen's Royal College. For him to take the view that cricket did not release but curbed human spirit is extreme. Yet Naipaul was rather insistent that cricket much like other social norms was an imposition and not a gift for expression of the natural spirit of the people.

From this perspective, the book is a serious study of the effects of colonisation on politics and people. On the personal level, men were reduced to role-playing, shifting between already defined roles between the native (read Trinidad) and mother (read British) societies. Ralph being an Indian is 'reduced' to getting a scholarship and going to England to study and marry there. When England offers no stable sources of income, Ralph returns to his island to lead the Indians. The newly de-colonised society reeks of racial animosities that colonisation has bred over 200 years of rule. Ralph becomes a successful land developer and a well-respected politician. Yet, he has to run away once the initial momentum of political independence has been lost. While the public craves for more participatory ownership over natural resources, the ex-colonial masters have little wish to relinquish their control over institutions. The book reflects the election mood in Trinidad in 1966–7 with Dr Eric Williams trying to defend his position while George Weekes led-opposition held rallies. Weekes was supported by C. L. R. James. In March 1965, the sugar workers went on strike. The PNM government passed the Industrial Stabilisation Act and declared the strike illegal. The 1966 elections also saw a bitter war between the various factions of the Democratic Labour Party. This war extended to the Capildeo brothers themselves—Rudranath and Simbhoonath. Eric Williams was able to win the 1966 elections due to a combination of factors including his successful exploitation of a poor opposition.

Naipaul saw the sorry state of affairs in Trinidad with public resentment running high and the opposition failing to pull itself together. He resolved once more that he would have nothing to do with politics. Walcott in his review comments: 'the supposedly hilarious incidents in *The Mimic Men* were sadder than the serious content of the novel, which was the chronicle of decline towards madness and anonymity that all of Naipaul's books record' (1967). From Walcott's point of view, even though the protagonist was a failed politician, he was still a successful writer and therefore not a failure. He did not read the book as a political novel. Trevor Sudama in his rebuttal published in the same newspaper highlighted the sombre mood of the elections in Trinidad reflected in the book and declared Walcott guilty of a political dispute with Naipaul. He asked why emergent societies cannot be criticised by their writers. While Walcott had criticised Naipaul for his aversion to the carnival, Sudama defended Naipaul stating: 'a detached appraisal of this phenomenon [carnival] may well conclude that far from being a supreme, strenuous effort at mass happiness, it is in fact a supreme, strenuous effort at mass mimicry—the admission of a society that it can express itself through mimicry' (1967). The idea that mimicry could be used for self-expression was a much later development in postcolonialism.

By 1968, Naipaul declared that he no longer felt that he knew Trinidad (Rouse 1968). He had been away from Trinidad for 18 years now. By this time in his life, Naipaul had come to believe that he could live exclusively by writing. He saw his greater acceptance in America as a sign that he could move away from colonial politics and its aftermath. This is reflected in his next venture, *The Loss of El Dorado*, which is a history of Trinidad written from a non-colonial and non-nationalist paradigm.

The Loss of El Dorado (1969: 2001)

The Loss of El Dorado is written around the time that Trinidad had achieved its independence from the British and is about two previous transfers of power in Trinidad, one from the Amerindians to the Spanish, the other from the Spanish to the British. The first was precipitated by Sir Walter Raleigh's raid on Trinidad and South America in 1595 and his inexplicable return in 1617. The second was the launch of a British sponsored revolution across the Spanish South American empire in 1801. The historical account ends in 1813, long before the emancipation of slaves and the arrival of Indian indentured labourers on the shores of Trinidad. Naipaul claimed that the book was a history of Trinidad based upon 'documents—originals, copies, prints— [he found] in the British Museum, the Public Record Office, London, and the London Library' (1969: 2001, p. 357). It is divided into three parts: Part I covering the period 1592 to 1618; Part II covering the period from 1633 to 1797; and Part III covering the period from 1797 to 1813. The nature of travel in the seventeenth and eighteenth century ensured that letters/orders were read at least six months after they had been written and dispatched. It also meant that any decision of the King was implemented with a customary delay of anywhere between six months and two years. By 1797, the three revolutions, American (1775–83), French (1789) and Haitian (1791–1804) had left Trinidad confused as a Spanish colony under British administration.

Nana Wilson-Tagoe writes that Trinidad's history between 1633 and 1776 appears in the book as 'the conflict between the colonial simplicities of settler planters and the complex moral drive of metropolitan radicals' (1998, p. 56). Both the practice and abolition of slavery were colonial missions. But the book does not account for the white conquistadors alone. According to Bridget Brereton, Naipaul was convinced that 'the erasure of the past, the failure or refusal to develop well researched and reasonably objective historical narratives were key indices of underdevelopment and intellectual impoverishment for any people, nation or region in the world' (2018, p. 90). Trinidad had never been written about and found very little mention in colonial records. Having identified this as a gap in his own understanding about Trinidad, Naipaul researched the history of it in colonial libraries since Trinidad had no established library of its own. Helen Hayward argues that 'the story it tells adds up to nothing, and goes nowhere. The work describes no momentous achievements, and its account falls into separate parts' (2002, p. 86). Naipaul made the same point when he said that the history of Trinidad was non-existent in Britain because 'nothing was created in the West Indies' (*The Middle Passage* 1962: 1981, p. 19).

The problem with *The Loss of El Dorado* is that it is a history without a nationalist perspective. In his travels to India, Naipaul had discovered a number of monuments, mostly reminders of the earlier colonial and Muslim rule over India. There were no big temples in Northern India, the heartland of the Hindus. This made him realise that the monuments always belonged to the victors and never to the defeated. The Muslim rule in India had systematically destroyed the Hindu temples and palaces leaving the majority of Indians feeling lost. This later became the theme of *India: A Wounded Civilization* (1977). However, in the context of Trinidad, he realised that the Spanish and the British did not commemorate their rule in Trinidad either by building monuments or writing its history. Trinidad's position was peculiar because it did not exist either in the discourse of the victor or the defeated. Trinidad appeared and disappeared in the colonial archives as a point of discovery by self-styled conquistadors, Columbus in 1498, Raleigh in 1595 and Francisco Miranda in 1806. Each discoverer presented Trinidad as El Dorado, the elusive city of gold, that perhaps never existed but whose grand legend was kept alive to serve their own ambitions. In the Foreword to *The Loss of El Dorado*, Naipaul points out that later settlers, the Africans and the Indians, including his own extended family, never displayed any desire to learn or preserve the history of Trinidad: 'All this seemed so settled and complete it was hard to think of Chaguanas being otherwise' (1973, p. 13). The same point is later reiterated in one of the essays, 'Columbus and Crusoe,' published in the collection, *The Overcrowded Barracoon and Other Articles*. Naipaul questioned the iconic positions of Columbus and Crusoe as the typified discoverer and the coloniser in Western and Caribbean histories. By questioning their place, Naipaul wanted to wring Caribbean history free from the shackles of British colonial myth-making. *The Loss of El Dorado* is Naipaul's most sincere attempt at providing Trinidad with a history.

The book had been commissioned by an American publisher, Little, Brown and Company, who rejected the manuscript because Naipaul had turned what was supposed to be a purely historical account, a sort of guidebook on the city of Port of Spain, into a convoluted tale of colonial greed and racial partisanship. The publisher rejected the book because he had 'wanted only a book for tourists' (Atlas 1987, p. 102). The rejection led to a second nervous breakdown and Naipaul's retreat to Wiltshire. Knopf and Deutsch later approved and published it (French 2008, p. 263). Clyde Hosein (1969) in his review of the book for the *Trinidad Guardian* wrote: 'There is a distance felt, no matter how close the names of places are for us; or how dearly the name Port-of-Spain, or for that matter, Raleigh, ring in our consciences of things [...] one would have hoped that his book would have provided us with a far deeper insight into the 200 years between the two separate parts of his book since very much happened between the two periods of great significance to the final turn of events.' The book has found appreciation only amongst academicians in Trinidad and Tobago who recognise it as an essential part of their historical bearings, but not among the local people.

The locals do not consider Raleigh or Miranda as their ancestors nor link them in any way to their heritage. They see themselves as inheritors of the island but not its history. The book's failure to capture local imagination springs from Naipaul's unwillingness to write a nationalist account. The information provided is far too discursive, shifting from one point of view to the next. Rather than viewing colonialisation as a redeeming civilisational intervention, Naipaul saw each colonial intervention as adding to the mix of confusions. The British Governors governed the plantations according to Spanish laws. But this co-mingling of colonial interests is lost not only because of poor record keeping but also because there is little folk memory of Trinidad being the El Dorado. It highlights the many confusions that colonial authorities brought to the islands. The book commemorates the People of First Nation. The Santa Rosa First People's Movement is stronger at the present time and the Trinidad and Tobago's Government announced a one-time holiday on October 13, 2017 to celebrate their contributions to Trinidad and Tobago. It must be remembered that Naipaul wrote the book against the backdrop of the civil rights movement in America when calls were being made to go 'Back to Africa.' Naipaul knew that there could be no going back. He was strengthening his own relationship with Trinidad.

Mimicry and Representation

Naipaul was a pioneer in defining mimicry as a creative response to dealing with the harsh realities of the postcolonial world. If Naipaul was critical of mimicry, he was equally responsive to efforts to break through the cycle of mimicry and mis-representation. By becoming a writer, Naipaul knew that he had broken through the divide that separated the portrayer and the portrayed. The cross-over position between the 'us and them' led him to experiment with genres and subjects as he increasingly positioned himself outside of his protagonists. As Naipaul watched himself create these characters/ protagonists, he also shows awareness that his British readers assessed the previously colonised people as poorly equipped to handle political independence.

Gordon Rohlehr in 'Articulating a Caribbean Aesthetic' says: '"mimicry" in that novel [*The Mimic Men*] is more than simple copying of other people's stuff. It is the result of the attenuation and destruction of will through historical process, the loss of the capacity for choice and the possibility of selfhood and because of these things, the openness of the psyche's shell to every chance, opinion, fashion and style, and the replacement of willed choice by role playing' (1992a, p. 9). This 'role playing' was inevitable on the one hand, and was a result of extreme labour, on the other hand. Naipaul, having worked so hard to get a scholarship to go to London, could not look upon the man in the tropics in an English suit as a poor imitation of colonial lordship. There is a scene in *A House for Mr Biswas* where Mohun Biswas arrives in his Prefect car (1961, p. 511) wearing an English suit. By this simple gesture, Mohun distances himself from the world of agriculture and pronounces himself a city man. There is a similar photograph of Seepersad Naipaul wearing an English suit and standing against his car (French 2008, 170). To a Britisher, this character appears a tragic figure grandiose in his limited success or a comic figure belittling his achievement. To a Trinidadian, he appears both as a figure of achievement and ridicule. He appears as an achiever who has successfully turned his back on his agricultural background and a long history of torture and violence. He also appears ridiculous for standing in boots too big for him. Was the Indo-Saxon or the Afro-Saxon less ridiculous if he wore the suit in the tropics than in London? Was the English suit inextricably linked to a racial and class identity that was denied to the colonised? While in the Caribbean, Ralph was one of the very few 'chosen' scholarship winners; in England, he was part of a large immigrant population that had come there post-World War II. For Naipaul, mimicry was a stage, a rite of passage, through which all must pass in order to become critical of their colonial pasts. Naipaul himself passed through this rite of passage when he fictionalised Trinidad in 'A Flag on the Island' and *The Mimic Men*. While the first four books were organically linked to Trinidad and to Naipaul's father's writings, Naipaul broke from his past in the 1960s.

In 'The Problem of the Problem of Form,' Rohlehr argues: 'There is a clearly discernible link between the early wit of Naipaul's *Miguel Street* which reinforced itself by, and was a comment on the ballad calypso; the grotesque comedy of *A House for Mr Biswas*, and the confessional absurdism of *The Mimic Men*. Each phase represents a movement along a continuum, from a detached, but still participatory perception of the secular/ oral paradigm, towards an increasingly abstract, literary and modernist model' (1992b, 27). He argues that Naipaul brought the Western existential crisis within the ambit of Caribbean subject hood. Looking from the other side, Peter Kalliney argues that the BBC *Caribbean Voices* programme and the Bloomsbury group played a crucial role in providing Caribbean writers such as Naipaul, Selvon, Brathwaite, and Lamming with a literary atmosphere and access to a reading and writing audience and a publishing industry. This literary exchange allowed 'modernist tropes of urban alienation [to be ...] readily adapted to representations of migrants suffering racism, deracination, and poverty' (2007, 96). No matter how we view the Caribbean writers' incorporation of British modernist crisis, Naipaul always remained clear that he felt an outsider to London society.

By writing about Trinidad in the way that he did, Naipaul garnered a lot of local criticism. He looked at this criticism creatively taking it to be a sign of affecting the raw nerves of his readers. Naipaul was convinced that writing should be provocative in order to be effective. Yet, not all his fellow writers in the Caribbean shared this view. Most thought that in the new post-independence era, artists/writers/academics should strive towards nationalist goals. But Naipaul played the fool. He refused to be bogged down by nationalist agendas. He made a reputation for himself as a picaroon, that is, as somebody who could deliberately play the fool. He knew that as long as he could keep replicating his writing success, he would be respected locally in spite of his disparaging remarks regarding Trinidad. This became a habit and he played himself up as the habitual offender.

During the 1960s, he and Pat went to live in East Africa for a year. Pat accompanied Naipaul on all his travels and copied out notes in the libraries. Patrick French points out that Pat kept a diary that recorded her anxieties about not having children. Together Pat and Naipaul built a narrative that Naipaul did not want children because it would impede his travels, his writings, and his creativity. In 1968, they looked for a home in Canada but returned to England with Naipaul deciding that he was to make England a base for his writings (French 2008, 276; Ramchand 2018a, 33). They returned to England in 1971 and went to live in Wiltshire, post his second breakdown. Overall, the 1960s were an exciting but confusing times for the Naipauls. Trinidad's independence, his travels to India, his long stay in East Africa, his growing popularity in America, his consideration of Canada as a possible home and his return to England made it all busy. And, at the end of it, we see a more mature Naipaul emerging from the shadows of his father and his absolute refusal to be overshadowed by any person or agenda.

Chapter 4

DISPLACEMENT ACROSS BORDERS IN THE 1970s

People with causes inevitably turn themselves off intellectually (Naipaul in conversation with Michener 1981, p. 71).

I have divided the 1970s writings into two sections: the first section deals with *In a Free State*, the Black Power Movement, 'Michael X and the Black Power Killings in Trinidad' and *Guerrillas*; the second section deals with the impact of the Black Power Movement on Naipaul's writings with a focus on *The Return of Eva Perón, India: A Wounded Civilization* and *A Bend in the River*. The 1970s saw Naipaul establish himself as an independent writer with a steady income and readership in England and America. The readership in the Caribbean remained steady but small. Political unrest in Trinidad that finally took the shape of the Black Power Movement had many political and cultural ramifications. It had a personal dimension for Naipaul and his relationship with Trinidad. There are clear indications that Naipaul began to feel alienated from the Trinidad he knew as a child.

The 1970s were also undoubtedly the busiest, controversial, yet most rewarding time for V. S. Naipaul. In 1970, the Trinidad government awarded him the Hummingbird Gold Medal. In 1971, Naipaul received the Booker Prize for *In a Free State*. The advent of the new academic disciplines of Commonwealth Literatures and/or New Literatures in English at British universities and other places established Naipaul as a writer of repute. His popularity in academic and intellectual circles led to many book-length studies being written about him. At least six book-length studies, Paul Theroux's *V. S. Naipaul: An Introduction to his Works* (1972), William Walsh's *V. S. Naipaul* (1973), R. K. Morris's *Paradoxes of Order: Some Perspectives on the Fiction of V. S. Naipaul* (1975), Landeg White's *V. S. Naipaul: A Critical Introduction* (1975) and Robert Hamner's *V. S. Naipaul* (1973) and *Critical Perspectives on V. S. Naipaul* (1977) further established his stature within English literature. In 1977, V. S. Naipaul switched publishers, choosing Secker and Warburg with Gillon Aitken as his agent. After all, he was aware that Paul Theroux and even

84   V. S. NAIPAUL OF TRINIDAD

his younger brother, Shiva Naipaul, had received better remunerations for their first books. But he was unhappy with the new publisher for calling him a West Indian writer and returned to Deutsch later.

It is an enigma that, though Naipaul never agreed to be called a regional writer, in popular imagination, his prospects of winning the Nobel Prize remained linked to his birth in the Caribbean. Though the *New York Review of Books* commissioned him to write articles about South American countries and he travelled to yet new territories in this phase of his writing career, the impetus for all his writing remained his involvement with the contemporary political scene in Trinidad. Naipaul visited Trinidad many times during the early 1970s, often on his onward journeys to Argentina and New Zealand. On one of these visits to Trinidad in 1972, he met his father's brother and sister. On another occasion in his travels to Argentina, he met Margaret Murray nee Gooding who was to become his mistress and companion on many of his travels through the 1970s and 1980s. According to Patrick French, Naipaul 'could string her along and mistreat her, with her abject consent' (French 2008, p. 320). Margaret disagrees with such an interpretation of their relationship but has not provided her version yet. After their first few meetings in Argentina, Margaret went to meet Naipaul in Morocco. His relationship with Margaret Gooding caused a permanent rift in his relationship with Pat. In 1973, Pat went away to live in Kensington. In 1975, Margaret accompanied Naipaul to Zaire. In 1978, Naipaul decided to go and live in the United States of America with Margaret, taking up an assignment at Wesleyan (French 2008, p. 389). But midway, he sent Margaret back. Similarly, Naipaul went with Margaret to Iran and Pakistan but sent her home from Kuala Lumpur (Malaysia). In her place, he called Pat to Indonesia to continue with his journey and his writing. Slowly, Naipaul fell into a pattern in his relationships. He would go on travel with Margaret but return to England and stay with Pat while he wrote. This was to continue for the next 20 years.

Naipaul's relationship with Margaret caused disquiet and alarm among Naipaul's friends, Pat's friends and even the Naipaul family in Trinidad. There came a time when Naipaul expected his family to receive Margaret in Trinidad. However, his mother refused to meet Margaret and this led to discord between them (French 2008, p. 380). According to Savi Naipaul Akal, Savi refused to house Naipaul and Margaret because she had young children and it was embarrassing for her to explain to her children the relationship between Uncle Vido and Margaret (Akal 2018, p. 171). Henceforth, Naipaul stayed with his elder sister, Kamla, when visiting Trinidad. Kamla had returned to Trinidad with her children while her husband had stayed back in Jamaica during the race riots in the early 1970s. There might have been other reasons, besides race riots, for Kamla to come back to Trinidad because she never went back. She built a house on land given to her by her mother in the village of Felicity in north-central Trinidad.

The Overcrowded Barracoon and Other Articles (1972)

I break the chronological discussion of Naipaul's book publication history here. This is because I find it easier to discuss Naipaul's discursive essays in conjunction with thematic issues related to his writings in the 1970s in general. In some of the essays in *The Overcrowded Barracoon and Other Articles*, Naipaul assesses and highlights political uncertainty in India and the Caribbean. These pieces are interspersed with a section on England, which describes his position as an outsider and a section on America and the decline of the West. The book has four sections titled 'An Unlikely Colonial,' 'India,' 'Looking Westward' and 'Columbus and Crusoe.' We have already referred to 'Cricket' in relation to *The Mimic Men* and 'Crusoe and Columbus' in relation to *The Loss of El Dorado*; 'Looking Westward' is discussed in relation to *In a Free State*; 'Power' and 'The Overcrowded Barracoon' inform the discussion on the Black Power Movement. The seven essays dealing with India and his essay on Africa are dealt with in relation to *India: A Wounded Civilization* and *A Bend in the River*, respectively. This ensures continuity of thought because Naipaul travelled widely in the 1960s and 1970s.

(i) The Booker Prize and the Black Power Movement

In a Free State (1971)

The book, *In a Free State*, is a collection of three disparate stories about displacement, with a prologue and an epilogue that define the narrator's travels. In the 2011 Picador Preface, Naipaul narrates how Diana Athill, his literary editor at Andre Deutsch, wanted to publish only the third story as a separate publication, but Naipaul insisted that the stories had to be published together and were essentially companion pieces. This book, perhaps Naipaul's most successful, won the Booker Prize silencing those critics and academicians who had been keen to declare him a part-time wonder from the tropics. The Booker Prize was not without its share of controversy. A panel member, Malcolm Muggeridge, had resigned slightly before the announcement, citing the fact that he felt 'nauseated and appalled' at the submissions because the new writers were more experimental than his expectations. He was replaced on the panel. Naipaul's reputation had been so solidly built as a picaroon that Diana Athill was apprehensive that he might actually refuse the Prize. She perhaps did not understand that the Trinidadian 'smart-man' would never refuse the prestige and the prize money of £5000. The Prize is now worth a whopping £50,000. Further, for Naipaul, perhaps a bittersweet connection to the Caribbean made him accept the Prize. The Booker Prize was instituted in 1968 by the Booker Trust. Ironically, the Booker family had made its wealth from the sugar industries in British Guiana. The irony that the recipient of this award was a descendant of the indentured brought to the Caribbean by the sugar estate owners would not have escaped Naipaul.

In the prologue to *In a Free State*, the narrator focuses on his travel across the Mediterranean from Piraeus to Alexandria by ship. He sees a tramp on the ship wearing a pastiche of colours who is constantly bullied by a set of Libyan businessmen. The tramp calls himself a citizen of the world and gets his revenge by locking the businessmen out of their own cabins. The following three stories are loosely linked. The first story is about Santosh, a lower-class servant from India, and his settlement in Washington, D.C. after escaping from his benign Indian employer, his independent stint as a cook and his marriage to a black woman. The second story, 'Tell me who to kill,' is about an unnamed narrator who follows his younger brother from an island in the tropics to England in search of money, success and family but is severely disappointed on all counts. In this tale, Naipaul fell back into using Trinidad locutions (as pointed out by Pat and qtd. in French 2008, p. 287). The third story is about two colonials, Bobby and Linda, who travel from England to Africa in search of the self. Naipaul envisions the characters in personal crises in spite of all their presumptions about the world. This is the first of the many portrayals of Africa that we come across in Naipaul's writings. In an interview with Adrian Rowe-Evans, Naipaul criticises writing that romanticises tribal customs: 'The idea that all the things which have been presented to Africa have somehow been already assimilated and appropriated by Africa, is the most hideous type of conning' (1971, p. 28). In the story, he attacks the assumptions made by Bobby and Linda about themselves, about each other, about Africa and about their place in Africa.

The three stories of travel and displacement have a tone of disappointment in spite of the individual successes of the protagonists. Santosh, at the end of his narration, stands before a mirror contemplating death; the unnamed narrator waits for his death following his disappointments in England, where he is presently in jail for killing; and Bobby and Linda contemplate their bleak future in Africa as Africans fight for their independence. Misra (2017) analyses the book for its use of the mirror as a literary trope. The epilogue is about the narrator's journey to Egypt, where he sees the local boys begging for money from tourists by playing hungry and poor. It is reminiscent of a scene from *The Mimic Men* where tourists on board throw things in the water for local boys to retrieve. The narrator comes to a realisation that there is no pristine vision and every society has had a long history of displacement and violence. Similarly, no story is complete by itself. Each story is borne out of previous experiences and lends itself to newer interpretations by its successors. Thus, Santosh's story has meaning by itself and by what precedes and follows it. Read by itself, Santosh's story is about his disassociation with the land of his birth and with America, where he is always a new entrant and never a member of its society. His fears of pollution do not allow him to completely conform to his new environment. Read in the context of the prologue, Santosh's story highlights how a traveller severs ties to his family, caste, religion and nation only to feel dislocated and homeless even in Washington, D.C., 'the capital of the World.' Read in the context of 'Tell me who to Kill,' Santosh is a stereotypical immigrant who seeks a new life in the centre of the world without realising the ensuing compromises. Read in the context of the whole assembly of stories, Santosh's story is one of adaptation, ingenuity, opportunism, success and disappointment beyond success.

This book became an emblem of Naipaul's interest in writing about the world. Centres of power are shown to be empty shells that promise much but deliver little. In the first of the three stories in *In a Free State*, Washington, D.C., burns in the background with the civil rights movement. In the second story, 'Tell me who to Kill,' London with its racial violence remains hidden in the background. In 'In a Free State,' the whole colonial enterprise hides the violence, inherent in its dispensation in Africa. It comes to the fore only in the final moments, when Bobby is beaten by the rioters. Naipaul highlights the inability of the centre to fulfil its promises of freedom, equality and brotherhood.

It could be said that Naipaul projected his own disenchantment with politics in Trinidad to America, England and Africa in *In a Free State*. His writings began to identify patterns of human behaviour, cycles of violence and the inevitable disenchantment with life and its processes. He weaved together seemingly disparate stories, and anyone who saw the stories as separate entities failed to see the larger picture. The book is an interesting admission of the interconnectedness of the world as borne out of his many travels. Around this time, he definitively began to present himself as someone who saw the larger picture, who saw the connections between places and peoples and who could not be contained or defined by any piece of land or property or nation. This eventually fed into a narrative of the exile and the cosmopolitan that became popular at this time.

Within a similar thematic context, Naipaul presents four articles on different aspects of Western civilisation and its decline in the section titled

'Looking Westward' in *The Overcrowded Barracoon and Other Articles*. 'Looking Westward' is a reference to the shifting of the power centre from England to America. For Mr Mastuda, a Korean immigrant in Japan, the West or America stands for freedom and non-attachment. While the East interprets freedom and non-attachment in metaphysical and religious terms, America interprets them in materialist terms. Naipaul proves that the West does not stand up to these ideals when he mentions in the postscript that three years later, Mr Matsuda works as a lorry driver. Is he really more free? With 'Steinbeck in Monterey,' Naipaul explores the gap between a writer's world and its commemoration by the public. Steinbeck had commemorated Monterey at a certain time but the later generations had commercialised both Monterey and Steinbeck for material gains. Does the writer have control over his meaning? On Norman Mailer's political campaign trail, Naipaul sees compromise writ large as the politician bows down to white supremacist attitudes of his electorate. Is the writer freer than the politician? This theme is further reinforced when Naipaul meets the exiled politician Jacques Soustelle, who doubles up his career as a politician with that of an anthropologist. Soustelle advocates the incorporation of the colony of Algiers into France. Is finance the only problem in integrating cultures? Coming from the small island of Trinidad, where he saw races and communities fight ugly political wars taking refuge in 'purist' visions, Naipaul was equally, if not more disheartened at watching a replay of racial politics in America and elsewhere. Naipaul often described himself as politically neutral, but his disinterest in politics was not due to his lack of interest but due to his cynicism about his personal intervention. It was a slow recognition on his part that if England had failed to hold its centre, America had not grasped it either. America had become the world leader in technology, yet its democracy, peddled as the world's oldest, was racially flawed. Naipaul's thoughts on America and the 'West' are important in the context of his later formulation of the concept of a universal civilisation and his writing in *A Turn in the South*.

Naipaul's disappointment with America ran almost contrary to his increasing popularity in America in the 1970s and 1980s. In the interview with Rowe-Evans, Naipaul said that his writing brings out his truer self, one that looks 'for the seeds of regeneration in a situation' (1971, p. 30). He also said that he was not only different from British writers but also American writers because he was bereft of affiliations: 'I come from a small society; I was aware that I had no influence in the world; I was apart from it' (1971, p. 31). So, he recognised that there were advantages to being from a small society that is only 'a dot on the map' of the world. Yet in the same interview, when Rowe-Evans questions him about his adoption of a metropolitan point of view, he says: 'I can't help thinking that I might have had much greater success, been much better understood as a writer, if I had been born in England' (1971, pp. 32–3). In an interview with Jim Douglas Henry, Naipaul recounted his urge to leave Trinidad, saying: 'I saw myself as leaving the rather empty, barren place where I was born and re-joining the old world' (1971, p. 23). His statement could be interpreted in various ways: by referring to Trinidad as an empty, barren place, he is perhaps mocking his interviewer who takes the writer at his word. The fact that Trinidad was neither empty (home to its many migrated populations) nor barren (production of sugarcane) calls out the West for believing his word about his simple beginnings and hence his greater achievement. By positioning himself as the guileless, innocent immigrant from a former colony which had no institutions, he was only playing himself. The *Trinidad Guardian* played its own role by re-publishing an article from *The Observer* in London, which misrepresented Trinidad and the East Indian community into which Naipaul was born. It stated:

> They were, of course poor, but they were also Brahmins, the highest caste in Hindu society and essentially aristocratic, more so than most of the Maharajas.
>
> His father worked at the *Trinidad Guardian* and also published a collection of short stories.
>
> …His mother, emerged, once her children had grown up, as a forceful business woman.
>
> She now owns and manages a quarry.… ('An Area of Brilliance,' 1971, p. 5)

The critic misrepresented Naipaul as belonging to a secure and influential family, while Naipaul had always emphasised his humble background. It also presented Naipaul as a successful writer, well-settled in his Wiltshire cottage with a loving wife and no children to bother him. Trinidadians would have seen through this misrepresentation of one of their own. Anyway, Naipaul was certainly not at the end of his career, and his life was to see some unprecedented upheavals.

Black Power Movement in Trinidad

The 1970s saw the rise of the Black Power Movement in Trinidad and elsewhere in the Caribbean. On the one hand, the conservative narrative in the United States of America viewed Black Power as a destructive and violent phenomenon that undermined the achievements of civil rights

90 V. S. NAIPAUL OF TRINIDAD

(Quinn 2014, p. 4). On the other hand, according to Walter Rodney, the Guyanese academic and activist, Black Power in the West Indies meant:

- the break from imperialism, which [was] historically white racist;
- the assumption of power by the black masses in the islands;
- the cultural reconstruction of society in the image of the blacks (Quinn 2014, p. 2).

It was the first serious challenge to governance in the post-independence Anglophone Caribbean. The February Revolution or Uprising in Trinidad was led by a coalition of parties and organisations that comprised the National Joint Action Committee (NJAC), the National Union of Freedom Fighters (NUFF), Pivot, Young Power and the United Movement for the Reconstruction of Black Dignity (UMROBI). The February Uprising lasted for 55 days, from February 26, till the declaration of political emergency on April 21, 1970. The coalition of parties organised assemblies to generate public support and organised marches throughout Trinidad under the banner, 'Indians and Africans Unite.' The local conditions indeed warranted that the leaders of the Black Power Movement in Trinidad seek the support of Indo-Trinidadians in their fight against the state. They vented their anger against 'neo-colonial' political leaders like Eric Williams. Geddes Granger, who later took up the name Daaga, was the leader of the Nationalist Forum (NJAC). On March 4, 1970, Granger led a march from Port of Spain to Caroni 'to liberate their minds from domination of the racist capitalist ideology of White Western civilization' (Pantin 1990, p. 58). According to Raoul Pantin, the movement garnered public interest because the local business community was apprehensive about its role in the newly formed state, the government was largely unresponsive, the banks and the clubs were still dominated by the creoles and the carnival was projected as a poor Black festival (1990, p. 37). The marches and demonstrations received such huge public support that Eric Williams imposed an emergency before another march could be held on April 21, 1970. The East Indians were not fully integrated into the Black Power movement and were often the victims of the rioting that occurred. The general view is that, though the Indians in Trinidad sympathised with the movement, they were not convinced that its leaders were fighting for their cause. While most commentators see the Black Power movement in Trinidad as an ethnically Afro-centric affair, some others see it as the coming together of Africans and Indians against the government in place. According to Brinsley Samaroo, the Afro- and Indo-Trinidadians had always come together in all working class movements, such as the 1884 Mohurram Massacre and later, the 1937

Oil and Sugar Workers union strike under Uriah Butler and Adrian Rienzi. It was precisely because the Afro- and Indo-Trinidadians did not unite that Eric Williams, the then Prime Minister of Trinidad and Tobago, was able to put down the revolution with force. According to Raffrique Shah, one of the lieutenants who mutinied against Williams, though the two major ethnic groups had a common background in working-class struggle, they could not come together because of their different cultural- and middle-class aspirations (1988, p. 1). In the newly published Eric Williams' last manuscript, *The Blackest Thing in Slavery was not the Black Man* (2022), Williams belittled the rise of the Black Power movement in the Caribbean to the literary protests inspired by the *négritude* movement in the Francophone Caribbean. He also saw a link between Black violence against the Indians in places such as Uganda, Malaysia and Ceylon and racial violence in Trinidad, Guyana and Suriname. All the latter countries have substantial Indian populations, who are variously seen as nation-builders and/or as unwanted beneficiaries of resources over which the descendants of the enslaved should have the first claim. In Eric Williams' assessment, the Black Power Movement was heavily influenced by the Black Americans since it mimicked 'Afro-hairstyles, dashikis, attacks on the "Establishment" and the "White Power Structure," designation of the police as "fuzz" and "pigs," [and] rejection of "conventional politics"' (2022, p. 217). The movement was finally crushed by the imposition of Emergency and the killing and jailing of the movement's main leaders. Williams described it as 'minimal violence.'

Naipaul was in and out of Trinidad during this time and had a ringside view of the phenomenon that garnered enough public support to propel the government of the day to order a violent crackdown upon the protestors. With political independence, power shifted to local elites, who seemingly continued to perpetuate colonial interests while advocating socialist ideals of equality and freedom. This bred discontent against the popular and democratically elected government. It was further fuelled by the fact that the unemployment rate was particularly high at 30 per cent (Hassan 1986, p. 116). Naipaul had earlier said that a writer should be apolitical and never take sides. Yet he continued to assess political unrest in the Caribbean, Mauritius, Argentina and India in his journalistic pieces. In a piece titled 'Power' (originally written in 1970, later published as part of *The Overcrowded Barracoon and Other Articles* in 1972), Naipaul linked the Black Power Movement in Trinidad to the carnival, which he called the 'original dream of black power' (1972, p. 247). He characterised the Black Power Movement in the United States of America as 'the protest of a disadvantaged minority which has at last begun to feel that some of the rich things of America are accessible, that only self-contempt and discrimination stand in the way' (1972, p. 248).

He contrasted the movement in the United States with the movement in the Caribbean:

> After the sharp analysis of black degradation, the spokesmen for Black Power usually become mystical, vague, and threatening. In the United States this fits the cause of protest, [...]. In the islands it fits the old, apocalyptic mood of the black masses. (1972, p. 248)

Naipaul further argued: 'Black Power as rage, drama and style, as revolutionary jargon, offers something to everybody: to the unemployed, the idealistic, the drop-out, the Communist, the politically frustrated, the anarchist, the angry student returning home from humiliations abroad, the racialist, the old-fashioned black preacher who had for years said at street corners that after Israel it was to be the turn of Africa' (1972, p. 248). Naipaul commented on the futility of such a movement against a Black government in power. He was convinced that the Black Power Movement in Trinidad merely fed off the vocabulary of dissent and dissatisfaction provided by the Black Power Movement in the United States. He refused to recognise the possibility of the coming together of Afro- and Indo-Trinidadians in their struggle for political, social, economic and cultural empowerment. By comparing the movement with the carnival, he belittled the movement, saying that the Caribbean societies 'will continue to be the half-made societies of a dependent people, the Third World's third world' (1972, p. 250).

The piece 'Power' appeared in summarised form in the *Sunday Express*, dated October 11, 1970, under the title 'Vidia Naipaul looks back in Blackness.' The editor invited comments. Earl Lovelace, a writer himself, hit out at Naipaul for his dismal vision (1970). He said that 'Naipaulian attitude of despair' saw the movement as a trap, while he saw it as part of the 'world-wide call for human dignity, rights and freedom:'

> His [Naipaul's] thesis of discouragement and hopelessness is consistent with his own alienation and discouragement which is perhaps the most damaging affliction to come out of that education which disoriented colonised individuals from their selves and indoctrinated them into a culture which fails to accord them true human equality and security in the deepest psychological sense.

Fred Hope (1970) voiced his opinion on somewhat similar lines to Lovelace, saying that 'we must reject any assumption that ours is a perpetual limbo.' The diverse responses of Naipaul and Lovelace to the Black Power Movement characterise their different positions in relation to their writing. Lovelace places his audience in Trinidad, is able to seek and believe in the relevance of the movement for Trinidad, and has a vision for its future. In his version, Naipaul writes for a British audience, has no hopes for politicians in England or the world in general, and offers no comforting vision to his readers.

Naipaul also expresses a similar opinion regarding the Black Power Movement in an article titled 'The Overcrowded Barracoon,' which is on Mauritius. Mauritius was a plantation colony established by the Dutch and, ruled by the French and later, by the British. Mauritius gained independence in 1968 and Naipaul visited it in 1971. Its population was two-thirds Indians, more of a majority than a minority. Naipaul characterised the population as such:

> The large estates, the big commission agents and the sugar factories are white (though there are many Indian landowners and there is an Indian aristocracy of sorts); rural labour is Indian; mulattoes are civil servants; Negroes are artisans, dockworkers and fishermen; Chinese are in trade. (1972, p. 257)

He could have been describing Trinidad. While the empire had engineered the almost empty islands into sugar plantations, travel writers more recently embarked on a plan to portray them as 'lost paradise' (1972, p. 257). Naipaul is at his best when he writes: 'Mauritius is a conservative, wife-beating society and the government doesn't want to offend anybody' (1972, p. 261). The Prime Minister, Sir Seewoosagur Ramgoolam, came from a rural background, educated himself in England, became a doctor and returned to work as a trade union leader before becoming its first prime minister. Justifying his own lack of activism, Naipaul stated that for the majority of the people 'real power is unobtainable; and politics is the opium of the people' (1972, p. 264). Naipaul twists a popular phrase from Karl Marx, who opined that religion was the opium of the masses. Naipaul declares that Mauritius was 'an agricultural colony, created by empire in an empty island and always meant to be part of something larger, now given a thing called independence and set adrift, an abandoned imperial barracoon, incapable of economic or cultural autonomy' (1972, p. 270). Naipaul reiterated similar opinions on British Honduras, St. Kitts and Anguilla in the Caribbean in other articles. In these essays from *The Overcrowded Barracoon and Other Articles*, Naipaul analysed these island states run by pseudo-educated new elite chieftains who valued themselves more than their people. Together, these essays highlight the inability of the new Caribbean leaders to rule their states efficiently and their overt dependence upon the West, in most cases, America, for assistance in marketing their islands as ideal 'sun and sand paradise' destinations.

Naipaul's own working position is unclear because his criticism of those in power equivocates with his recognition that the opposition was poorly organised. In Naipaul's opinion, Black Power slogans were used by the local leaders to scare off political poachers, rather than ordinary white people (1972, p. 260).

In an interview with Ian Hamilton (1971), Naipaul described the American Black Power Movement as 'a bogus sort of television revolution' with little political value elsewhere. He said that the West Indian Blacks were 'people without any representation in the world whatsoever,' neither in England nor in their own countries. Yet his political statements were ambivalent. He said that England's interest in American Black Power Movement was false because they did not look after *their own* Blacks. He denied that the groups received any empowerment linking their own small 'mutinies,' to use Naipaul's own vocabulary, to a larger Black Power movement across the world. He also denied Trinidad its heroes, not recognising Stokely Carmichael in America or Makandal Daaga in Trinidad. Michael X could have provided leadership in England, but he ran back to Trinidad, fearing prosecution in England. Later, he was indicted and prosecuted for deaths on his farm in Trinidad.

In the interview with Adrian Rowe-Evans, while talking about the Black Power movement in Trinidad, Naipaul noted 'revolutions can come about very easily in undeveloped societies' but 'the result of the revolution is nothing' (1971, p. 29). He recounted how in 1836, an ex-slave named Daaga thought he could walk back across the Atlantic Ocean to Africa, which led to a mutiny that was quelled. A 100 years later, the pattern of the messiah who showed the way was repeated and failed. Here he was referring to Uriah Butler and the oil workers' strike in Trinidad in 1937. He put Eric Williams in the same bracket as a messiah promising change, revolution and salvation in the late 1950s. Many indeed saw Eric Williams as 'God.' According to Naipaul, the Black Power Movement in Trinidad was another such promise: 'Black Power is a great mirage, and I fear it will end badly' (Rowe-Evans 1971, p. 30).

In yet another interview, this time with Eric Roach in Trinidad, Naipaul repeated the same thoughts, adding: 'Black Power adherents always talked in vague abstractions. They had no idea of the weakness of the unskilled in the modern worlds' (1972, p. 38). He did not view Trinidad as an under-developed country because 'we have an educated and fairly advanced consumer society' (1972 p. 38). Such contradictions underlie all his writings in this decade. His apathy towards the African and pan-Caribbean causes and his criticism of the Black Power Movement had long-lasting impacts on Naipaul's reputation both in academic and popular circles in the Caribbean.

'Michael X and the Black Power Killings in Trinidad' (1980a: 1981)

Michael X was a poor representative of the Black Power Movement in the Caribbean but was its most popular leader in England. Naipaul's long article was written in the early 1970s but published later, after long legal delays in London in 1980. The article is presented as a journalistic true account of the life of Michael X, alias Michael de Freitas, alias Abdul Malik of Trinidad. In the first part of the book, Naipaul establishes the basic facts of the case. In the second part of the book, he deals with the background of Michael X and in the third part, he deals with the trial of Michael X in Trinidad in the present tense. Naipaul was not in Trinidad during the 1970 February Uprising but came back later to attend the trial of Michael X. In fact, his wife Pat attended most of the trial proceedings while he was visiting Argentina for his work for the *New York Review*.

In 1957, Michael X, then Michael de Freitas of mixed African and Portuguese ancestry, had gone to England at the age of 24. In Notting Hill, he was a pimp, drug pusher and gambling house operator, specialising in slum properties and West Indian tenants. In 1967, he was incarcerated for a year for making an anti-white speech. In 1969, he established a commune in Islington with the help of several white benefactors. He arrived in Trinidad in January 1971, much after the 1970 February Uprising, under the Muslim name of Abdul Malik to establish an 'agricultural commune' and a 'people's store.' Over the course of the next year, there were many cross-cultural visitors to the commune from America and England. Hakim Jamal visited the commune with his girlfriend, a 27-year-old middle-class British divorcee, Gale Ann Benson.

Within a year of his arrival, a series of killings took place: Benson was killed on January 2, 1972; Steve Yeates drowned off Sans Souci on February 13, 1972; Joseph Skerritt was killed, and his grave was discovered following a fire report on February 15, 1972. By the time the graves were discovered, Malik and Jamal were already on the run separately in Guyana and America. Naipaul is critical not only of Malik and Jamal but, more importantly, of the white benefactors and their interests in the Black Power Movement. The so-called black leaders had a cult-like following due to their ability to get white money: 'Malik claimed that he was the best-known black man in the world; and Jamal appeared to agree. Jamal's own claim was that he himself was God. And Gale Benson outdid them both: she believed that Jamal was God' (1980a: 1981, pp. 5–6). Ironically, Naipaul tells us, Michael continued to receive money from white benefactors in spite of the discovery of the graves, his run, his capture, his trial and his hanging: '[…] for Malik and his well-wishers abroad […] Negroes existed only [so] that Malik might be their leader' (1980a: 1981, p. 22).

In the second of the three parts, Naipaul delves into how 'Malik became a Negro' in London: 'He was everybody's Negro, and not too Negroid' (p. 24) of mixed birth. Michael successfully presented himself as a painter, a Negro poet, writer and even a teacher of 'basic English.' He led a flashy lifestyle, travelled in chartered planes, met with the American leaders of the Black Power Movement, Nigel Simmons and Stokely Carmichael, and managed donations from white benefactors. In contrast, Naipaul exposes Michael X as a fraud, who had only two original ideas: 'one was that the West Indian High Commissions in London paid too little to their nationals. The other, more bizarre, was that the uniform of the Trinidad police should be changed' (1980a: 1981, p. 24). Naipaul also criticises Michael X's autobiography, apparently ghostwritten by an Englishman, on two counts: first, Michael's views were racist because he wrote that an Anglo-Saxon was ever suspect of all kindness done by the African and a Jew always looked for ways to make money; second, Naipaul criticised the portrayal of Michael's mother. On the one hand, she was concerned with appearances; on the other hand, she was a 'drunkard, hysterical, quarrelsome, wearing appalling Negro-coloured clothes' (1980a: 1981, p. 27). Naipaul interpolated this information with his own knowledge that 'In Trinidad, [...] she was a stranger with a "red bastard"' (1980a: 1981, p. 28) who poured boiling water on her husband in bed. He uses this information to highlight and deflate Michael X's failed efforts in starting up Racial Adjustment Action Society (RAAS).

Part three of the book brings the reader up-to-date with the activities of Michael X in Trinidad. Naipaul informs us that Michael X recreated Trinidad as an impoverished land where a black leader fleeing political persecution set up an 'agricultural' commune with 'despairing blacks' (1980a: 1981, p. 51). Michael X completely hid the fact that Trinidad was an oil-rich country with a standard of living equalled in South America only by Venezuela and Argentina in the 1970s. By successfully marketing his agricultural commune with his talk of worms, cabbage, silt and aridity, Michael X came back from Canada loaded with a Humber Super Snipe and a Jeep. Patrick Chocolingo of *The Bomb* was the only newspaper editor who gave him space while he was slighted by Raoul Pantin of the more popular *Trinidad Express* (1980a: 1981, p. 52). Chocolingo, too, was soon able to see through the shallowness of Michael X. However, this was all in hindsight. Gale Benson was killed on January 2, 1972. Simmonds returned to England in mid-January. Jamal and Kidogo left for the United States on January 20, 1972. On February 9, 1972, Malik received a notice to vacate his land, and he left for Guyana with his wife and children on February 19, 1972. Benson's grave was discovered on February 24, 1972, and Michael was hanged in May 1975 after a lengthy trial.

The narrator concludes: 'Malik's career proves how much of Black Power—away from its United States source—is jargon, how much a sentimental hoax' (1980a: 1981, p. 74).

By all accounts, Michael X is a poor representative of the Black Power Movement in Trinidad. During this time, the Caribbean saw a large influx of black leaders from the United States of America and the United Kingdom who visited the Caribbean in the hope of gaining more support back home. Naipaul was generally wary of imported vocabulary and imported heroes. He deliberately chose to misjudge the Black Power Movement in Trinidad with Michael X as a representative figure. On the flip side, one has to remember that his primary audience were the British, and it was his aim to expose the triviality and smallness of the so-called 'messiahs' in Britain. The British progressives saw Michael X as somebody who could change the destiny of the 'poor people in the Third World.' Naipaul attacked such myopia and orientalism through his corrective narration of how the Caribbean saw Michael X as a conman par excellence: 'To the Trinidad crowds Malik had become a "character," a Carnival figure, a dummy Judas to be beaten through the streets on Good Friday' (1980a: 1981, p. 24). The narrator makes it amply clear that Michael X was a fugitive from law: in Britain, he had many cases of extortion on his head; in Guyana, he was on the run for murder. Naipaul informs the reader: 'Michael de Freitas, Michael X, Michael Abdul Malik, and now Mr Thompson, Mr Lindsay, Joseph, George. So many names, so many personalities, so many ways of presenting himself to the people: that was his talent' (1980a: 1981 p. 14).

Towards the end of his narrative, Naipaul reinforces his own literary credentials by informing the readers about his discovery concerning Michael's involvement in Gale Benson's murder. In a novel being written by Michael X, Naipaul discovered the exact moment when the point of view swiftly changed from that of Lena Boyd-Richardson (loosely based on Gale Benson) to Sir Harold (loosely based on Michael X). To Naipaul, this sudden change in point of view implied that Lena had been murdered. The narrator announces, 'An autobiography can distort, facts can be realigned. But fiction never lies: it reveals the writer totally' (1980a: 1981, p. 67). Naipaul was himself inspired to write a fictional account about the murder of Gale Benson in *Guerrillas*.

Guerrillas (1975a: 2011)

In his 2011 Picador Preface to *Guerrillas*, Naipaul mentions his frequent journeys and the political crisis in Trinidad that forms the background to this book.

The story of the rise of Michael X interested him because Michael X 'had a myth in England and Trinidad; he was in touch with distinguished liberal people; he had ideas of racial reform that could appeal (in the late 1960s) to black and white' (Preface 2011, p. vi). What Naipaul did not mention was that this 'myth' was perceived differently in England and Trinidad. For the British, Michael X was the poor Black man's leader, while for Trinidadians, he was the 'smart-man.' The book concentrates on the events of three months preceding the killing of Gale Benson and the breaking up of the dream of the commune, leading to the trial of Michael X. *Guerrillas* made a significant impact in America, establishing Naipaul as a writer of repute.

According to Patrick French, 'Underlying Vidia's [V.S. Naipaul] reaction was a personal antipathy to figures such as the "honorary prime minister" of the Black Panthers in the United States, Stokely Carmichael, alias Kwame Ture, a former Tranquillity pupil. More irritating still was Michael de Freitas, alias Michael X, who had displaced Vidia as the most famous Trinidadian in England' (2008, p. 292). Naipaul had gone to Tranquillity Boys School in Trinidad. Further, French points out that, like V. S. Naipaul, Michael X and Hakim Jamal were published by André Deutsch. André Deutsch had even come to Trinidad to meet Michael X in September 1971 (French 2008, p. 285). Thus, Naipaul was making a point to his close circle of friends when he wrote about Michael X in Trinidad.

The book *Guerrillas* opens with the commune in a state of deterioration, with many 'boys' leaving because agriculture is a heavy-handed skill that they did not wish to practice. Even though the commune is a disaster, it still generated money from its British and American benefactors, who felt that they were doing the right thing by promoting agricultural and educational farms/ schools that provided skills to the poor. James Ahmed (Haji) or Jimmy keeps up the pretence, saying, 'I'm not subversive. I'm the friend of every capitalist in the country. Everybody is my friend. I'm not going out on the streets to change the government [...] I'm no guerrilla' (1975a: 2011, pp. 20–1). This sums up James's (and by extension Michael X's) philosophy since he is dependent upon the money of the capitalists and their paradoxical belief in the socialist ideals of the commune. However, the idea is impractical because the weather is far too hot and the largely black working class aspired to an easy life. Agriculture, especially within the ex-plantation colonies in the Caribbean, was seen as a regressive step that reminded them of slavery. Coupled with this flaw, Naipaul makes James confess to his own deception: 'Out here he [James] is a controversial figure, no one is indifferent to him, he is discussed in every quarter. For the ordinary people, the common people, he is like a saviour, he understands and loves the common man, and that is why for the others, the government people and the rich white firms and people of that ilk he is something else, they're scared of him and they queue up to give him money' (1975a: 2011, pp. 32–3). Naipaul points out the irony behind the white benefactors, secure in their own class, race and nationality, funding a cause against their own white race and community. A little later, he informs us that old firms like Sablich's, 'great slave traders in the old days, they now pretend that black is beautiful [...]' (1975a: 2011, p. 36). The reference to Sablich's could easily have been the Booker's who had made their money from the sugar estates in British Guiana and later became the sponsors of the Booker Prize.

Jane feels a commune is a perfect cover-up for the guerrillas, indulging in her own fantasy regarding helping the 'poor blacks' fight their wars. For Jane, the whole commune is an idea that appeals to her middle-class sensibility: 'At the back of that vision lay the certainties, of class and money, of which, in London, she had seemed innocent' (1975a: 2011, p. 97). Her white skin is passport enough to let her in through immigration. It leads to a situation later where there is no record of her trip to the island because her passport was never stamped on her entry. Jane had followed Roche to the island in what seemed to be a noble cause: 'In London Roche had seemed to her an extraordinary person; [...] He had appeared to her as a doer; [...]. He had just published a book about his experiences in South Africa' (1975a: 2011, pp. 42–3). The literary angle is important because the books appealed to the white middle-class sensibility of academic intellectualism. However, on the island, Roche acted as a 'refugee' (1975a: 2011, p. 45), running away from a world of action and passively instigating boys to join Jimmy's commune: 'Every morning he thought I've built my whole life on sand' (1975a: 2011, p. 98). Naipaul makes the point that though James, Jane and Roche were all part of England's progressive intelligentsia, on the island, their activism turned to pure rhetoric, which failed to deliver effective improvement and empowerment to the common man.

Meredith Herbert, a local politician, journalist and radio jockey, exposes James as Jimmy Leung, a boy who lived down the street and came to be a 'plaything' of the British. He plays a game with Jane, Harry de Tunja and Roche, asking them what they would like to do if they were given a chance. Jane wants 'lots and lots of money' (1975a: 2011, p. 143), Harry wants to get his wife back, Roche wants more sex and Meredith wants the gift of rhetoric. The game reveals that, 'The life being described is the life the speaker lives or a life he has already lived' (1975a: 2011, p. 148). The truth strikes them as they drive back to their houses. Naipaul uses the game as a literary device to reveal the true character of each of his protagonists. The self-revelation leads to each character taking hold of their lives, drawing the book to a close.

The absence of Stephens, so innocuously mentioned by James early in the book, becomes a turning point. Stephens' body is found, and James is able to build 'one hell of a procession' (1975a: 2011, p. 177), taking the body through the streets of the capital and instigating riots. Everyone becomes a guerrilla, but no lives are lost as Meredith, as minister of security, regains swift control. In a radio interview with Meredith, Roche confesses that an agricultural commune is 'anti-historical. All over the world people are leaving the land to go to the cities [...]. The land is a way of life' (1975a: 2011, p. 207), and its time is over. Jane is killed by an act of personal hatred, but the murder is justified as an act against a class and a gender.

Jane's innocuousness, James's ruthlessness and Roche's neutrality in the dénouement of the book create a dismal picture of the proponents of the Black Power Movement. Diana Athill concluded that Naipaul had used Gale Benson inaccurately in order to make a point about middle-class white girls (French 2008, p. 333): 'I'd never disliked anything in his books until *Guerrillas*, in 1975. It was based on people I knew and he'd got the woman completely wrong' (Athill 2018, p. 103). Furthermore, Athill had become friends with Jamal but believed Michael X was a conman (French 2008, p. 293).

Naipaul has been severely criticised for his portrayal of a shallow-minded Jane. To all his critics, Naipaul said that *Guerrillas* was humorous: 'You should hear me read it' (Meighoo 2018, p. 84); 'Do you know Guerrillas is full of jokes? If I had read Guerrillas aloud you would be roaring with laughter. Really' (Mukherjee and Boyers 1981, p. 87). I doubt whether anybody can read the dismal book to evoke laughter. Perhaps, the book can be read more successfully as Naipaul's criticism of Britain's failure to imbibe racial and cultural diversity. Ryan Durgasingh analyses the book for its experiments in stylistics, where each character is presented from his or her own point of view. Naipaul clearly experiments with writing through multiple points of view that are not his, cannot be his and that he had never attempted before. He writes as a man of mixed birth, a woman and a foreigner about a territory close to his heart. Harold Barratt defends Naipaul's presentation on grounds of the reality of race relations in Trinidad because 'differences in shades of colour within the same racial group are as crucial and important as differences between the various races' (1983, p. 67). Michael X could never have been a populist leader in Trinidad because of his lighter skin tone. Even Jane expected somebody more negroid, while James looked 'distinctly Chinese' (1975a: 2011, p. 8).

John McClure, in his analysis, criticises Naipaul's lack of participation in an Afro-centric vision for the Caribbean: 'While *Guerrillas* makes it clear that the neo-colonial bourgeoisie cannot lead society forward, it also rejects, for the Caribbean at least, the chance of positive social change through revolution' (1978, p. 12). He argues: 'The reader learns nothing of the well-organised student and labour groups that played an important role in the 1970 revolution' (1978, p. 14) and that Naipaul limited the scope of the change to 'Jimmy's tourist-poster vision of rape and reconciliation, Jane's image of a fearless lover, Roche's camp nightmare, Meredith's fantasy of security—these dreams shape the dreamers' personal histories, condemning them to act out again and again ill-conceived programs of rebellion' (1978, p. 14). Hence, the 'revolution [is felt] as a threat rather than a promise' (1978, p. 16). Lawrence Scott supports this view, wondering why Naipaul's books 'indict guerrillas for their pretensions rather than indict the imperialism that drove them to insurrection' (2011, p. 167). Selwyn Cudjoe complains that Naipaul denies the possibility of any revolutionary 'activity at any given level and to treat it as a squalid farce whenever it appears' (1979, p. 8). Jeremy Taylor takes the attack further saying that 'Over the years, he [Naipaul] has called people monkeys, infies (inferiors), bow-and-arrow men, potato eaters, Mr Woggy' (2002, p. 45) since 'he sees himself as a diagnostician, not a therapist' (2002, p. 47). Angus Richmond gives a biographical twist to Naipaul's understanding by arguing that Naipaul's early childhood within an enclosed East Indian world led to his alienation towards the oilfields workers' vibrant political struggle of the 1930s and the 1940s: 'that Naipaul was never close to the spirit of the labour movement in the West Indies, [...and] the absence of any genuine empathy with Afro-Caribbean' (1982, p. 126). Based on a reading of *The Middle Passage* and *Guerrillas*, Richmond attributes Naipaul a nihilistic view because of his failure to see 'history as a revitalising process that is continuous' (1982, p. 133). Richmond contends that Naipaul's guerrillas are not 'linked to the guerrilla fighting of organisations such as FRELIMO in Mozambique, the MPLA in Angola, SWAPO in Namibia, the FLN in Algeria, or Fidel Castro's bearded men from the Sierra Maestra' (1982, p. 134). However, Richmond's argument falls flat when he equates Naipaul's criticism of Michael X to Naipaul's criticism of the 'Negro' character in general. Most of these critics equate Naipaul's criticism of Michael X with his criticism of Black Power Movement in Trinidad.

Naipaul was far too discerning to equivocate. He knew that Michael X did not represent the movement. He correctly records that: 'There were daily anti-government marches in Port of Spain; revolutionary pamphlets appeared everywhere, even in schools; sections of the regiment declared for the marchers' (1980a: 1981, p. 43). These were 'spontaneous, anarchic outburst[s]' (1980a: 1981, p. 43). In reality too, the Black Power Movement in Trinidad was a long-drawn movement, with the NJAC organising marches and meetings on March 12, 24, 28, 29, April 1, 4, 6 and 9 in 1970. These marches attracted government attention and even a police firing that resulted in the death of an activist. Michael X came to Trinidad in January 1971, that is, much after the movement had lost its momentum. In order to emphasise the marginality of Michael X in the Black Power Movement in Trinidad, Naipaul highlighted that Michael's speech to the striking bus drivers had little effect, and Randolph Rawlins, a left-wing Trinidadian journalist, was bored with his rhetoric.

Most critics obscure the fine lines between leaders like Makandal Daaga, who had little time to address Western audiences or seek finances, and those 'fake' leaders like Michael X, who built their personal empires around the British interest in the movement. Naipaul insisted that the Black Power Movement was an American movement with American roots and was a poor imitation in its avatars in Britain, the Caribbean and elsewhere. Taking this position, he failed to write about it as a homegrown movement and as a genuine expression of anger and anguish against a corrupt and insensitive administration. While many critics feel that he did not read race relations in Trinidad correctly, on the contrary, he read it too accurately to realise that the projected call for unity against the Eric Williams government failed because the Indo-Trinidadian and Afro-Trinidadian political leadership could not find common ground. Yet he deliberately chose to write about Michael X to unnerve the supporters of the movement in Britain. This was where his age-old strategy of addressing his primary audience in Britain while speaking to his people in Trinidad and the Caribbean failed for the first time. He chose to focus too intensely on the role of white elites in the guerrilla-like revolution. In Naipaul's eyes, guerrillas failed to attack the system, and their constant nagging only made the system stronger and plunged the countries into never-ending cycles of violence. This was certainly a point of interest for him in his travels to Argentina, Uruguay and Paraguay.

Guerrillas and 'Michael X and the Black Power Killings in Trinidad' were Naipaul's last engagements with the politics and happenings in Trinidad for a long time to come. After the Black Power Movement, Naipaul seems to have changed gears and started to look for his subjects elsewhere. Naipaul did not write directly about Trinidad for almost the next 20 years. His next book about Trinidad was *A Way in the World*. However, Trinidad was never far from his mind. The so-called failure of the Black Power Movement ossified many of Naipaul's beliefs: first, he did not believe in the socialist ideals of setting up a welfare state (he always suspected that state largesse led to the suppression of individual efforts); second, he did not believe that any revolution could change the system in place (especially one that did not have a larger vision and a concrete plan for change); third, he refused to believe in guerrilla warfare (primarily because he believed that violence was an emotional outburst and had little to do with constructive change). All three notions were put to the test in his travels now.

(ii) The Impact of the Black Power Movement

It is no secret that Naipaul, as a young boy, felt politically, socially and culturally marginalised in the multi-cultural and multi-racial society of Port of Spain. But he had experienced equal, if not more, marginalisation in England, India and Africa, where he had gone on to live for some lengths of time. This led to a reassessment of his own growing-up years in Trinidad, where, though he felt marginalised and there was an inherent and persistent sense of violence, violence that had seeped into relations between brothers and sisters, fathers and sons, there had been no consistent perpetration of violent attacks by one community over the other. The protests, even the protests in the Black Power Movement, were directed against those in power and not against each other. But Naipaul felt at odds with the Black Power Movement in Trinidad. He had not been in the country for over 20 years and was out of touch with local politics. He could not grapple with either violence or empty rhetoric about a sudden transformation of society through a regime change or faith in the coming of a messiah. Hence, rather than focus on the moral question, Naipaul chose to focus on the racial and class hypocrisies of the white benefactors. The white benefactors projected their own racial prejudices (such as Black is poor, or, alternatively, Black is beautiful) onto local communities and felt they were doing a good deed by supporting people such as Michael X. Ironically, by targeting this group, Naipaul distanced himself from his own readers who were sympathetic to the Black Power Movement and found favour with conservatives who did not support the Movement. This 'new readership' sustained his reputation as a conservative writer through the next two decades. The academia for their part, had moved on from 'New Literatures in English' to discourses on migration and displacement. Naipaul remained academia's favourite because of his thematic emphasis on migration, displacement and 'nihilism.'

The Return of Eva Perón (1980b: 1981)

In 1943, in Argentina, Juan Perón usurped power as a military dictator, later legitimising his coup through two consecutive electoral victories in 1946 and 1951. In 1952, his wife Eva, who had become hugely popular, died and her body was embalmed. Subsequently, in 1955, Perón was exiled from Argentina after another military coup. He spent the next 17 years in Spain. 'The Return of Eva Perón' is about the return of Juan Perón with his wife's embalmed body to Argentina, since in public memory, Eva had been transformed into a saint and Juan a benign ruler who had nationalised many strategic industries and institutionalised socialist schemes of welfare.

Cathleen Medwick writes: 'The dead, embalmed, miraculously undecayed Eva Perón [became] the image of Argentina, "magical, debilitating," petrified by its own dream' (1981, p. 59). Naipaul travelled to Argentina in April 1972. He noted that Argentina, in spite of its rich agricultural and mineral resources, was struggling with an inflation rate of 60 per cent, political instability and social breakdown. The guerrillas were threatening and killing executives of companies, the army and the government personnel who were seen as enemies of the people. Naipaul found it extraordinary that the public, who had sent Perón into exile, were now awaiting his return so anxiously.

Naipaul met the writer, essayist, poet and translator Jorge Borges in Buenos Aires, and using his insights into Argentine history, he attempted to analyse the current political strife in Argentina with its five major groups: the military rulers, the Peronists, the communists, the bourgeoisie and the guerrillas. In his bid to understand the revolutionary strains, Naipaul's narrator befriended a priest and several civil rights lawyers as well. Yet he failed to see how Peronism, with its firm belief in class differences between the rich and the poor and its commitment to developing a welfare state, could help a flagging economy. As in Mauritius, an over-emphasis on the development of a welfare state only led to the destruction of older ways of life without replacing them with sustainable alternatives. In Mauritius, the welfare state encouraged young men to sit around clubhouses drinking, sulking and looking elsewhere for a future. In Argentina, it led the young to take up arms while awaiting the return of Perón as their 'messiah.' Peronism had grown out of a promise of wealth to the workers against the bourgeoisie, yet it was Perón's earlier largesse that had severely depleted state resources, leading to the present civil war. Over the years, Peronism had alternatively become 'protest, despair, faith, machismo, magic, espiritismo, revenge' (1980b: 1981, p. 119). In fact, Naipaul's narrator says that the Argentinians believed that 'if you kill the right people, everything will work. Genocide is their history' (Hardwick 1979, p. 47). Hence, Naipaul is convinced that public faith is misplaced.

Uruguay and Paraguay are similarly analysed. Naipaul believes that politicians and would-be politicians exploit the poor and the simple-minded because the general public lacks a historical perspective. Colonialism had robbed the colonised of their sense of history, leading to a dysfunctional relationship between man and his environment. The ecological approach is quite different from the exploitative one, where people treat land as a possession and an unlimited resource for food. Naipaul was years ahead of the now-in-vogue anti-climate change brigade. Naipaul's adventures through the politically unstable states in the Caribbean and Latin America reinforced his sense of impending doom for the ex-colonies. Long-term colonial rule had destroyed the traditional economies and placed the newly independent

DISPLACEMENT ACROSS BORDERS IN THE 1970s

states at the mercy of their ex-masters. We see a continuation of this theme in his next venture, *India: A Wounded Civilization*. However, before that, I document his visits to Trinidad in 1975 for a conference and later to receive a doctorate from The University of the West Indies. He also republished a set of stories written by his father in 1976.

The first conference on East Indians in the Caribbean (1975)

Naipaul, in a keynote address at the first conference on East Indians in Trinidad in 1975 organised by The University of the West Indies, attacked Trinidadians for not questioning a colonial vision of themselves: 'England is selling itself, its history, its achievements. Trinidad sells only its "picturesqueness," its "cosmopolitan" population, and such tourist concepts harden simplicities and ignorance' (1975b, p. 1). Since nearly four hundred years of colonisation had failed to produce a stable, self-sufficient economy, the newly independent nations in the Caribbean were left to rely upon tourism as their only self-sustainable industry that required little immediate investment from the respective governments. This often led the islands to conform to the 'sun and sand paradise' narrative that had been built by the colonial rulers. It also led to the local population, by and large, remaining ignorant of their history. Naipaul praised the conference as a 'first Indian attempt at self-examination [... as an] intellectual response to cultural loss' (1975b, p. 3). He argued that Indians came to Trinidad from a 'pre-revolutionary and rather static society' (1975b, p. 3) and became 'colonial almost without knowing it' (1975b, p. 4). He urged the East Indians to examine their lives without falling for racial and often cultural definitions of 'authenticity' (1975b, p. 8) and to emphasise continuity rather than see the 'distance between the past and the present' (1975b, p. 6). Naipaul gave this same advice to most other countrymen in his travels. However, the press reports during his visit were not favourable. One newspaper report stated: 'Naipaul didn't interpret the Indian world in a way the people could understand and feel, and when they wanted a bright wide beam of his insight all they received was a sharp little penlight into some corners' ('Naipaul Failed his audience' 1975). Another report stated: 'Asked [...] whether cultural integration was possible in Trinidad & Tobago, with the separate cultures of the various ethnic groups merging into one, Mr Naipaul replied: "I can't talk at that level. You make it sound like a bowl of soup. You make it sound trivial"' ('Heckling at UWI as Naipaul ignores "frivolous"questions' 1975). The overall feeling was that the people looked for simple answers to complex problems while Naipaul only spoke in intellectual riddles. Bhoe Tewarie in a much later column in the *Trinidad Sunday Guardian* acknowledged that Naipaul was not the most popular of writers in the Caribbean: 'On one occasion, at a writer's conference in Jamaica, he was subjected to strong verbal abuse by a university student; On another occasion, invited to speak at a conference at the St. Augustine Campus of The University of the West Indies, and having delivered a thoughtful and sensitive address, he was booed by a boisterous section of the audience' (1992). Naipaul must have been disheartened by the public response. Yet, in the same year, he received an honorary doctorate from The University of the West Indies ('Naipaul comes for doctorate' 1975). Naipaul was doubly aware that he needed to find a place for Trinidad in his literary creative sphere, but he was also determined that he would not idealise or romanticise his place of birth.

Naipaul perhaps found solace in the fact that his father had also received criticism from the locals when he published his book, *Gurudeva and Other Indian Tales*, in 1943. In the book he got Andre Deutsch to publish now, Naipaul made some changes. He removed two stories, 'Sonya's Luck' and 'Gopi' and added five stories: 'They named him Mohun,' 'My Uncle Dalloo,' 'In the Village,' 'The Engagement' and 'The Gratuity.' In the foreword, the younger Naipaul recalled that his father had received a couple of angry letters from fellow Indians who thought he had written damagingly about the Indian community. He had also received a letter from a 'religion-crazed Muslim' (Foreword 1976, p. 7). He went on to tell his father's story:

> From a vision of a whole Hindu society he moved, through reformist passion, which was an expression of his brahmin confidence, to a vision of disorder and destitution, of which he discovered himself to be part. At the end he had nothing to claim, it was out of this that he created comedy. (Foreword 1976, p. 20)

Perhaps Naipaul's assessment of his father is not accurate, but that is the beauty of portraits. Naipaul's foreword is noteworthy for his stated allegiance to other writers from the island: 'What is true of my father is true of other writers of the region; *we* all in different ways discover that we stand nowhere' (Foreword 1976, p. 22; *emphasis added*).

India: A Wounded Civilization (1977: 1978)

While, *An Area of Darkness* was a personal response to India, *India: A Wounded Civilization* was an intellectual response to the core values of Hinduism. India was an ancient civilisation, and Naipaul's ancestry made it almost impossible for him to distance himself from his travelling persona. His response was emotional: 'I felt India only as an assault on the senses' (*The Overcrowded*

Barracoon and Other Articles, 1972, p. 41). India was a cause of pain 'for which one has a great tenderness, but from which at length one always wishes to separate oneself' (*The Overcrowded Barracoon and Other Articles*, 1972, p. 46). But while in *An Area of Darkness*, he saw the dirt and the squalor, now he says, 'I have learnt to see beyond the dirt and the recumbent figures on string beds, and look for the signs of improvement and hope, however faint' (*The Overcrowded Barracoon and Other Articles*, 1972, p. 42). Naipaul felt that Indians were too conceited and did not take any measures to reduce poverty in India. He found the Indian middle class distancing itself from a larger, poorer and dirtier India. This was as true of the Indian bourgeoisie as for its political leaders and its writers.

In *The Overcrowded Barracoon and Other Articles*, the section titled 'India,' contains seven essays that were later made part of *India: A Wounded Civilization*. In 'Jamshed into Jimmy,' Naipaul wrote about how the new bourgeoisie in Calcutta had adopted the colonial 'spirit of plunder,' taking on the attitudes of the conqueror and continued to indulge in upper-class lifestyle club-sports such as golf and swimming in a poor country. In 'Indian Autobiographies,' Naipaul judged Mahatma Gandhi, P. L. Tandon, Mirza Ismail and Nirad Chaudhuri as intellectual failures because they failed to engage with the impact of British rule on Indian society. He gave the example of the Victoria Memorial that stood in the middle of the Calcutta grounds as a sterile reminder of the presence of the British in India in the nineteenth and early twentieth centuries. He failed to comprehend why Chaudhuri and Mahatma Gandhi supported the institution of caste within the folds of Hinduism. Naipaul summarised these visionaries as hypocrites who wanted to become 'occidentals' in their 'spirit of equality, freedom, work and energy, and at the same time Hindu[s] to the very backbone in religious culture and instincts' (Naipaul quoting Vivekananda 1972, p. 70). Naipaul could not understand how Indians could continue to claim the supremacy of Indian spiritual discourse over western discourse (India is East) while acknowledging that Western civilisation had superior science and technology. From the rundown palace of an erstwhile prince to an assembly of Maharishi Mahesh Yogi to his travels to primary schools and a health centre in the Indian hinterland, Naipaul came across a number of Indians who refused to acknowledge the pathos of their situation. In spite of Indians taking pride in being an ancient civilisation, its people repeatedly failed to analyse the reasons for its present state of poverty and thus failed to take affirmative action. Their reliance on magic 'complement[s] a shallow perception of the world, the Indian intellectual failure, which is less a failure of the individual intellect than the deficiency of a closed civilisation, ruled by ritual and myth' (1972, p. 86). Later in the same essay, he expresses hope that the political unrest across India will bring about positive change. In the last essay, 'The Election in Ajmer,' Naipaul follows the fortunes of two candidates from the bifurcated arms of the Indian National Congress party led by Morarji Desai and Indira Gandhi, respectively. Sabotage and distribution of free liquor precede election day. Taken together, in the seven essays on India, Naipaul concludes that Indians refused to intellectually engage with their own civilisational history.

Soon after, he composed *India: A Wounded Civilization*, where he narrativised these disparate thoughts and experiences from India. While Europe had seen continuous human development over the last 1000 years, India and Indians had to adapt to the 'fact of defeat' (Wheeler 1977, p. 39). Against this background, Naipaul analyses the opposition rallies and the proclamation of a political emergency as signs that rural India was waking up to the challenges of a new nation. In Naipaul's view, his own identity as an Indian, a Trinidadian and a Hindu were bound up as a whole. Yet among Indians, he saw no sense of a racial or national identity, just a longing for a lost pride. In a reaction that has overtones of his response to the Black Power Movement in Trinidad, Naipaul found that the opposition was intellectually poor and therefore, in spite of the public mobilisation, incapable of bringing about a change. Just as the Black Power Movement lost its momentum once disarmed by the state apparatus, Naipaul foresaw the failure of the Indian opposition to bring about a change in India. He was certainly not unsympathetic to Eric Williams and certainly 'not unsympathetic' to Indira Gandhi (Wheeler 1977, p. 42).

It is also important to remember that all of Naipaul's visits to India happened against the backdrop of India's wars, first with China in 1962 and then with Pakistan in 1965 and 1971. Though nationalism united the people, it also pushed them into an intellectual stupor. For someone like Naipaul, who grew up with a belief in the agency of the self, it was an enigma to pull away from traditional Indian society, inclusive of caste and the joint family system. In Trinidad, the Indo-Trinidadians defined success through investments in agriculture, business and education (Brereton 2010, p. 226). Naipaul felt a need to understand the complexities attached to the appeal of Hinduism among Indians through nearly a thousand years of 'foreign' rule in India, through the passage over the *kala pani* for the indentured, and through religious conversions in Trinidad. In a 1999 interview with Tarun Tejpal, Naipaul said that he was particularly struck by the absence of Hindu monuments in north India. By looking deeper into history, Naipaul realised that the Muslim invasion was far more intrusive and destructive than the British colonial rule in India. The Muslim invasion and their continued attacks for over eight centuries left Hindus in a state where very few demands were made on the individual. The colonial takeover merely extended the 'foreign' rule. The monuments it produced, much like the Victoria Memorial in Calcutta (now Kolkata), were sterile. In another interview with Andrew Robinson, Naipaul argued that though both Chaudhuri and he saw the empire as a reforming influence in India, they differed in their vision for the future of India: Chaudhuri predicted a bleak future while Naipaul saw a possible regeneration (1990, p. 112). Naipaul was to later see the Hindu resurgence in India as a creative corrective force.

In an attempt to avoid any analyses of contemporary politics in India in either *An Area of Darkness* or *India: A Wounded Civilization*, Naipaul chose to focus on Hinduism. Naipaul's relationship with Hinduism is discursive and controversial. He saw the philosophy of karma as a 'Hindu killer' (*India: A Wounded Civilization* 1977: 1978, 17) and interpreted it as a philosophy of 'nondoing, noninterference, social indifference' (*India: A Wounded Civilization* 1977: 1978, p. 15). With the help of Sudhir Kakar, an Indian psychologist, Naipaul linked the feeling of failure in Indians to the philosophy of karma. Dilip Chitre rightly argues that Naipaul uses 'Dr Sudhir Kakar's reported hypothesis about the Indian mind [specifically, 'underdeveloped ego'] as a single conceptual key that explains everything from Gandhi to the Shiv Sena, a Maratha farmer's new life style to Jayaprakash Narayan's mind style, Vijay Tendulkar's plays to Ananthamurthy's *Samskara*, R.K. Narayan's novels to recent Indian history' (1977: 1978, pp. 177–8). Dr Kakar analyses the Indian character as indecisive, unsure and craving for security of the family, clan and community. Naipaul quotes the psychologist in much detail because he supports his own analysis that Indians were psychologically incapable of understanding their history or literature and hence practiced what he calls 'instinctive living.'

Through his repeated visits to India, Naipaul began to realise that Trinidadian society had made him un-Indian. This distinction lay not in his physical features nor in the outer vestiges of dress or manner, but in cultural differences. In an essay 'East Indian' in the section 'An Unlikely Colonial' in *The Overcrowded Barracoon and Other Articles*, Naipaul distinguishes himself from Indians at large. In the article, first published in *The Reporter* on June 17, 1965, Naipaul recalls meeting an Indian from India aboard a flight from London to Paris. The man drinks and eats 'meats of all colours,' while informing him that he was a teetotaller and a strict vegetarian at home. In contrast, Naipaul, belonging to the East Indian community in the West Indies, does not drink hard liquor and avoids meat. Years later, he meets another Trinidadian at the Gymkhana Club in Delhi, and they both agree that Trinidad is far ahead and more developed than India.

110   V. S. NAIPAUL OF TRINIDAD

The twin meetings showcase a popular attitude among Indo-Trinidadians towards India. Naipaul emphasises that in Trinidad, India not only evokes an ancient civilisation but also evokes visual images of 'famine' and 'teeming millions' with 'tiny houses, tiny poor fields, thin stunted people, a land scratched into dust by an ever-growing population' (1972, p. 36). Instead, they in Trinidad had recreated 'an India without caste or the overwhelming pressures towards caste' (1972, p. 37). This India was better than the physical India he was now visiting.

A Bend in the River (1979: 2011)

Naipaul's interests in the 1970s clearly lay with the political, economic, social and cultural unrest in the newly decolonised nation states. Naipaul's reputation as an Africa basher had been built with his book *In a Free State*, with critics such as Laban Erapu finding his portrayal of Africa too confusing with its presentation of the '1966 revolution in Uganda in which Dr Obote, then Prime Minister, not President, ousted King Freddie' (1972, p. 71) and using combinations such as 'Mubende-Mbarara (something like Edinburgh-Oxford)' as place names (1972, p. 72). Anthony Appiah went further to define what he called the 'Naipaulian fallacy' as the tendency to understand Africa 'by embedding it in European culture' not realising that it is Europe that is 'ignorant of Africa (and not because Africa is ignorant of Europe) that Africa needs explaining to Europeans' (1984, p. 146). However, the issue of an audience is a tricky one in literature. Since Naipaul believed a writer could never lie in fiction, one can only assess if a character like Salim could exist outside Africa.

At the time Naipaul visited Zaire, Joseph Mobutu was the president. In the essay 'A New King for the Congo: Mobutu and the Nihilism of Africa,' he analysed the political crisis in Zaire (first published in *The New York Review of Books*, June 26, 1975). In most of the official documents and press releases, Mobutu was shown wearing a leopard-skin cap and carrying an elaborately carved stick. He claimed to have the support of the spirits of the ancestors. Naipaul was interested in knowing why Mobutu, part of an educated new elite in Zaire, claimed a chieftaincy and a quasi-mystical justification for his rule. He realised that 'the dream of an ancestral past restored [wa]s allied to a dream of a future of magical power' (1980b: 1981, p. 212). But in this process, the country's more recent Belgian and Arab pasts were pillaged and ruined. Naipaul was weary of such cultural investments in ancient mythology because he saw 'the general corruption, the jobs not done, the breakdown of municipal administration in Kinshasa, the uncleared garbage, the canals not disinfected [...] the vandalised public television sets and telephone booths [...]' (1980b: 1981, p. 213). In 1973, Mobutu tried to forcefully push away foreign investors and 'nationalised all businesses and plantations belonging to foreigners—mainly Greeks, Portuguese and Indians—and had given them to Zairois. Now, a year later, he had decided [...] to entrust them to the state' (1980b: 1981, p. 189) sending the Zairois back into the bushes. As Naipaul travelled to Bomongo, he noted: 'The bush [was] a way of life; and where the bush [was] so overwhelming, organised agriculture [was] an illogicality' (1980b: 1981, p. 199). The attempt at modernisation frequently led to economic disasters. These events form the backdrop to Salim's struggles in *A Bend in the River.*

The events of *A Bend in the River* are based on a fictitious, newly independent nation in Africa. The title is reflective of change and movement in the course of the river as it meanders its way out of the continent. It points to a meeting ground where civilisations have traditionally thrived since time immemorial. Naipaul points out three things in his 2011 Picador Preface to the novel: that the name Metty was from Trinidad, where it referred to a person of mixed race, and the overseer at the Petit Valley was called Metti (French 2008, p. 33); two, that the narration came to him in a dream about the President's Big Man (Preface 2011, p. ix); and three, in spite of the publisher's fears, the book was a major success. According to Linda Blandford, Naipaul received an advance of $25,000 for the book, which was not high and normally associated 'with a competent biography or promising second novel' (1979, p. 51). The book is divided into four parts titled 'The Second Rebellion,' 'The New Domain,' 'The Big Man' and 'Battle.'

The book opens with the now hugely popular line, 'The World is what it is; men who are nothing, who allow themselves to become nothing, have no place in it' (1979: 2011, p. 3). The phrase 'The World is what it is' was later used in the title of Naipaul's authorised biography by Patrick French. The implied fatalism is immediately cut through by calling on the importance of action in the lives of men. Salim, the protagonist, is an African of Indian Muslim descent who makes the journey from the coast to the middle of the country to a small town to set up his shop. He is accompanied by Metty, his African slave companion, who is of similar age. The theme of young men coming to terms with independence (political and personal) is carried forward in the portrayal of Zabeth's young son, Ferdinand, a local of African tribal descent who seeks power through education and industry. Much like *Guerrillas*, Naipaul tells the story through three characters and three points of view: Salim, the coastal 'intruder', Metty, the under-privileged and Zabeth, the local tribal. However, unlike *Guerrillas*, where the points of view compete with each other, here the omniscient narrator backs Salim.

Salim soon achieves moderate success and decides to visit London. The London of this book is distinctly different from the London of *Mr Stone and the Knights Companion* and *The Mimic Men*. While Mr Stone had hardly noticed the colonials on the streets of London, and while Ralph felt totally ignored, Salim's London is a multiracial multicultural hub—'Koreans, Filipinos, people from Hong Kong and Taiwan, South Africans, Italians, Greeks, South Americans, Argentines, Columbians, Venezuelan, Bolivians, lot of black people who've cleaned out of places you've never heard of, Chinese from everywhere' (1979: 2011, p. 274). By the time Salim returns from London, political changes have been effected, all his assets have been confiscated and he is designated a foreigner and a mercenary in spite of his family being in Africa for a few generations. London is now his only refuge.

The book is interesting in drawing linkages between India, Africa and Europe. For Salim, India is his past, Africa is his present and Europe (or specifically London) is his future. The Indians had never made any attempt to become a part of African culture. The fault lay not just with the Indians but also with the Africans, who guarded their beliefs as passionately as the Indians. While independence brought new opportunities for the Africans, it also meant adjustments for the Indians. Salim realises that Metty thinks he is his lawful heir. It takes him time to realise that the Arab and Indian traders by enslaving the Africans had failed to look after their aspirations. When Metty realises that Salim wants to liquidate and sell his businesses, he informs the police and Salim has to run to save his life. In the meanwhile, the 'bond' between the Africans and Europeans is also broken when Father Huisman is killed. It is Ferdinand who comes to the rescue of Salim because their friendship had not been based on economic exchange but on mutual respect and affection.

Naipaul's choice of Salim as a narrator allows him to view Africa from a particular point of intimacy and distance. Salim's history emphasises his distance from the State. The Indians never took any interest outside of their trade. Though the political happenings are presented from a very personal and young point of view, there are points in the book where there is a more mature narrator at work. For example, when Salim contemplates the postage stamps, scientific innovations that he reads about in magazines, or the role of Europe in writing his history, the narrator is a mature person who has read more and has a more comprehensive view of the world than Salim. The double vision enhances the experience of reading the book as social history.

The relevance of the book's subject to the Caribbean is little explored. Because the theme of homecoming was popular during the 1970s, the fate of Indians in African countries was left largely unexplored in the Caribbean.

DISPLACEMENT ACROSS BORDERS IN THE 1970s   113

Naipaul was unable to understand the violence perpetrated on Indians in Africa with a neutral eye. Undoubtedly, politics and race relations in Trinidad had been challenging, but the Indians, who were a minority, were never denied basic rights in Trinidad. Though many Indo-Trinidadians migrated away from their country of birth, the situation was never as bad as in Africa. It perhaps led Naipaul to critically analyse his own stand with regard to people like Eric Williams, who had taken political control at independence. Thematically, the book is linked to Naipaul's own experience as an East Indian in an Afro-dominated society. Naipaul was to explore more aspects of the Caribbean in Africa in his later books in the 1980s.

Kenneth Ramchand lists some of the features of the literary works that accompanied the négritude and négritude related movements in the USA, Europe and the Caribbean in the 1920s, 1930s and 1940s that talked back to the systematic denigration of Africa, Africans and African cultures that had been constructed by the practitioners of slavery and other capitalist enterprises to justify their exploitative behaviours. These literary works by Africans promoted awareness of African technological advance; offered corrective accounts of the African past; celebrated 'Africa as a cultural matrix; ...[exhibited] a pride in blackness; [emphasised] a contrast between [the African's] harmonious way of life and a decadent White civilisation lost in materialism; and a joyful proclamation of the sensuous and integrated African personality' (1970: 2004, p. 105). Naipaul's vision of Africa is a particular version of this Africa and adds the Indian to its complex cultural mix. By recognising the presence of the Indians, the Arabs, the Belgians and other foreigners in Africa, Naipaul wants the Afrcians to come to terms with their own history. Rather than destroying the remnants of foreign buildings, Naipaul wants Africans to document and accept the colonial presence and their contribution to the present day Africa. For him, any investment in a 'pure past' was bound to fail because traditional knowledge and traditional crafts had been destroyed and there was little to gain by denying the advancements in science, medicine and modern technology. Naipaul saw value in accepting the past and moving forwards by reviving the world of Zabeth. Ferdinand, without the values of Zabeth, was no better or worse than the erstwhile coloniser. Naipaul was to make one more attempt at retrieving the Africa of Zabeth in his last book, *The Masque of Africa*.

Challenges and Misrepresentation

Naipaul was writing about Trinidad during the first half of this decade and coming to terms with his severance from a contemporary Trinidad in the latter half of this decade. Trinidad had strangely become the mirror in which he did

114   V. S. NAIPAUL OF TRINIDAD

not see himself, just as his father could not see himself in the mirror during one of his bouts of depression ('Prologue to an Autobiography,' 1984, p. 82). His major theme was decolonisation and its debilitating effects on newly independent states, which were left to govern themselves with little economic support from the ex-colonisers. On a broader level, according to Lilian Feder, Naipaul's chief concerns were:

> lack of education and training in the development of natural resources, long exploited by colonizers; the absence of preparation for independence and consequent wide-spread poverty; retreat to fantasy when there are no established institutions to provide social cohesion and solutions to economic problems and social conflict; the rise of despots who amass great wealth by robbing populaces denied participation in government, opportunities for financial security, cultural enrichment, a sense of their own dignity, the freedom to develop their own abilities and talents, to pursue their "vocation," and thus their particular version of "happiness." (2001, p. 79)

Till the 1970s, Naipaul had indeed concentrated his energies on dealing with the effects of European decolonisation on newly independent countries. Some critics like Selwyn Cudjoe saw a pattern in Naipaul's portrayal of Africa and Africans from *In a Free State* to 'A New King for the Congo' to *Guerrillas* to *A Bend in the River*: 'The bush be[came] a metaphor for the backwardness and stupidity of all colonial peoples' (1988, p. 153). According to Timothy Weiss, Naipaul sought 'to appropriate the word *guerrillas*, to remove it from leftist, 1960s and 1970s discourse about revolution, strip it of its progressive connotations and 'populate' it with meanings that grow out of his understanding as Trinidad Indian and as exile [...]' since the Black Power movement in Trinidad had failed to bring about social change (1992, p. 182). Weiss's position to see guerrillas as progressives naturally contrasted with Naipaul's stand that these guerrillas acted in their own personal interests. In contrast, Helen Hayward argues that there was no 'explicit moral condemnation' in *Guerrillas* (2002, p. 149). Naipaul, in his early books, portrayed Trinidadians beyond the scope of moral judgement. If we continue to see the suspension of moral judgement as a key element in Naipaul's fiction, then *Guerrillas* too makes no overt statement regarding the actions of these individual characters. Read from a more apolitical stance, Kerry McSweeney argues that the island is 'seen almost entirely from the point of view of transient whites; representatives of its East Indian community, the macro-subject of Naipaul's first three novels, appear *en passant* only in one scene, and the novel's three principal foci—sex, race and a white, outside point of view—are the very elements which in 1958,

Naipaul said that, for reasons of artistic integrity, he was not able to use in making his Trinidadian subject matter more appealing to the non-West-Indian reader' (1976, p. 75). He further added that *The Mimic Men, In a Free State* and *Guerrillas* had mixed sexual, political and colonial concerns (1976, p. 79). While this may be true for the latter two novels, *The Mimic Men* is written from a much closer, first-hand insider point of view. An outsider could not have written such a poignant account of island politics.

Critics were also offended by Naipaul's portrayal of women. Helen Pyne-Timothy focuses upon the portrayal of women in *In a Free State, Guerrillas* and *A Bend in the River,* constructing her argument on the words spoken by Roche in *Guerrillas,* where he describes women as vague, unrealistic in their expectations, incapable of realising their expectations on their own, 'reeds in the wind' or later as 'sea anemones waving (their) tentacles at the bottom of the ocean' who must attach themselves to men for definitions of self and purpose (1984, p. 3). Pyne-Timothy argues that except for Zabeth who was celibate, Linda, Jane and Yvette were European women who were 'victimised, sexually used, abused, beaten, degraded' (1984, p. 13): 'We are in the presence of the Eves and Delilahs, the temptresses and the adulteresses, the foolish virgins and the whores' (1984, p. 14). As mentioned before, Naipaul's world was a masculine world, but race and class considerations significantly altered his characterisation of women. The charge of being a misogynist was levelled against Naipaul and fed on the charge of his being a racist and a conservative.

Many critics compared his portrayal of Africa to that of Conrad. Naipaul himself recognised that he owed Conrad a debt because Conrad had been metaphorically where Naipaul was now. In an article titled 'Conrad's Darkness' published in *The Return of Eva Perón, with the Killings in Trinidad* (first published in *The New York Review of Books,* October 17, 1974), Naipaul confessed: 'To take an interest in a writer's work is, for me, to take an interest in his life' (1980b: 1981, p. 238). According to Naipaul, 'in fiction he [Conrad] did not seek to discover; he sought only to explain' (1980b: 1981, p. 239). Based upon his analyses of Conrad's personality and his writings, Naipaul concluded: 'And so the world we inhabit, which is always new, goes by unexamined, made ordinary by the camera, unmediated on and there is no one to awaken the sense of true wonder. That is perhaps a fair definition of the novelist's purpose, in all ages' (1980b: 1981, p. 245). Naipaul endorsed this definition of a writer's function.

For the first time, Naipaul faced a backlash from his so-called 'primary' audience in England and his 'true' audience in Trinidad. Further, from the 1970s, Naipaul began inculcating the idea that his kind of writing would not have been possible in any other place except England. Increasingly, it was American interviewers (Elizabeth Hardwick, Cathleen Medwick, Charles Michener and Mel Gussow) who saw him as a wannabe Englishman. Linda Blandford says: 'It is somehow impossible to reconcile this careful, formal man fussing over wines, cheese, old furniture—all the patina of breeding and background—with the child he must have been, poor in a colonial country, the outsider in a white and black West Indies' (1979, p. 52). In America, Naipaul could play the maverick, the English dandy, because he was now financially sound. The Americans, with their lack of knowledge about the Caribbean, were also more likely to believe that Naipaul had given up his Trinidadian identity. Michener asks, 'Is his acerbity that of a dark-skinned man's too-zealous conversion to Western tastes?' (1981, p. 72). Would Naipaul have approved of these interviewers viewing him as an English dandy? Definitely not. But Naipaul was now writing for an American audience. The theme of going back—looking for one's roots—was, to use a more contemporary term, 'trending', and his last book fell squarely into that category—a young male hero looking to put down his roots in Africa with his personal faith in intelligence, endeavour and enterprise. Financially, *A Bend in the River* was Naipaul's most successful publication.

Chapter 5

THE IMPERIAL VISION
OF THE 1980s

By the 1980s, V. S. Naipaul (as an extrapolated creation from his books) was well established in England and America and supported by his personality that was abrasive, rude and selfish. He had bought a dilapidated dairyman's cottage, in Salterton, up the valley from Wilsford Manor in England. After getting it fixed, he moved into Dairy Cottage in 1982. Naipaul's reputation in America bloomed in the aftermath of the Vietnam War, when the Americans began warming up to colonial writing (French 2008, p. 252). An early and seminal anthology, *Critical Perspectives on V. S. Naipaul*, edited by Robert Hamner, was published in 1977. It contained fourteen essays that gave full representation to Naipaul, with critics, both from the Caribbean and elsewhere, quoting from his newspaper articles, interviews and short pieces. The anthology enhanced Naipaul's reputation as a self-fashioning writer because most of the critics quoted from his journalistic pieces to endorse him as a postcolonial satirical writer who rejected 'Hinduism and the colonial society into which he was born' ('Introduction' 1977, p. xvi). Meanwhile, *The New York Review of Books*, which had turned into 'the house journal' of 'America's liberal intelligentsia' (French 2008, p. 281), welcomed V. S. Naipaul. Naipaul began a new phase in his career where he stayed in England but catered to the tastes of an American audience (the new West). The writings of the 1980s are imbued with American concerns, whether through his travels to Iran, where the Americans had been expelled from, Grenada, which the United States had invaded and occupied, or the American South. Naipaul was determined not to return to Trinidad. It had never been a real option. Yet the more he tried to get away, the more he felt connected to the early world of his childhood in Trinidad. All his attitudes and all his analyses reverted back to those early memories.

The decade began with Naipaul travelling to the non-Arab Muslim world of Iran, Pakistan, Malaysia and Indonesia. This was a path-breaking journey for Naipaul. His Indian travels had led him to analyse the slow death of Indian civilisation. He now analysed the Islamic civilisation, not in its birthplace but in countries which had subsequently adopted Islam, suppressing their own histories and civilisations. In many ways, it defined his global perception since, for the first time in his travels, he also wished to be identified as a Hindu from a nondescript part of the world instead of only putting on the garb of an English traveller. He found that both Islam and Christianity had spread through the world by a combination of military, political and social forces. However, as he once lovingly commented, 'Not that Christianity hasn't done harm, but that Christian idea of love, added to the Roman idea of laws, of contracts, is what has made Western civilisation' (Michener 1981, p. 71). In his travel writing, he contrasted this Western civilisation which, to his mind, emphasised law, rationality and love, with the Islamic civilisation, which only required faith. In his mind, the Islamic world was a closed civilisation akin to the contemporary Hindu world, while the Western Christian world was an open civilisation absorbing ideas from all possible sources.

On the personal front, Sati, Naipaul's younger sister, died in November 1984. In 1985, Shiva, his younger brother, died at age 40. In 1987, Kamla, his elder sister, suffered a near-fatal heart attack. She survived, but the unfortunate incidents brought the family together in Trinidad. They shared their old memories in a deeply contemplative mood surrounding death. Naipaul found comfort in Hindu philosophy. In a purely reflective mood, he published the twin narratives, 'Prologue to an Autobiography' and 'The Crocodiles of Yamoussoukro.' He finally left Andre Deutsch for Viking in 1986. In 1987, Naipaul bought an apartment for Margaret in Buenos Aires. In 1988, Naipaul travelled to India with Margaret. And in 1989, Pat was diagnosed with breast cancer. She never fully recovered.

In a spoof published in the *Trinidad Express* (1981: 11), under the title 'A House for Mr Naipaul by V. S. Biswas,' the writer parodied Naipaul's fears about Trinidad even as Trinidad welcomed him. He even hinted at the possibility of the state buying the Hanuman House to house the National Foundation of Arts and Culture. In the piece, Naipaul is welcomed at the airport by the ruling People's National Movement (PNM), but he is too scared to address their rally entitled 'How PNM Education Creates Writers.' The article goes on to mention that the PNM decided to give Naipaul a house since he professed to have none. However, this recognition sent Naipaul running, hijacking a plane to take him back to England. While the government is fully committed to house Mr Naipaul, Mr Naipaul is scared stiff of staying in Trinidad. The article humorously summarises the relations between the then-ruling party of Trinidad and V. S. Naipaul. There was even an answer to this article in the *Trinidad Express* (Caulfield 1981). The opposition to Eric Williams was growing strong, and both the PNM and the opposition

THE IMPERIAL VISION OF THE 1980s 119

coalition National Alliance for Reconstruction (NAR) party frequently used references to Naipaul's writings to highlight the poor state of affairs. Reporting from London, Hugh Lynch highlighted how Naipaul's name got dragged into the discussion of Trinidad and Tobago not offering dual citizenships (1985).

Charles Michener published his interview with V. S. Naipaul in the *Newsweek* in 1981. This was a feature article highlighting Naipaul's 17 books, prefaced by epigraphs from Irving Howe, Edward Said and an Author's note. Written soon after the publication of *Among the Believers*, the article highlighted Michener's own position while he was ostensibly speaking with V. S. Naipaul. Michener interpreted Naipaul's early books as satires: '*The Mystic Masseur* is a breath-taking sustained black joke: what seems a charming tale of the slippery rise of a harmless quack becomes the chilling expose of a complete charlatan [...] *The Suffrage of Elvira* is a broader satire about the coming of "democracy" to Trinidad, which ends as a quietly shattering comedy of community self-destruction [...] [and *A House for Mr Biswas* as] the mimicry of a more successful culture' (1981, pp. 67–8). Compared to these, Michener labelled Naipaul's writings in *In a Free State*, *Guerrillas* and *A Bend in the River* as examples of 'a modern master' (1981, p. 72). This is completely at odds with how the Trinidadians read the early books, as highlighted in the previous chapters. Michener saw an alternative structure at work, whereby he implied that England was more civilised than Trinidad or any other previously colonised state. However, I contend that while Naipaul continued to live in England, he never compared any other society to the British because the society was not his to own.

The *Trinidad Express* republished Michener's article on November 29, 1981, along with photographs of an infant V. S. Naipaul with his parents and Michael X. It mentioned that Naipaul was the first Trinidad- or West Indian-born person to be honoured by an international news magazine in this manner, with the exception of Cuba's Fidel Castro. For the next four months, an open discussion ensued between readers in various newspapers defending or criticising Naipaul. Andrew Johnson quoted Jan Carew as calling Naipaul the 'Gungadin of Caribbean Literature' explaining that he was 'liked in the court of the master but hated among his own people' (1982). Johnson wrote against the 'Naipauls and the Walcotts and the neocolonials' who had failed in large measure to take West Indian art and culture to the most crucial phase of liberation. Anthony Milne wrote in defence of Naipaul, stating: 'Vidia Naipaul is, of course, perfectly correct. We do live in an unsophisticated, anti-intellectual, inefficient, and corrupt little island' (1982a). The Gungadin of Kipling's poem sacrificed his life while serving his English masters. Naipaul served no master as he made in-roads into the English landscape and literature.

Moreover, in Trinidad, the real powerhouse of discussion was the exchange of letters to the editor. One of the letters stated: 'As an ardent reader of the *Express* 'Letters to the Editor' page, I get the impression that every so often Vidia Naipaul uses foreign press interviews during Nobel Prize selection time to make a variety of disparaging remarks about the country and region of his birth and upbringing' ('Naipaul—Snob provocative artist, or what?' 1981). Another stated: 'Engrossed as many of us are in his outright and distasteful description of this country as a "bush" country, there has been strangely little scrutiny of the more profound meaning of his peculiar honesty' (Taylor 1982). A third stated, 'bush has become a symbol, a symbol opposite to "tapia" [...] tapia, [...] means building from below, it means to grow from native materials [...while] "Bush," on the other hand, means anything which is a copy from the grand capitalist master of the north' [presumably cosmetics, inferiority among countrymen, weak education, transportation and professionalism] (Maharajh 1982). Naipaul couldn't have agreed more because he, too, had elsewhere, interpreted the 'bush' in Trinidad as 'the breakdown of institutions, of the contract between man and man. It is theft, corruption, racist incitement' (Hardwick 1979, p. 47). Another letter stated: 'For this is a problem of Third World writers: the politico-socio-economic condition of their countries usually impels them to take a side—usually the left—and this makes many of them, as useful and brilliant as some are, chiefly propagandistic, thus bastardising their art' (Cowie 1982). Naipaul was well-defended. The article by Michener was also later republished in *Conversations with V.S. Naipaul* edited by Feroza Jussawalla (1997, pp. 63–74).

A second controversy erupted when Dr Basil Ince, External Affairs Minister and Senator, in an address to the 20th Annual Conference of the San Juan Constituency of the PNM, mentioned that 'one of the great sons of our soil, perhaps the greatest writer in the English language, has turned his back on us.' Dr Ince never mentioned Naipaul by name but stated that: 'He doesn't recognise the fact that he is what he is because of where he was born; that the pulsations that emanate from this country moulded him and shaped his personality and perceptions. He writes about us with cruel disdain and scorn. He is totally alienated from his homeland. He regards his birth in this country as a cruel accident and he has denied it of meaningful identity' ('Writer shows disdain for Land of his birth—Ince' 1982). Again, there were various letters to the editor defending Naipaul. One of them by Iere Siboney [incidentally, Iere was the first name of Trinidad and Siboney was a tribe of the First Nations People; hence, the writer was projecting him/her/self as one of the People of First Nation] said: 'But, of course, why not attack Mr Naipaul; he is an intelligent scholarly son of the soil, who because of his international status as the greatest novelist in the world today,

THE IMPERIAL VISION OF THE 1980s

poses a threat to the People's National Movement. Maybe Dr Basil Ince envisions his probable return to this country and consequently another Dr Rudranath Capildeo in the making' (Siboney 1982). Another letter by J. P. Jaikarran of County Caroni said: 'If Naipaul looks at his country in this way, what are the social conditions which shape his vision? Are those conditions there or not there? Dr Ince should first address himself to that issue […]. Trinidad society is a frustrated one. Given this circumstance, what should one do? Laugh at the people? Drown oneself in sorrow? Escape in alcohol, or say, "Work over, back to fete?"' (1982).

Among the Believers: An Islamic Journey (1981: 1982)

Globally, this book is perhaps the most controversial of all Naipaul's books. It was an important turning point in his career because it defined him for years to come. It is also important to understand this book because it lays bare his thesis on universal civilisation. Building further upon his reputation as a conservative, racist and hater of new nation states, it added Muslim-hater to his litany of faults. Most critics saw Naipaul as an apologist for the colonialists. But Naipaul continued to play up his particular position as an East Indian from the West Indies and a Brown Sahib in a world defined by the Whites. In this particular book, Naipaul went further to position himself as an East Indian *Hindu* from the West Indies.

Naipaul travelled to Iran in 1979, the same year that saw the publication of *A Bend in the River*. Naipaul, after his stint at Wesleyan, was looking to re-invent himself. He had already written 16 books, numerous essays and he had most recently added teaching to his portfolio. Iran had just undergone an Islamic revolution with the overthrow of the Shah of Iran, and Americans had lost big strategic and economic interests there. Naipaul made adjustments to the persona of his narrator to reflect his limited knowledge about Islam: 'Muslims were part of the small Indian Community of Trinidad, which was the community into which I was born, and it could be said that I had known Muslims all my life […] My own background was Hindu […] Islam, going by what I saw of it from the outside, was less metaphysical and more direct than Hinduism […]' (1981: 1982, pp. 11–2). The narrator makes it clear that he knew about Islam in the most general way and was oblivious of their religious practices. By highlighting his Hindu background, he emphasised that he was neither a westerner nor a Christian, and that was why he was equidistant from both the Islamic Revolutionaries and the Americans. At this early point in the narrative, Naipaul summarised his thesis: 'Islam was a complicated religion. It wasn't philosophical or speculative. It was a revealed religion, with the Prophet and a complete set of rules. Islam, almost from the start, had been an imperialism as well as a religion' (1981: 1982, p. 7).

The Islamic revolution had been proclaimed as 'the rule of Ali again: the dream of the society ruled purely by faith' for the establishment of the *jame towhidi*, the society of believers,' hence the title of the book (1981: 1982, p. 30). But the narrator finds it intriguing that 'cars, radios, televisions [...] were considered neutral; they were not associated with any particular faith or civilisation; they were thought of as the stock of some great universal bazaar' (1981: 1982, p. 33). This is a moot point in Naipaul's writing about what he later deemed 'our universal civilization.' Naipaul's narrator first associates science and technology with western civilisation, then disassociates western civilisation from its said universality, and finally remembers the medieval times when the Islamic civilisation had dominated much of Asia, Europe and Spanish America. This larger, more expansive view of the history of the world provided Naipaul's narrator with a vision similar to that of Conrad at the beginning of *Heart of Darkness* when he mentioned that England had once been a colony. It could be argued that this larger, expansive view was part of Naipaul's Hindu philosophy, but he would have had to read a huge amount of literature to arrive at this vision within the Hindu fold. Elsewhere, he had informed us about the distrust that existed between Hindus and Muslims in Trinidad (notably in *The Suffrage of Elvira*). However, he now suppresses any knowledge of this animosity under the garb of curiosity for the unknown. He plays himself as an innocent, curious Hindu traveller in an uncertain Islamic world.

Naipaul also frequently lapses into playing the English traveller as he brings forward the contradictions inherent in the Iranian revolution. He expresses his doubts over how the Ayatollah could be the 'voice of God'; and criticises how communists helped bring about a revolution that essentially installed an Islamic leader. He also goes on to criticise the Islamic Republic of Pakistan for obliterating its own Hindu and colonial history, the welfare state in Malaysia and the agricultural communes in Indonesia for turning their back on their traditional societies. Naipaul's narrator-traveller keeps reminding his readers about his difference from them: 'with one corner of my mind I approached Iran through classical history and felt awe for its antiquity—the conqueror of Egypt, the rival of Greece, undefeated by Rome; and with another corner of my mind I approached it through India, where, at least in the northwest, the idea of Persia is still an idea of the highest civilisation' (1981: 1982, p. 41). Naipaul disassociates himself from his own interpreter, Behzad in Iran when he realises that he had introduced him as an American writer to Shirazi. The narrator comments: 'it would have served my purpose better—to get Shirazi's response to me as a man without religion,

THE IMPERIAL VISION OF THE 1980s

and as a man of an idolatrous mystical-animistic background' (1981: 1982, p. 51). He immediately withdraws himself from reporting on this meeting and focuses upon 'the great medieval Muslim world, the great universal civilization of the time' (1981: 1982, p. 53). In Pakistan, he highlights the obliteration of local history: 'All this history [reference to 1947 riots, migration, regionalism, formation of Bangladesh, Mr Bhutto's execution] all this secular failure and pain, had been conjured away by the logic of faith' (1981: 1982, p. 86). This is the main theme in this section of the book that explores the failure of the welfare state with its attendant rhetorical emphasis on Islam: 'Wouldn't it have been better for Muslims to trust less to the saving faith and to sit down hard–headedly to work out instructions?' (1981: 1982, p. 91). His visit to a successful welfare state like Malaysia brings no comfort either because the people seem to be longing for an era gone by. In contrast, Indonesia was experimenting with de-schooling and agricultural communes. The narrator informs us that though Indonesia, like Malaysia, is an Islamic state, its 'pre-Islamic past [...] showed as a great civilisation' (1981: 1982, p. 298). He recounts Indonesia's pre-Islamic Buddhist and Hindu pasts, the Islamisation of Indonesia from the thirteenth to the sixteenth centuries, its subsequent subjugation by the Dutch for more than 350 years, the Japanese invasion during the Second World War, the declaration of Independence in 1949, and the anti-communist military coup in 1965. Recollections of the mass killings of 1965–6 were still fresh in public memory, and the narrator emphasises why Islam answers the need of the people: 'the new Islam, the Islam that is more than ritual, that speaks of the injustices done to Allah's creatures and of the Satanic ways of worldly governments: the Islam that makes people withdraw, the more violently to leap forward' (1981: 1982, p. 300). He senses unrest because people were losing their traditions that connected them to the land that they cultivated. He had similarly analysed the Black Power Movement's failure in Trinidad as a failure of the agricultural commune.

The narrator brings up his Hindu past to point out how the new generations were losing their traditional understanding while he had maintained his:

> *Indrapura*, "Indra's city," was painted on the bus in front of us; and *IndraVijaya*, "The victory of Indra," was on many shops. But this Indra was no longer the Aryan god of the Hindu pantheon. To Prasojo, as well as to the driver of our car, this Indra was only a figure from the Javanese puppet drama. Prasojo began telling me a local Muslim legend of the five Pandava brothers, who represented the five principles of Islam. And I don't believe Prasojo had an idea of the true wonder of the legend: the story he was telling me came from

the ancient Hindu epic of the *Mahabharata*, which had lived in Java for fourteen hundred years, had taken Javanese roots, and had then been adapted to Islam. (1981: 1982, p. 319)

Naipaul's narrator establishes that he sees beyond what the locals tell him. Unlike his travels through Iran, where he was unable to read posters, here he is able to understand and interpret the references to Hindu mythology even better than the locals. This is a significant development for Naipaul, who had never before acknowledged his Hindu background to this extent. He had merely referred to his Hindu background summarily as a point of difference. Here, he becomes its expert. He also sees cross-cultural exchanges as the tale of the five Pandava brothers is accommodated within Islam as one of its five principles. He foresees a greater threat coming from a seemingly more normative Arabic Islam, which demands complete submission to its principles at the cost of destroying traditional ways of life.

There is calmness in his activities in his travels across Indonesia, where his attitude is neither confusing (as in his meeting with Khalkhalli in Iran), confrontational (as in his meeting with Nuzrat in Pakistan), or persuasive (as with Shafi in Malaysia) but explorative and discursive. Pat had travelled down to Indonesia and this had a calming effect on Naipaul. He begins to outline his thesis. The obliteration of history leads to the falsification of hopes in the present. Also, there is an unqualified acceptance of the universal civilisation of the West as something that could be made to serve them without disturbing their faith:

> The West or the universal civilization it leads, is emotionally rejected. It undermines; it threatens. But at the same time it is needed, for its machines, goods, medicines, warplanes, the remittances from the emigrants, the hospitals that might have a cure for calcium deficiency, the universities that will provide master's degrees in mass media [...] Rejection, therefore, is not absolute rejection. It is also for the community as a whole, a way of ceasing to strive intellectually. It is to be parasitic; parasitism is one of the unacknowledged fruits of fundamentalism [...]. (1981: 1982, p. 168)

This thesis is repeated later in his essay 'Our Universal Civilisation.'

Critical reception of the book

It is said that Naipaul's reputation in the West was cemented because of his writings on Islamic countries. In my view, Naipaul came to terms with

THE IMPERIAL VISION OF THE 1980s 125

his own identity while travelling through the Islamic world. Repeatedly, in this book as also in *India: A Wounded Civilization* and *A Bend in the River*, he emphasises how the more orthodox societies never seem to recognise the contradictions inherent in accepting the advances of western science. Even the guerrillas in Argentina did not see that they used the most modern guns, manufactured and sent from the western world, to further their cause against the westernisation of Argentine society. Though Islam claims to be 'a complete way of life,' its followers use western science and technology as though advancements in science had no ideological assumptions. The individualism of the Western Christian world propels the scientific community to invent and modernise our daily lives. Unlike Islam, Western Christian civilisation allows even non-believers to imbibe its technologies and its value systems without religious conversion. He gives the example of Mahatma Gandhi, whose values he says were really Victorian (Levin 1983, p. 97), and of himself, who could read the New English Bible without adopting Christianity (Michener 1981, p. 73). At a personal level, his travels through the Islamic world revived and reconciled him to his Hindu heritage. The trajectory of his development is clear: in Iran, he wishes that he was recognised as a 'man without religion,' (1981: 1982, p. 51); in Pakistan, he discovers an older pre-Islamic history that revives his faith; in Malaysia, he begins to see continuity of faith amidst change; and in Indonesia, he begins interpreting Hindu symbols from his own heritage in Trinidad.

Naipaul's book, placed in a larger context, fed into Samuel Huntington's 'The Clash of Civilisations' theory that saw the 'dominating source of conflict' in the new world as cultural, that is, between 'nations and groups of different civilisations' (1993, p. 22). Edward Said denounced Naipaul for having betrayed himself and his upbringing by pushing the neo-colonial agenda about the failure of the Islamic states of Iran, Pakistan, Malaysia and Indonesia. Said deemed that Naipaul neither knew the languages nor the subject of Islam. For Naipaul, 'the sorry state of African and Asian countries who are sinking under poverty, native impotence, badly learned, unabsorbed Western ideas like industrialisation and modernisation' cannot be explained by 'National Liberation movements, revolutionary goals, the evils of colonialism' (1998: 2018, p. 118). Further:

> The West is the world of knowledge, criticism, technical know-how and functioning institutions, Islam is its fearfully enraged and retarded dependent, awakening to a new, barely controllable power [...This] is the fate of the converted, people who have lost their own past but have gained little from their new religion except more confusion, more unhappiness, more (for the Western reader) comic incompetence, all of it the result of conversion to Islam. (1998: 2018, pp. 119–20)

126 V. S. NAIPAUL OF TRINIDAD

Although Naipaul's efforts to understand Islam were disproportionate to his aversion to understanding a different religion and culture, he defended his views forcefully, repackaging them for a lecture at the Massachusetts Institute and in his later book, *Beyond Belief.*

In Trinidad, *Among the Believers* generated little controversy as compared to the *Newsweek* interview. Jeremy Taylor, in his review of *Among the Believers*, pointed out that Naipaul gave numerous examples of Islamic scholars, students and fundamentalists who take the West for granted:

> His tacit assumption—that these paradoxes invalidate the aspiration behind Islamic fundamentalism—is wholly western; most western reviewers have sounded oddly comforted by Naipaul's book, as if it were some sort of reassurance that the Islam of Khomeini and Gaddafi was not after all the threatening monolith it appeared to be, and was simply the old familiar ragbag of dreamers and crackpots, idealists and ideologues, marching around in circles, albeit colourfully. (1981, 25)

Taylor concluded: 'Naipaul's *Among the Believers* is, as always, a good read, but that conclusion, in the end, explains nothing.' (1981, p. 25). Parsuram Maharaj writing for the *Trinidad and Tobago Newsday*, post Naipaul receiving the Nobel Prize, however, argued:

> The early novels *The Mystic Masseur, The Suffrage of Elvira, The Middle Passage* and *The Loss of El Dorado* gave no clue as to the intellectual evolution of Sir V. S. Naipaul, especially as an Indian and Hindu voice in the international arena [...] Decades later *Among the Believers* and *Beyond Belief* firmly planted V. S. Naipaul in the Indian and Hindu intelligentsia. (2001, 10)

Riza Khan, reviewing the book in a Letter to Editor said that Naipaul is like 'anybody who visits Northern and Southern Ireland to get a view of fundamentalist Christianity. Both people in Ireland are Christians, and they are killing one another, which I am sure in no way has anything to do with Christ's teaching' (1982). Three different readers, three different readings from within Trinidad, each representative and partisan in its own way.

Globally, most writers (Walcott, Kincaid, Al Young, Ishmael Reed, Shelby Steele, Salman Rushdie, C. J. Wallia and Bharati Mukherjee) contended that Naipaul's audience was 'the white insecurities market' or right-wing Western people (Winokur 1991, p. 121). Dinesh Mohan interpreted *Among the Believers* as feeding into the West's fear of Islam: 'Until the seventeenth century the "Ottoman peril" lurked alongside Europe to represent for

THE IMPERIAL VISION OF THE 1980s 127

the whole of Christian civilisation a constant danger. This danger still appears real to the West, and the Palestinians, Libya's Gaddaffi, the Iranians—and now Naipaul's writings—are used in the West to keep alive the dreaded image of Islam' (1982). However, Mohan did make a comment whose truth cannot be denied: 'It is only his fame and talent which distinguish him from most of the characters he writes about.' According to Scott Winokur, the book later became a cornerstone for the West's understanding of Islam: 'Reporters turned to Naipaul this winter when they wanted a leading cultural figure to make sense of Saddam Hussein' (1991, p. 120–1). This image was further validated when he was conferred the Nobel Prize following the 9/11 attack on the twin towers in 2001.

Finding the Centre (**1984**)

Naipaul followed this deeply controversial book with a contemplative one. *Finding the Centre* is a combination book of two narratives, 'Prologue to an Autobiography' and 'The Crocodiles of Yamoussoukro.' In the 1984 Andre Deutsch published Preface to *Finding the Centre*, Naipaul writes, 'both pieces are about the process of writing. Both pieces seek in different ways to admit the reader to that process' (1984, p. 9). Narrating the genesis of these two pieces, he writes that the initial idea came to him in 1967 and developed in 1972 when he visited Trinidad, trying to write about 'his literary beginnings' and 'the imaginative promptings' of his 'many-sided background' (1984, p. 9). In 1977, he visited Venezuela to meet Bogart, and in 1981, on the promptings of an American editor, Richard Locke, he wrote the first piece. The second is about the writer's need to seek 'new people and new relationships' (1984, p. 10). In the first piece, Naipaul the writer and Naipaul the narrator are one, while in the latter piece, the distance between the two is tangible, even though both articles are written in the first person. The narrator confesses to being a colonial in 1960, 'travelling to far off places that were still colonies, in a world still more or less ruled by colonial ideas' (1984, p. 11). He knows that he now moves in a world that is no longer colonial, and travel becomes 'the substitute for the mature social experience—the deepening knowledge of a society' (1984, p. 12). The tone is reconciliatory, theorising about the genesis of writing about worlds that the writer professes to know and not know.

In the first piece, Naipaul describes the moment when he became a writer while sitting with a typewriter in the freelancers' room at the BBC. From his memory, he created 'the white–negro–mulatto town' (1984, p. 18) through the eyes of a young boy who was Hindu and Indian. He confesses that Hat was modelled upon a Port of Spain Indian, 'descendants of South

Indians, not Hindi–speaking, and not people of caste' (1984, p. 18). Bogart was modelled after a relative from his extended family belonging to Punjab, India. His own writing was modelled after his father, Seepersad Naipaul's writings: 'It was my private epic' (1984, p. 43). He describes his early life in the town of Chaguanas, and confesses: 'The ambition to be a writer was given me by my father' (1984, p. 33). His father's stories 'celebrated elemental things, the order of the working day, the labour of the rice fields, the lighting of the cooking fire in the half–walled gallery of a thatched hut, the preparation and eating of food' (1984, p. 42). In his quest to find his centre, he found his father's writings at the beginning of his creative universe. However, he found his centre disintegrating when he realised that his reformist father had once fumbled.

Seepersad Naipaul, while working for the *Trinidad Guardian*, once reported that Hindus did not get their cows vaccinated because they were superstitious. This angered the local community leaders, and he was sent death threats privately. He was asked to sacrifice a goat in order to appease the gods that he had angered in his over-enthusiasm. In the 1970s, a journalist sent V. S. Naipaul an article from the 1933 *New York Herald Tribune* regarding Seepersad Naipaul having participated in the ritualistic sacrifice of a goat. Naipaul researched the *Trinidad Guardian* of the time and realised that the incident had happened in June 1933 and had been widely reported within Trinidad. This probably led to Seepersad Naipaul feeling publicly humiliated and having his first bout of depression. Naipaul realised that his father presented himself as a social reformer in his writings but was no revolutionary. He idealised his father, yet he now saw him as a publicly humiliated man who receded from public life after this incident. His attachment to his father had defined his relationship with Trinidad for much of his life. This was a crude shock. Similarly, Bogart, whose presence at a certain time and place gave him the material for his first book, busted the myth of the carefree, smart man who went on sea adventures.

Having explained how his known world had crumbled before his eyes, he now focuses on an unknown part of his world—the Ivory Coast. In the accompanying piece, 'The Crocodiles of Yamoussoukro,' Naipaul's thematic concerns remain the same as the first piece, albeit with a difference because he has no personal connection to the people or the place. The difference between Naipaul the writer and Naipaul the narrator is back in place. The title refers to the presence of man-eating crocodiles in the moat surrounding the palace built by President Houphouët-Boigny in his village. The significance of the crocodiles is never fully explained either by President Houphouët-Boigny to his electorate or by Naipaul to

THE IMPERIAL VISION OF THE 1980s 129

his readers. He chooses two women, Andrée and Arlette, to be his guides in Ivory Coast. This is a departure from his usual narrative self, that is, to use women as his interpreters and helpers. It is also the first time that he positively recognises his connection to a larger Caribbean space since both Andrée and Arlette were recent migrants from the Francophone Caribbean.

The narrator acknowledges that Africa 'has always been in its own eyes complete, achieved, bursting with its own powers' (1984, p. 92). It remains hidden and unknown to him because he wants to approach it through a Western lens. Professor Niangoran-Bouah, working on the science behind drums, reveals that the drum is not merely music but mimics 'human speech: a trained singer could re-discover, in a particular passage of drumming, a poem, an incantation, a piece of tribal history, a story of victory or defeat' (1984, p. 169). The narrator notes that the Africans consider the Western civilisation lesser because the Westerners, in spite of their superior technological and scientific advances, do not know or believe in the world of energy, ancestors and spirits. Through this insight, Naipaul, the narrator, reaches his own understanding about Afro-Trinidadians: 'To the outsider, to the slave-owner, the African night world might appear a mimic world, a child's world, a carnival. But to the African […] it was the true world: it turned white men to phantoms and plantation life to an illusion' (1984, p. 162). This is a reworking of his position in *The Loss of El Dorado* where he refused to recognise the African world of spirits as real. It is also a reworking of his position in the essays 'Power?' and 'Michael X and the Black Power Killings in Trinidad.' In those two articles, Naipaul's narrator saw the Black Power Movement in Trinidad as another extension of the fantasy of the carnival where the existing state was maintained in spite of the reversal of the roles of the oppressor and the oppressed for a brief period of time. Naipaul's narrator acknowledges that, though he may not understand, he shall not question the legitimacy of those beliefs. There is no evidence to suggest that he reworks his position on the Black Power Movement in Trinidad, but a recognition of African beliefs does reveal a reworking of his position on traditional animist religions around the world. He recognises the legitimacy of rituals, not only as community gatherings of inclusion and recovery but also as sustaining and creating communities by themselves. William Ghosh reads 'The Crocodiles of Yamoussoukro' from within the sphere of Caribbean intellectual debates but finds Naipaul reinforcing the Western discourse on Africa. He reads Naipaul as part of a veritable line of Caribbean travellers to Africa from George Lamming to Maryse Condé, tracing the development of 'the idea of Africa' in the Caribbean. For Ghosh, 'the African "reality," Naipaul suggests, is unavailable not just to imperial, but to Caribbean eyes' (2019, p. 188).

130   V. S. NAIPAUL OF TRINIDAD

As I read it, Naipaul continued to highlight the mediated nature of reality and our limitations in knowing it. From not recognising interpreters in his writings to recognising interpreters as possible interventionists who colour meanings in *Among the Believers* to now using interpreters with whom he has a *natural* affinity, the trajectory is reconciliatory. The two pieces together recognise that the writer cannot know but must always strive to know the truth.

Critical reception in Trinidad

In an interview with Bernard Levin before the release of this book, Naipaul stirred a controversy when he said that he being born in Trinidad 'was a great mistake': 'I didn't like the climate. I didn't like the quality of light. I didn't like the heat; I didn't like the asthma that gave me. I didn't like a lot of the racial tensions around me [...] I didn't like the music; I didn't like the loudness. I just felt I was in the wrong place [...] I didn't like my family' (1983, p. 92). Hugh Lynch, writing from London in his *Trinidad Express* column, reported on Naipaul's interview with Levin, adding: 'Mr Naipaul always does, in fact such interviews, give every sign of intense cogitation, his face going into contortions and his words emerging—often at long intervals—with all the normal difficulty of water from a tap in present-day Trinidad' (1983). The metaphor emphasises Lynch's displeasure at hearing Naipaul speak so despairingly about Trinidad. Another critic, though equally critical of Naipaul in another instance, felt that by inviting self-criticism in his interviews, Naipaul shielded himself from 'false empathy and sentimentality' (Cadogan 2007).

Finding the Centre was favourably received in Trinidad with an article by Nisa Khan reviewing the 'Prologue to an Autobiography' (1984). Wayne Brown in his review summarises the book with the comment: 'Naipaul is far more prone than he was to withhold pronouncement in favour of description, judgment in favour of elucidation' (1984). Wayne Brown in a series of three articles published between July and August 1984, analysed Naipaul's writing: 'Apart from one tentative feint (*The Mimic Men*) into the heady air of metaphysics, his development since *Miguel Street* has been relatively straightforward—a steady descent into the Nietzschean nightmare of idealism and misanthropy [*In a Free State* and *Guerrillas*], followed by an equally steady climb back towards the grassy plains where ordinary folks live [*A Bend in the River*].'

Naipaul's writings were becoming calmer and more mature. In two different articles published in the *Trinidad Express*, one dated November 2, 1986, and the other dated February 22, 1987, Naipaul praised the writings

THE IMPERIAL VISION OF THE 1980s 131

of Neil Bissoondath ('Keeping faith with the Naipaul Legacy' 1986) and Shiva Naipaul ('The Brothers Naipaul' 1987), his nephew and his brother, respectively. Naipaul was known to be condescending towards fellow writers, but in these cases, he made exceptions for the family. The feeling may have been occasioned by the family's grief over the loss of Sati (Naipaul's younger sister and Bissoondath's mother) and Shiva so soon after her. The reconciliatory tone is even more evident in the following book, *The Enigma of Arrival*.

The Enigma of Arrival (1987)

The Enigma of Arrival was published as 'a novel in five sections.' However, many critics, such as John Thieme, Gillian Dooley and Vijay Mishra, read it as an autobiographical travel book. Naipaul had arrived in England at the age of 18. He was now 55 years old. The book is an account of a colonial writer coming to terms with the England of his imagination in real time and place. I contend that the book is about a traveller's extended stay in a country, and, throughout the book, the narrator fashions himself as a newcomer to those surroundings and therefore builds his identity as an outsider to Wiltshire, if not England.

According to Kenneth Ramchand, none of the other writers of the so-called 'New Literatures in English,' the Indian, Australian or Canadian writers, made London their centre in the same manner as the West Indians did (Ramchand, Personal Communication, November 23, 2019). The West Indian writers of the 1950s not only wanted to be published in England but to also migrate and settle there. The Notting Hill Riots, which ran from August 30 to September 5, 1958, were a reminder of the racially charged political atmosphere against the policy of open immigration from places such as the West Indies. The poor white working Londoners saw the newly arrived West Indian immigrants as competitors in the workplace and as polluting their lives, cultures and neighbourhoods with their drinking, smoking and brothel cultures. West Indians flocked to London in search of better living conditions, money, ambition and recognition, and London remained an integral part of the West Indian 'escape route.' Writers from the Caribbean were put in a double bind: they were expected to embrace an Anglicised personality while opening themselves up for racial and class-forward attacks on their use of the English language, tone and mannerisms that hid their 'essentially exotic' peasant backgrounds. Whether the West Indian peasant (as spoken of by George Lamming in the 1960s) was a repository for anti-colonial or post-colonial subjectivity (as read by British critics) or could he really represent a vast West Indian multi-racial, multi-cultural psyche remains a contentious formulation even within the Caribbean.

132 V. S. NAIPAUL OF TRINIDAD

Naipaul's depiction of England was a mix of emotions because he owed his recognition and literary career to England, yet he never felt welcomed in British society. In his early essay, 'London,' Naipaul tells us that though he had been living in London for eight years [at that time] and was convinced that his Trinidad was 'a simple colonial philistine society' (1958b: 1972, p. 9), he felt lost because he knew that his books could only be truly appreciated by those who knew the region he wrote about: 'Without that knowledge it is easy for my books to be dismissed as farces and my characters as eccentrics' (1958b: 1972, p. 11). His sense of disillusionment with the then-contemporary literary scene in London led him to declare that his eight years in England had granted him 'the Buddhist ideal of non-attachment' (1958b: 1972, p. 16). This 'non–attachment' referred to his response to the social world of England and not to his writing. Naipaul was always fiercely attached to his writings and defended them till the end. In another essay titled, 'Jasmine,' Naipaul tackled the problem of the use of the English language and its literary tradition. He claimed in this essay: 'The English language was mine; the tradition was not' (1964b: 1972, p. 26). His stay in England had made 'English writing more truly accessible, [but] it had made participation more difficult' (1964b: 1972, p. 28). Naipaul came to a realisation that all literature including English literature, were provincial or regional. They were written in dialogue with their literary traditions and local mythologies, and these meanings were available only to the local readers.

Naipaul came to this conclusion because he realised that the place of India in the imaginary of the Indo-Trinidadians was vastly different from how it was seen as just another colony in England. Similarly, London had been imbued with meanings of success unavailable to those Britishers who were perhaps born in London. London was a place to escape to for the narrator in *Miguel Street* and Anand in *A House for Mr Biswas*, an administrative centre in *The Mystic Masseur, The Middle Passage*, and *An Area of Darkness*, an ageing society in *Mr Stone and the Knights Companion*, a place of psychic breakdown and rehabilitation in *The Mimic Men*, a colonial centre unable to sustain its immigrants in 'Tell me who to Kill,' and a lost space full of immigrants in *A Bend in the River*. It was later to be depicted as a conduit/ study centre in *Half-a-Life* and *Magic Seeds*. However, this book is not about London, rural England or his settling down but about adopting and adapting the English language for speaking about the colonies. In order to do this, the writer must fully understand the language in its context.

The book opens with Naipaul's narrator reflecting on the English language as it rains for the first four days. Naipaul's narrator creates a distance between himself and the 'new' place, which he subsequently begins to describe by adjusting the points of view, seasons and light of the day. Naipaul's narrator, as opposed to the omniscient narrator, returns to the same scene over and over again, adding details that had escaped his eye in the first, second, or even third excursions through references to literature that defined his mental picture of England while growing up in Trinidad. The task is huge considering that most post-colonial writers in the colonies read English literature from Chaucer to the Victorians in a stereoscopic manner as a single discourse at a given time, envisioning an England in the absence of a physical referent. The England produced in the colonised spaces through a reading of English literature contrasts sharply with present-day England, and the migrants must negotiate the present through images set in the past. As the narrator walks through Wordsworth's lake districts, he is aware that the romantics' vision is no longer available because of the introduction of modern conveniences such as roads, buses, tractors, and machinery. In spite of this, he explores the countryside with a deep understanding that literature exerts greater power when placed in its proper context.

In the second section, 'Journeys,' Naipaul's narrator bridges the gap between the narrator and the writer. For Naipaul, the scene in de Chirico's painting in *The Enigma of Arrival* (1987, p. 105), with two figures on the quay and the ship a little way beyond, evokes a scene where the traveller returns to board his ship to go back to where he had come from, but the ship has already left. The travel experience has changed him, and he cannot return. The painting not only makes for a great title for his book but also helps him look 'anew' at his past portrayals of England and his use of the English language. Just like the traveller in the painting, the ship has left Naipaul's narrator in England, and he cannot return. He compares the storyline to the one he was then writing, later published as 'In a Free State.' The scene haunts him because it is loaded with meanings. It is a further surprise to him to know that the painting has been given meaning and its title by a poet and not the painter. Thus, Naipaul is able to give meaning to England and its depleting rural landscape even though he was not born there. Naipaul, then, accommodates his presence within this England: 'To get anywhere in the writing, I had first of all to define myself very clearly to myself' (1987, p. 168). Each journey undertaken between England and Trinidad 'was to qualify the one that had gone before, one response overlaying the other' (1987, p. 161). He goes on to say how '[e]very exploration, every book, added to my knowledge, qualified my earlier idea of myself and the world' (1987, p. 168). Repeatedly, the focus is upon his knowledge and reading of English literature and his ability to mould the English language to accommodate his presence there. The book does not decode England; it merely makes space for the non-native narrator to write in his presence.

134   V. S. NAIPAUL OF TRINIDAD

In the third section of *The Enigma of Arrival* called 'Ivy,' Naipaul secures his position in the England countryside against the disintegrating world of the Landlord: 'This empire explained my birth in the New World, the language used, the vocation and ambition I had, this empire in the end explained my presence there in the valley, in the cottage, in the grounds of the manor' (1987, p. 208). But the empire has already fallen apart. The times have changed. Thus, Jack, Jack's father-in-law, Pitton, the landlord, Mr and Mrs Phillips, Brenda, Les and the farm manager, are all intrusions into the lovely English countryside with its trees and animals. While the landscape has adjusted to accommodate the narrator, these people, whom the writer initially thinks belong there, are revealed to be rather out of place. Jack was a recent entrant to the village; Pitton will soon return; the landlord will die. Naipaul's main concern is the contradictory status of his writing position that is both English and non-English, colonial and postcolonial. Thus, the book is a deep-seated contemplation of a non-native English writer's position within England, English writing and the traditions of English literature. Naipaul lays claim not only to language but also to the tradition of English literature that he has read in a particular way and which now allows him to place himself within that tradition.

In a review, Bernard Levin called Naipaul an 'inquiline,' that is, a lodger, and also an animal that lives in another's nest. Andrew Robinson informs us that Naipaul liked the word (1992, p. 132). Closer home, in an article, Romeo Kaseram found that Naipaul's new book, *The Enigma of Arrival*, only reinforced his beliefs that the islands were wastelands in which nothing grew. What is new is that he has realised that 'the central city too is like the wasteland from which he fled, and contains the final decay from where the Caribbean's desolating colonialism emanated' because 'He does not see the emergence of an originality from the desolation which he denounced, which made him into a writer' (1987). This assertion is somewhat faulty. At the end of the book, Naipaul recounts his visit to Trinidad to attend a ceremony following the death of Sati, his younger sister. The reader watches Naipaul's narrator turn his gaze *not away* from himself but on his Indian Hindu inheritance in the West Indies. Naipaul realises the calming influence of rituals as well as the disconnect of the ritual from the earlier earth rites. Conducted on a terrazzo floor in a modern house, the rites seem inauthentic. Yet the family desires the rites to be performed. Naipaul now notes the difference between *his* Trinidad and the present one: 'None of the Indian villages were like villages I had known' (1987, p. 385). He even appreciates a cousin who compresses history by drawing a link from Columbus to Queen Isabella to the Indian indentured (1987, p. 386). Towards the end of the book, he acknowledges that his trip to Trinidad and his participation in the Hindu rituals led him

THE IMPERIAL VISION OF THE 1980s   135

to expel his own fears of death. Though the book itself is about a writer's adjustment into an established society and the incorporation of his writing into the English tradition, the last section is devoted to his visit to Trinidad. Trinidad becomes the source of his release from stasis. Naipaul realised that the more he tried to get away from Trinidad, the more he remembered it as the source of all his thought processes.

A Turn in the South (1989)

The final book in the 1980s was *A Turn in the South*, about his travels through the southern states of America. The *Trinidad Guardian* reported that Naipaul was in the Nobel race again in October 1988. Naipaul was now faced with a new challenge of 'visiting' America. Naipaul had been visiting America since the 1950s; he had taken a ship from New York on his way to Oxford; he had frequented America for literary assignments; he had been writing for the *New York Review* for more than a decade; he had spent a year teaching at Wesleyan University; and he had covered the Republican Convention in 1984. Travelling to write about America posed a problem that was as grave as the one he had faced in 1961 when he had travelled through the Caribbean. He had played with the distance between himself and his narrator to the extent that they appeared to be one without admitting any other relation into the mix. He had done so in *The Middle Passage, An Area of Darkness, India: A Wounded Civilization,* and most recently in *The Enigma of Arrival*. He had admitted to the use of interpreters in his travels to Muslim-majority countries and to the continent of Africa. But now the challenge was based neither on ancestry nor coloniality nor language. He could not write as a British writer because he was neither nostalgic nor impressed with the American model of development. He did not see America as a British colony because the Europeans had settled there long ago and built up a civilisation. Further, England had by this time lost its place in the geo-political panorama, providing the figure of the English traveller with no added benefits. He fell back on his Indo-Caribbean heritage, but his racial and class background did not really provide him with a clear perspective. His lack of perspective was compounded by the fact that a typical Indian or Caribbean traveller viewed America as a dream destination, and settling down in America was perhaps seen as their greatest achievement. Naipaul, on the other hand, had decided in the 1970s that he would not live in America. Further, in all his previous travels, Naipaul had built his travelling persona as ideologically neutral and as an East Indian from the West Indies. In Trinidad, the Africans and the East Indians shared a history of colonial rule, discrimination and violence. Even the local white creoles had seen times of abject poverty because the colonial masters had drained Trinidad's economy.

All racial and ethnic classes in Trinidad felt the effects of a common colonial power. Thus, race relations in Trinidad had a very different 'felt' quality than in America, where the traditional elite white class had imported, exploited and actively discriminated against the Blacks for generations and continued to do so in spite of all the changes in their legal framework after the civil rights movement.

A Turn in the South is about Naipaul's travels through the seven southern cities of Atlanta, Charleston, Tallahassee, Tuskegee, Jackson, Nashville, Durham, and Charlottesville in the United States, undertaken over a period of four months. The book opens with Naipaul's narrator emphasising his outsider-ness to America. As opposed to the uncomfortable struggler in *The Enigma of Arrival* where it rains the first four days, in *A Turn in the South*, he is the self-assured traveller-writer-professional who lands in America with the name of a contact and soon finds his first lead in following Howard to his home, 'Howard had something neither Jimmy or I had, a patch of the earth he thought of as home, absolutely his' (1989, p. 3). Unlike Sitor in *Among the Believers* who also had a 'patch of the earth' to call his own, here it is Howard, a descendant of the African enslaved who were brought from Africa to till the land in the American Southern states. Soon, Naipaul realises that the 'patch of the earth' that was absolutely Howard's is more of a region than a specific piece of land. His mother lives in a new concrete house that is 'home' to her and Howard, though they grew up in another house nearby. The theme of change, decay and the passing of an era, begun in *The Enigma of Arrival*, is continued. The specificity of the patch of the earth is lost. Naipaul must re-evaluate what Howard meant by 'home' and what he himself means by 'home.'

The Southern states of America were the traditional plantation estates that lost the Civil War to the Northerners. The traditional estate households were destroyed, and the animosity between the White owners and the Black plantation workers fuelled a silent war, with each side claiming to have lost a secure way of life. Naipaul's lack of a personal dimension to his narrative (remember his earlier stated position that he travelled only to places connected to his place of birth) is compensated by his delight in connecting old chests of tobacco to slavery and West Indian farming practices. Dissanayake and Wickramagamage argue that Naipaul's narrative maintains a detached tone from the main current of events, letting 'the South articulate itself through what its people say and what its history reveals, limiting himself to a seemingly neutral observer' (1993, p. 119). It suits their thesis that once Naipaul has reterritorialised himself in England in *The Enigma of Arrival*, he is more 'appreciative of the "order and faith" of the South' (1993, p. 120). However, Rob Nixon attacks Naipaul's neutrality by arguing that Naipaul

THE IMPERIAL VISION OF THE 1980s   137

'accept[ed] southern Christianity as a necessary irrational compensation for the anguish and fractured order of the past' (1993, p. 164). This is unlike his Indian and Islamic writings 'where he condemns all forms of religion as stifling, sentimentality seduced by the past, irrational, and antiquated' (Nixon 1992, p. 165). Nixon makes a case for reading Naipaul as an indulgent racist. He quotes Arnold Rampersad to point out:

> the book displays an imbalance in the distribution of Naipaul's sympathies and attention to the point of bigotry. Transfixed by country– and western music's inventiveness, he remains silent about blues and jazz. White writers get a full billing as artists; black writers are scaled down to representatives of racial frenzy or despair [...] noble pathos of a vanishing past amidst white southern communities, but among black communities, he unearths self-violation and back-to-back dereliction. (Nixon 1992, p. 165)

In fact, Rampersad views Naipaul's narrator as a 'car window sociologist' (1990, p. 25), with the 'prevailing attitude of whites toward Blacks' (1990, p. 37). Rampersad, a Trinidadian settled in America, argues that the Blacks are not given adequate representation within the book, and someone like Naipaul should have made more efforts to correctly record the white supremacist attitudes.

While Naipaul's racism is nothing new to point out today, Naipaul himself shows this awareness when, in the preface to a 2011 edition, he confesses his poor political judgement, 'where history is so bad, impartiality [is] prejudice.' Telling both sides of the story is not to be apolitical. By 'balancing' Black Power Movement with White Supremacists, Naipaul makes both sides appear spurious, turning the position of the impartial spectator into a gimmick. The 'rednecks' have never experienced violent pain, as opposed to the Blacks who still feel racial tensions in today's America. Naipaul fails to present both sides of the tale but does succeed in exposing America as a racially divided society to an armchair traveller elsewhere. Naipaul does not subscribe to the myth of America being the great 'melting pot' where people from all over the world come to seek 'opportunities.'

Naipaul uses various registers, including his racial identity as an 'Indian' (1989, p. 6) and (1989, pp. 61–4), as an East Indian from the West Indies (1989, p. 33), as a Hindu (1989, p. 122) and as an English traveller for whom the racial question is 'new' (1989, p. 25). He uses these registers, disregarding his knowledge of the race riots in England in 1958 and of the Black Power Movement in England and Trinidad in the 1970s. He even disassociates himself from the figure of the much-travelled postcolonial traveller because

138 V. S. NAIPAUL OF TRINIDAD

none of these registers give him the necessary elbow room to develop a perspective and write about the Southern states of America, where racial violence was not a matter of attitude but a reality. The book is a failure in much the same way as *Mr Stone and the Knights Companion* because Naipaul fails to develop a perspective and situate himself within the book. *A Turn in the South* made a loss for Knopf (French 2008, p. 435), primarily because Naipaul had received a high advance payment from Knopf.

Naipaul's neutral stance is a far cry from his scathing analysis of racial tensions in Trinidad in 1967. In a soul-searching article published on May 4, 1988, in the *Trinidad Guardian*, Kenneth Ramchand re-analysed Naipaul's *The Mimic Men* in the context of political and racial tensions in Trinidad. He wrote:

> Naipaul's account of the secondary school days of Singh, Browne, Hok and Deschampneufs is a bold expose of the factors in our growing up that consolidate racial prejudice and ignorance, that prevent knowledge and self-knowledge. [...] And by clear implication, Naipaul is saying that unless the groups and individuals in our society examine themselves with the rigorousness with which Naipaul examines Singh in this novel, unless the self-searching is as thorough as this no matter what, all our attempts at unity at the political and cultural levels will be built upon rotting and dishonest and self-deceiving foundations. As the relationship between Browne and Singh is.
>
> Read and learn, Mr Robinson.
>
> Read and learn, Mr Panday.
>
> *And all you self-serving lackeys who encourage racial politics for your own narrow ends, tutorials can be arranged.* [end] (1988, 9)

Ramchand found Naipaul's 1967 novel still relevant in 1988, not because of its milieu or protagonists but because of the way it portrayed racial relations among the Afro- and Indo-Trinidadians. Naipaul could have presented a more easy-going portrayal of racial harmony between the two dominant races on the island, but that would have falsified the realities. The overt message at the end of the article was to Mr A. N. R. Robinson and Mr Basdeo Panday to shed racial animosities and come together in a power-sharing arrangement for the first ever non-PNM government of Trinidad and Tobago.

So, the question is why Naipaul preferred to fashion himself as ideologically neutral to racial inequalities and segregation as opposed to his earlier analyses? My guess is that Naipaul, first of all, wished to disassociate himself from his earlier first-person involvement in local politics. It also sprang from his (mis-)reading of popular attitudes. In a decade where

THE IMPERIAL VISION OF THE 1980s   139

Naipaul found it hard to shed his own memories to move forward with life (with the deaths of his younger sister and brother), he questioned nostalgic attitudes for a 'lost cause.' In a strange comparison, Naipaul's narrator compares the Confederate Memorial (1989, p. 100) to the revolutionaries in Iran. Just as the Revolutionary Shias had built monuments of defeat and indulged in dreams of returning to Islamic purity, the Southerners cherished the memorial. Either the war was wrong or the practice of slavery was wrong. To cherish nostalgia for a past way of life means to continue segregation and inequality. Added to this was the fact that the Confederate Memorial commemorates only the white Southerners. The continued segregation in churches leads to serious questioning of Christian ideals. In most Christian churches with predominantly Black followers, Naipaul's narrator notes that the whiteness of Jesus was either not interpreted or he was described as 'colorless' (1989, p. 121). As Rev. Bernyce says, 'You're born a Hindu. We are not born Christians. We are born Black' (1989, p. 122).

The book records the racial divide but fails to question it. However, the book is reconciliatory in manner because, for the first time, Naipaul recognises the value of music and religion as 'supports against anarchy' (Hussein 1994, p. 157). Naipaul was infamous for detesting the sound of the steel drum and for his dislike of religious rituals. But it seems that after his last visit to Trinidad, he had made peace with both music and religion. Naipaul's positive inclination towards understanding the appeal of a communal identity is palpable. Naipaul had always been a dedicated follower of individualism. He had associated community with backward attitudes that inhibited the growth of the individual. In this book, Naipaul moves away from his set thinking and views investment in communities with a positive outlook. The churches provide individuals with the means to cope with past violence when individuals fail to draw upon their own resources to do so. Naipaul begins to look at the community as a pillar of strength, sustaining the individual rather than impeding their growth. We see a further development of this thought process in the next book, *India: A Million Mutinies Now*. The two books, *A Turn in the South* and *A Million Mutinies Now*, have a common theme, that is, the relationship between an individual and their community. Although both books employ a single tone of voice to filter the views of their varied people (no use of creole or differing speech patterns), the latter book is more successful in integrating this theme with the vision of the narrator.

Naipaul's Turn towards Conservatism

Naipaul had turned introspective in the 1980s, searching for his internal ideal. Slowly, he came to accept his early upbringing in a large Hindu household as a definitive influence on himself. His worldview was defined around two points: one, that he was an East Indian from the West Indies; and two, that few people, except for those who shared his heritage, could understand his unique position in the world. Repeatedly, he felt that by putting his heritage at the forefront, he was able to connect with people at a level that was not possible if he were an Englishman. This also had to do with the fact that he was no longer travelling only through previously colonised British colonies but through Muslim-majority countries where he connected with people through his own cultural resources as a Hindu. Naipaul had begun to look upon Trinidad as an ideal society, though not in real time. He saw his own multi-racial and multi-cultural upbringing in Trinidad in the 1940s as an idyllic time when he remained unaffected by religious, racial and class divisions. He was too young to truly sense the simmering racial tensions, and at the same time, there was camaraderie between the races against their common enemy, the British Governor. He now acknowledged that his particular circumstances gave him a wide net for writing about the world.

Naipaul's acknowledgement of his Hindu background in *Among the Believers*, *Finding the Centre*, *The Enigma of Arrival* and *A Turn in the South* needs a qualification. A Hindu is a reference to a religion, a race, a philosophy and a civilisation. Naipaul had repeatedly noted in his early writings that he was born a Hindu, though he personally was not a man of faith. He also noted that distinction was important to him as he was an East Indian in the West Indies and an Indian in England. It must also be noted that Naipaul's definition of himself as a Hindu is an expeditious statement rather than a descriptive, decisive position. He in no way aligns himself with a larger Hindu community or a Hindu philosophy. The fact that he attended his sister's death ceremony or that one of his friends read passages from the *Bhagvad Gita* at his funeral ceremony does not make him a practising Hindu. In *Among the Believers*, he realised that he could have had a dialogue with Shirazi only if he had been introduced as a non-Christian writer. Naipaul was always happy to be introduced as an East Indian from the West Indies, and not as a Hindu, a Brahmin or an Indian. But few people knew about the West Indies let alone the legacies of the East Indian. Instead, his whimsical nature was interpreted as that of a high-caste Brahmin frowning on lesser mortals, but Naipaul had neither training nor faith in the rituals of the Sanatan Dharma to inculcate his Brahmanism because, by his confession, he had not undergone the thread ceremony. His father's reformist streak had made Naipaul a cynic. Yet he did eventually believe that the ambition to become a writer was something that had come to him because of his Brahmanical upbringing. Hugh Lynch, reporting from London on an interview given by Naipaul to Andrew

THE IMPERIAL VISION OF THE 1980s   141

Robinson, originally published in *The Illustrated Weekly of India*, quoted Robinson as saying that as Naipaul 'ages, he thinks he is probably becoming more of a contemplative, a Hindu: the feeling that life is an illusion is growing on him, but he is not really sympathetic to it,' just 'more resigned' (1987). The question in the interview was, 'What aspects of yourself do you feel to be specifically Indian?' And Naipaul's answer was:

> The philosophical aspect—Hindu I would say. Speculative and probably also pessimistic. What I mean by pessimism is not things turning out badly, but a pessimistic view about existence; that men just end. It is that feeling that life is an illusion. I've entered it more and more as I've grown older. (Robinson 1987, p. 108)

This quite fits into my argument that Naipaul's travels through the Islamic world and the personal tragedies through the 1980s brought him an increased awareness of his religious beliefs as a Hindu, even if this consciousness was awakened in the most general sense. Similarly, Hugh Lynch, a Trinidadian and a late immigrant to England, chose to focus on three aspects within Naipaul's interview: Naipaul's confession of being a Hindu, his rather unhappy childhood in Trinidad, and his writing as an 'escape from extinction, from being nothing, from being crushed.' (1987)

This was the first decade in which Naipaul failed to write a novel. All his writing was non-fictional, although he labelled *The Enigma of Arrival* a novel. For the first time in his life, he used the metaphor of life as a journey and all men as travellers dealing with change. By pushing back history by a few centuries, Naipaul analysed Islam as an imperial political force that was supported by the Islamic ideals of that era. That was an era of expansion of the Islamic civilisation from its Arab centre to as far away as India in the east, Spain in the north and Africa in the west. This led him to formalise his thoughts about 'Our Universal Civilization.'

Chapter 6

REDEMPTIVE JOURNEYS IN THE 1990s

V. S. Naipaul was knighted by Queen Elizabeth II in 1990. Many centuries ago, Sir Walter Raleigh received his knighthood from Queen Elizabeth I in 1585. Sir V. S. Naipaul was in a long line of those who received the Order of the British Empire from the West Indies, both pre- and post-independence. In 1989, he was also awarded the Trinity Cross by the Government of Trinidad and Tobago. He called the latter the 'greatest award' in his life. He was happy that he received this award before the announcement by the British Queen. It made the award special in a personal way. On his way back to London from Trinidad after receiving the Trinity Cross (now the Order of the Republic of Trinidad and Tobago), Naipaul spoke to reporters at the Diplomatic Lounge at the Piarco International Airport in Trinidad. Suren Capildeo, the son of Simbhoonath Capildeo and Naipaul's cousin brother, had recently voiced concerns regarding the continued political alienation of Indians in Trinidad. Naipaul, in response to a question, said: 'The seeds of that (political alienation) were sown a long, long time ago in the (19)30s and 40s with the extraordinary pettiness of Indian political life and I think we're paying the price of that pettiness' (Cuffie 1990, p. 1). He refuted the claims of racial hostility by stating, 'I don't see a lot of (racial) tension here. I see a lot more community of interest and culture than most places. We certainly share a language, we share pleasures, we share an economy very much. [...] I think a lot of it is in the head' (Cuffie 1990, p. 1). This was a rare instance of Naipaul speaking benignly rather than nostalgically about Trinidad.

In Trinidad, there is a distinct bonhomie between the different races and religions, and in general, a creolised culture exists. However, this bonhomie is intermittently broken, as it was when a coup was attempted and the Trinidad Parliament was held under siege for six days in July and August of 1990. The political coup was a simultaneous attack on the Trinidad and Tobago parliament, the police headquarters, the National Broadcasting Service, Radio Trinidad and the Trinidad and Tobago Television station. For six days,

144 V. S. NAIPAUL OF TRINIDAD

from July 27 to August 1, 1990, the Prime Minister of Trinidad and Tobago, A. N. R. Robinson, six members of his cabinet, and ten other persons were held hostage in the country's Parliament House while the city burnt. Soon after, when the government had been reinstated and the rebellion quashed, a booklet was brought out titled 'Dear Prime Minister: Letters to the Prime Minister of Trinidad and Tobago, August 1990.' The booklet contained letters of goodwill received by the then Prime Minister from various Heads of State and eminent personalities on the restoration of his democratically elected government. V. S. Naipaul's message finds a space here where he congratulates the Prime Minister, praising Robinson's show of 'courage, fortitude and abundant dignity.' Curiously, he also puts in a line: 'This may be a good opportunity for building Port of Spain along aesthetic lines' (1990, p. 77). Naipaul wanted the city to be developed and preserved as an aesthetically beautiful city, a memory and a past that he cherished.

By the 1990s, Naipaul was well-settled in England. His perspective on the world had enlarged to encompass a wider geography and a longer history. In an interview with Andrew Robinson, Naipaul insinuated that nobody had given him a job in England after completing his degree at Oxford, may be, because of racial prejudice. However, when one 'considers the racial politics of Trinidad and Guyana and the Caribbean islands; [...] the racial riots between Africans and Asians; [...] the massive "ethnic cleansing" that accompanied the creation of Pakistan—[... you should not] speak about racial prejudice [in England]' (1992, p. 131). In comparison to racial, religious and ethnic clashes in Trinidad, Guyana and India (here he overlooks his own benign vision of these societies), Naipaul felt England offered him peace.

Naipaul was, by now, making enough money to be quite settled in life. *The Enigma of Arrival* was published by Viking Penguin; *India: A Million Mutinies Now* by Heinemann. Naipaul simply went for the biggest deal offered. Naipaul received the first David Cohen British Literature Prize in 1993. He offered to write a book on his travels to Brazil, Chile, Venezuela and Argentina in 1994. Instead, he wrote about Iran, Malaysia, Indonesia and Pakistan in *Beyond Belief*. Towards the end of the 1980s and in the 1990s, Naipaul scholars published a number of book-length studies, including studies by John Thieme (1987), Harveen Mann (1986), Richard Kelly (1989), Selwyn Cudjoe (1988), Peter Hughes (1988), Timothy Weiss (1992), Rob Nixon (1992), Bruce King (1993), Chandra Joshi (1994), Judith Levy (1995) and Fawzia Mustafa (1995) and slightly later, Suman Gupta (1999). Naipaul was also part of a large number of books which analysed the themes of travel, home and homelessness in the postcolonial era. Some of these were written by Sudha Rai (1992), Sara Suleri (1992), Caren Kaplan (1996), Michael Gorra (1997), Holland and Huggan (1998), Purabi Panwar (2000), Casey Blanton (2002), John Clement

Ball (2003), Debbie Lisle (2006) and Carl Thompson (2011). While Cudjoe wrote about how Naipaul had shied away from acknowledging his Indo-Caribbean legacies and King invested in a new postcolonial world full of hope, Thieme caught the enigma that came to define Naipaul. According to Thieme, Naipaul gained critical praise from the metropolitan commentators and censure from the non-metropolitan commentators:

> For the former, he is a man with crystal clear lucidity of vision who unflinchingly exposes the shortcomings of 'developing' societies, which are in reality regressing back into savagery and unreason. For the latter, he is a man who has repudiated his origins and yet trades on them to allow him to propound a view of Third World society which would be deemed racist if it issued from the pen of a white writer. He thus ministers to the tastes of metropolitan market by reflecting its prejudices so well. (1987, pp. 193–4)

Rob Nixon made the most scathing attack, convinced of Naipaul's alliance with the West. Timothy Weiss was perhaps the first to point out how Naipaul constantly created an exilic world while remaining at the centre of all his narratives. Fawzia Mustafa's study highlighted Naipaul's use of multiple narrative voices while maintaining his own centrality and control over the narrative. Contrary to this, Gillian Dooley (2006) argued that Naipaul had to resolve issues between the man and the writer before he could write. They could not function independently of each other. Patrick French argued that a 'rising disillusion with the postcolonial project led to Vidia [V. S. Naipaul] being projected as the voice of truth' (French 2008, p. 394). This was independent of the charges laid by Edward Said and Derek Walcott, each claiming Naipaul's loyalty to the West lay in his betrayal of Islam and the Caribbean, respectively.

According to John Thieme (2002), Naipaul's displacement from the postcolonial canon happened largely due to the popularisation of Homi Bhabha's concept of hybridity that took postcolonial criticism by storm. He argues that the fulcrum shifted with Bhabha's work from a discourse on displacement (of which Naipaul was an excellent example and exponent) to a discourse on celebrating hybridity (in which Naipaulian criticism found little space and was overtaken by Rushdie's celebratory hybridity). Naipaul's use of the trope of displacement was predicated on the disjunction between traditional culture and modern living. Ironically, Bhabha had been working on a thesis on Naipaul when he formulated the concepts of hybridity and mimicry that were enabling and, hence, celebratory. But these critical developments did not affect Naipaul or his writing. Naipaul's writings

146 V. S. NAIPAUL OF TRINIDAD

published in the 1990s were reconciliatory journeys to India, Trinidad, Africa, Argentina, Guyana, Iran, Indonesia, Malaysia and Pakistan.

India: A Million Mutinies Now (1990a)

In the first book-length publication of this decade, Naipaul travelled through India and wrote about it for the third time in *India: A Million Mutinies Now*. India had always remained an important geographical pivot in Naipaul's writings. India at this time was on the brink of rapid changes in its society, polity and economy. On the economic front, liberalisation was leading India to become a market- and service-oriented economy. In an era of coalition governments, India saw the implementation of the Mandal Commission Report, which provided 27 per cent reservation to Other Backward Classes (OBCs) in educational and governmental sectors. This triggered massive public protests by the forward castes, leading to a gradual recognition of an aspirational middle class. Around the same time, there was a massive movement for the construction of a temple at the birthplace of Lord Ram in Ayodhya. Naipaul had come to recognise change as the basis of life and saw political unrest in India as a sign of the positive reclamation of a Hindu past.

Interestingly, in an interview before leaving Trinidad, where he had come to receive the Trinity Cross, Naipaul spoke about the revival of Hinduism in Trinidad as a 'passing phase' and 'a stage of growth' (Cuffie 1990, p. 1). Ravi-Ji of the Hindu Prachar Kendra, in a rebuttal printed in the *Trinidad Guardian* wrote: 'I must declare that Sir Vidia is no Maha Guru with a franchise on the outcome of man's destiny [... since] to assert that the Hindu renaissance is purely reactionary is to be equally blind or intellectually dishonest' (1990, p. 14). Naipaul saw the revival of Hinduism in Trinidad as part of a cyclical phase but refused to see it as intrinsic to Hindu beliefs or as connected with anything happening in India. Naipaul treated it as the 'flavour of the season.'

But in India, in 1989, Naipaul sensed an unrest among Indians that was to soon burst on the national scene. In this assessment of India, Naipaul's narrator is in a more self-reflective mood as he travels through India in an anti-clockwise direction (in *An Area of Darkness*, he had toured the country in a clockwise direction), recording socio-economic-political changes as little mutinies against the status quo. Naipaul began to see beyond the western emphasis on individualism to communal identity provided by caste, class, region, language, gender and religious attachments. This was in keeping with his own return to the Hindu community after the demise of his sister. Naipaul also shifted his focus from political and intellectual elites in *India: A Wounded Civilization* to working classes in *India: A Million Mutinies Now*. He recorded the lives of individuals who laboured on community development projects in spite of not being too well off. He met a lot of community leaders, small-time politicians and workers in non-governmental organisations, essentially people who were working within their communities. This is a big development from his investment in individualism. He moved away from the big-time politicians and the literary intelligentsia lodged in Delhi to seek out people who told him that India was changing.

To record change, Naipaul democratised the narrative voice, a technical innovation within the genre of travel writing that he first experimented with in *Among the Believers* but uses more successfully here. Naipaul claims that he allows the people to speak for themselves. Yet, it is evident that all voices are filtered through him and set in a single tone. In the book, it is sometimes unclear whether some of the Indians are actually speaking in English or if Naipaul is transliterating or using the help of an interpreter to translate, though it is amply clear that he is still 'colonising' the narrative. Naipaul endorses the critics who note the difference in the tenor of the book, along with the fact that Naipaul uses more direct speech. Naipaul himself says, '[...] the truth about India wasn't what I thought about India, it's what they are living through [...] the travel book for me has also been a process of learning' (Hussein 1994, p. 157). This indicates that since he was no longer struggling to find 'his' India, he was able to let other voices speak about their 'India.' It was not that he had become a less 'fearful' traveller to India since he still records his sense of recoil as he enters people's houses and refrains from eating with them. It is clear that English travel writing, in spite of evolving away from its colonial beginnings, still imposes a singular vision upon disparate objects, peoples and landscapes. The fact that Naipaul recognises the various revolutions taking place all over India is a marker of his own ability to perceive subliminal changes in society. However, the fact that he presents them in a singular tone is his own failure to bring nuances within the genre.

Bruce King (2003), Lilian Feder (2001) and Fawzia Mustafa (1995) believe that Naipaul's third book on India, *India: A Million Mutinies Now*, is a book where he has 'resolved' his relationship to India. However, in his review of *India: A Million Mutinies Now*, Bhikhu Parekh argues that Naipaul's:

> [...] picture of India remains not only partial but also partisan. He pays little attention to the tensions and struggles of rural India, the frustrations and agencies of youth, the widely acknowledged coarsening of the Indian sensibility as a result of aggressive capitalism, the deep fears aroused by half-a-dozen secessionist movements, and the dramatic decline in social and political morality. He also ignores the decay of almost all major institutions, the alarming increase in cases of rape and dowry death, the pervasive ethos of violence, the collapse of law and order in several

148   V. S. NAIPAUL OF TRINIDAD

parts of the country, the criminalisation of politics and the politicisation of crime, the populist gimmickry that passes for politics, the rampant corruption and the lamentable middle-class lack of social concern [...] (1990, p. 34).

Parekh does not share Naipaul's optimism about India and claims back *his* India by disowning Naipaul as a mere traveller. Naipaul was not new to such criticisms because they were part and parcel of travel writing conventions. Naipaul's first book on India, *An Area of Darkness*, had received similar angry reviews from Indians. The difference between the Indian and international critics stems from their own first-hand experiences, since in this book Naipaul appears more at ease with himself than previously.

In 1993, Naipaul received the David Cohen British Literature Prize in March. The response in Trinidad was a little lukewarm, though enough critics pointed out that he truly deserved the award. Judy Raymond categorically stated: 'Whether he liked it or not, Naipaul was bound to this place; anywhere else, he was an exile. [...] it's impossible to imagine Sir Vidia liming in a rumshop, and surely he'd die than play mas. [... but he wrote about Trinidad and these were accepted as] mainstream English literature and never dismissed as literary exotica' (1993). In another article, Kenneth Ramchand, taking a wider view of Naipaul's writings, stated nobody had 'written more feelingly about the disruption of African traditional life, the patronising attitude to their culture and values and the ways in which Africans are strangers in their own cities than Naipaul' (1993, p. 40). He criticised Naipaul's writing in *Guerrillas* because 'the experiments with characterisation, conversation and a shifting point of view make the novel unnecessarily tedious, and I find some of the violence distasteful because it serves no artistic purpose that I can discern.' However, he concluded: 'But a man who keeps on creating cannot be a man who does not believe in human possibilities.'

'Our Universal Civilization' (1990b); later published in *The Writer and the World* (2002b: 2011)

A collection of essays titled *The Writer and the World* (2002b) was brought out after Naipaul had won the Nobel Prize. It contained a number of his well-known essays, including three that were written in 1990–91 on 'Our Universal Civilization,' Argentina and Guyana. These three essays taken together can be read as Naipaul's thoughts on the similarities between communism, Catholicism, Islam and idealism. All of these '-isms' offer dreams of purity and universalism while societies are, in reality, mixed and non-egalitarian.

America has various institutes that call themselves 'free market think tanks' or 'public policy think tanks' that focus on expanding human potential, democratic principles, free enterprise, global leadership, legal reforms, health care, race and urban policy. During the 1990s, against the backdrop of the Iraq war, the Manhattan Institute hosted a number of speakers on the subject of the rise of Islamic fundamentalism. Naipaul's lecture, 'Our Universal Civilization' was part of this series and was published in *The New York Times* on November 5, 1990. In his role as a writer and an 'expert' on Islamic states, Naipaul again declared Islam to be an imperialistic religion while the West (the pertinent question would be West of what?) is portrayed as an open discursive civilisation. Cleverly, the Western civilisation is presented as universal and quietly dislodged from its British and Christian setting to the American institute. By displacing the West from England and Europe to America, Naipaul is able to weed away the ills and violence of colonial rule without taking up the racial cause. He distances himself from the postcolonial history of Christian missionaries working in the colonies, converting the ex-enslaved, ex-indentured and the ex-colonised to Christianity. He also disavows any knowledge of the systematic degradation of Indian civilisation under Muslim and British imperialist rules, the Persian history of Iran, the Buddhist and Hindu histories in Indonesia, the ethnic histories of small empires that were systematically Islamised in Pakistan, the Chinese and Indian heritage in Malaysia and the extermination of original tribes in the Caribbean. All the issues are brushed aside to present a clear picture of the West and the rest; the Western secular space and the Eastern religions; the universal West with its science and technology and the Eastern stasis.

The lecture is actually a brief summary of his book, *Among the Believers*. He begins his lecture by recounting his meeting with Linus, a young poet in Java who could not tell his mother that he wanted to be a poet because, for her, the arts were symbolic of their past achievements as a civilisation. Her civilisation was already 'too achieved, too ritualised' (1990b: 2011, p. 504), and 'all poetry had already been written' (1990b: 2011, p. 504). It is a reference to the Hindu epics that were part of Naipaul's heritage too. Yet, as stated in the later 'Reading and Writing,' the epics did not inspire him to write. They were ritualistically recited and were complete by themselves. They couldn't be added to. In this, Naipaul disregards the whole tradition of the 'katha,' where the reciter discovers new meanings and elucidates them for a local audience. He also disregards how the epics provided impetus to write the human story again and again. Naipaul reiterates that it was the Western civilisation that:

> both gave the prompting and the idea of the literary vocation; and also gave the means to fulfil that prompting; the civilization that

150   V. S. NAIPAUL OF TRINIDAD

enabled me to make that journey from the periphery to the centre; the civilization that links me not only to his audience but also to that now not so young man in Java whose background was as ritualised as my own, and whom—as on me—the outer world had worked, and given the ambition to write. (1990b: 2011, pp. 506–7)

He says that he could not have been a writer in the Islamic world, China, Japan, Eastern Europe, the Soviet Union or Africa. Further, he says, the non-Arab Islamic people had suffered a double colonisation, one by their religion, the other by the West. Summarising the translated text *Chachnama*, the account of the Islamic conquest of Sind in the eighth century, he concludes: 'there was no room in the heart or mind of these believers for their pre–Mohammedan past' (1990b: 2011, p. 508); 'the faith altered values, ideas of good behaviour, human judgments' (1990b: 2011, p. 511). Summarising Nahid Rachlin's *Foreigner*, which he had also done in *Among the Believers*, he concludes that the young woman scientist who gave up the American way of life to adopt the veil 'assumes that there will continue to be people striving out there, in the stressed world, making drugs and medical equipment' (1990b, p. 515). Naipaul writes that such a conclusion is intellectually flawed because it assumes that the West will continue to serve them while they are 'free' to follow the path of complete faith. Hence, the segregation of the West and the rest. Coupled with science and technology is the fact that the universal civilisation endows 'ambition, endeavour, individuality' (1990b, p. 516) and therefore does not generate fanaticism, while the closed world of Islam demands complete submission to a way of life that feeds fundamentalism because it does not value accommodation and adaptation as core values.

In more general terms, the lecture summarises Naipaul's thinking on the concept of universal brotherhood. In an earlier interview with Edward Behr, Naipaul said that this universal civilisation, once Islamic, is now Western:

I feel there's a great universal civilization at the moment which people would say is Western. But this has been fed by innumerable sources. It's a very eclectic civilization and it is conquering the world because it is so attractive, so liberating to people. What disheartens me is that there are certain cultures where people are saying, "Cut yourselves off. Go back to what you were." The Arabs, the Muslims, some Africans are doing this. This is a disaster [...] The mistake of Western vanity is to think that the universal civilization that exists now is a pure racial one. (Behr 1980, p. 48)

Bhoendradatt Tewarie argues that 'Naipaul sees fundamentalism of any kind as diametrically opposed to this universal civilisation' (2011, p. 199). Naipaul's essay complemented Samuel Huntington's 'the clash of civilizations' thesis. Both the Manhattan Institute, that hosted V. S. Naipaul, and the American Enterprise Institute, which hosted Samuel Huntington, are American public policy think tanks. In Naipaul's vision, the greatness of Western civilisation lies in its emphasis on the individual (a throwback to the classical tradition) because it is the individual who retrieves the world from the clutches of empires, communities, religions, philosophies and ideologies. But the essay was more or less interpreted as Naipaul's confession of being the spokesperson for colonial powers. The fact is that Naipaul blames Western civilisation for its vanity, but ironically, the point was lost on his Western audience at the Manhattan Institute of New York and elsewhere.

'Argentina and the Ghost of Eva Perón, 1972–1991' (1991a); later published in *The Writer and the World* (2002b: 2011)

Naipaul adds to his earlier essay on Argentina recounting the day in March of 1977 when he was arrested by the Argentine police on suspicion of being a guerrilla fighter (French 2008, p. 377). According to Savi Naipaul Akal, Naipaul was 'dragged off a bus with a gun to his head' (2018, p. 167). He was forced to lie on the floor, body-searched and thrown into a cell: 'Eventually, through the intervention, I believe, of the British High Commission, he was released from jail' (2018, p. 167). Margaret was with him, though Naipaul does not mention any companion. What he does mention is the fact that he did not take notes, perhaps, because he was too much in the thick of things instead of being the usual spectator. He was saved because he carried an African pipe, and the policemen did not think a guerrilla fighter would smoke such a sophisticated foreign item. He kept this sensation alive as he wrote, 'a long imaginative work set in a country in Central Africa' (1991a: 2011, p. 403)—no doubt a reference to *A Bend in the River*. He now returns to write about Argentina after a gap of 14 years yet there had been no change on the ground. The guerrilla fighters had become family men, with a new set of recruits filling in the role of the rebels. He meets one of the older men, an ex-guerrilla who had found 'his Catholic instincts coinciding with the ideas of the Left [...] The idea of the New Man, the idea of the revolutionary as an identity, the revolutionary confronting injustice' (1991a: 2011, pp. 409–10). He had said something on similar lines about the combination of Khomeini's cause with that of the communists in Iran. He was to say something similar in a more abstract way when discussing the creation of a narrator in *A Way in the World*. Naipaul felt more

152 V. S. NAIPAUL OF TRINIDAD

and more convinced that any movement that rode on momentum alone could not achieve anything for its supporters. This has been read as Naipaul's conservative turn, but it must be pointed out that it had been over 20 years since those movements began. Yet, there had been no monumental changes in the polity of either Argentina or Guyana. In Argentina, agricultural production had gone down, foreign trade had been nationalised, and taxes had become greater than rents sending inflation soaring. In Naipaul's analyses, the violence in Argentine society was deep-seated and could not be exorcised because guerrilla revolutionaries kept killing one set of elites only to be replaced by another set of ruling elites.

'A Handful of Dust: Cheddi Jagan and the Revolution in Guyana' (1991b); later published in *The Writer and the World* (2002b: 2011)

Naipaul's writing on Guyana (earlier British Guiana) is a tribute to Cheddi Jagan, who was born to Hindu East Indian parents and was the first person of Indian descent to head a government outside the Indian subcontinent. The title of the article is taken from Evelyn Waugh's *A Handful of Dust* (1934), in which the protagonist goes on an expedition to British Guiana in search of a lost city. The theme of the lost city deep in the Amazon forests held the British imagination captive even in the twentieth century, when much land had already been colonised. Cheddi Jagan won three consecutive elections, but Winston Churchill removed his democratically elected government because he feared that Jagan would establish the first communist state in the New World. In retrospect, Naipaul's narrator surmises that since Marxism came to the New World 'without its history' (1991b: 2011, p. 491) and 'without a literary culture' (1991b: 2011, p. 495), it forced Jagan into an attitude that was non-negotiable. The 'ideas of surplus value and the universal class struggle' (1991b: 2011, p. 486) had an almost universal appeal during the time that Jagan was growing up. However, the British government preferred to establish a Forbes Burnham-led government in 1964. Subsequently, with independence, 'Every important industry—bauxite, rice—was taken over by the African-controlled government; and the government gave jobs, or created jobs, for its supporters [... leading to] racial tyranny' (1991b: 2011, p. 487). This led to more than a third of the Guyanese population, mainly the Indo-Guyanese, moving abroad over the next 30 years, to the United States and Canada. Cheddi Jagan remained out of power for 26 years before returning as the President in 1992. Politics aside, Naipaul had enjoyed the hospitality of the Jagans when he visited Guyana in the early 1960s.

Naipaul analyses the idea of change and difference, much in keeping with his mood in these years. At the beginning of the essay, Naipaul's narrator emphasises the connection between Guyana and Trinidad: '[British] Guiana had always been a land of fantasy. It was the land of El Dorado; it was the site of Jonestown commune' (1991b: 2011 p. 485). Thus, in popular imagination in Britain, Guyana was a land of adventure and romance, and it was the land that held hidden treasures. However, for the Americans, it was also the land where Jim Jones, an American cult leader of the People's Temple, had established his agricultural commune and where the century's worst mass suicide and murder took place in the late 1970s. Shiva Naipaul, his much younger brother, had explored the commune in his book, *Journey into Nothing*. Michael X had run away to Guyana before he was arrested and brought back to Trinidad for the trial for killings on his farm. Naipaul notes that the death of one Michael X or Jim Jones does not secure the lives of many other innocents. The lure of the lost city and deep forests is something that Naipaul explores again in *A Way in the World*.

The three essays written close to the publication of *India: A Million Mutinies Now*, which was favourably received by the Western media, further established Naipaul as a conservative writer who wrote in favour of maintaining the status quo because he hated change and bloody revolutions. He was seen to position himself against the Islamic revolution in Iran, the Argentine guerrillas and Jagan's Marxist politics. Such critics refused to look at the local conditions that Naipaul contextualised. Naipaul saw no value in bloody revolutions because they failed to bring about momentous changes either in society or politics. Guerrilla warfare had been going on in Argentina for over 20 years and had led to no positive change. Naipaul was to use this aspect later in his novel, *Magic Seeds*. Slow social changes were stronger and lasted longer than sudden changes in the status quo. This was Naipaul's reflected position.

A Way in the World (1994)

Naipaul's travels to Trinidad at this time resulted in the book *A Way in the World*. The book is a mixed genre compilation that was marketed with a subtitle 'A Novel' in the United States and 'A Sequence' in the United Kingdom. It is a series of seemingly unconnected narratives regarding Naipaul's relationship with Trinidad. After much travelling through the world, he settles upon the little 'patch of the earth' he once called home. Like *The Enigma of Arrival*, *A Way in the World* is a narrative written by a constructed self. And like *The Enigma of Arrival*, *A Way in the World* is more about Naipaul the writer than Naipaul the narrator. I would go to the extent of saying that he wrote this book in the spirit of the 1980s, when he was writing more discursively in *The Enigma of Arrival* than in the 1990s, when he wrote from a more detached point of view as in *India: A Million Mutinies Now*.

154   V. S. NAIPAUL OF TRINIDAD

A Way in the World is a combination book of seven separate narratives about his subjects, his fellow Trinidadians, his reviewers in England, his archival work and his experiments with forms of writing. The book is about Leonard Side, Blair (loosely based on Walter Rodney), Lebrun (loosely based on C. L. R. James) and Foster Morris (loosely based on Arthur Calder-Marshall), as well as the early European travellers to Trinidad: Christopher Columbus in 1498, Walter Raleigh in 1618 and Francisco Miranda in 1806. There is no singular subject or single narrator in the book. All the male protagonists, while successful at the beginning, are found, in the final analysis, to be too vain to acknowledge their failures. His reviewers, Lebrun, a fellow Trinidadian author and activist, and Foster Morris, an established British author and reviewer, had each chosen to read his early novels as flights of fantasy. While Lebrun had reviewed his writings positively, marking their subversive quality, Morris had commented on his lack of truthfulness. Both had chosen to ignore humour and irony, which were essential elements in his writing. They had ignored the effort required to write about Trinidadians for a British audience without making them look too exotic or too stupid. Naipaul remained unsatisfied with their reviews even as he survived to write again and again, each time re-inventing himself and expanding his sphere of writing. Unlike Columbus, Raleigh and Miranda, each of whom refused to give up their quests for India, El Dorado and a South American revolution, Naipaul acknowledged that, beyond a point in time, he could no longer write only about Trinidad. Travel replaced social experience and provided him with the 'impetus' to write about the world at large. By overlapping the concerns of the writer with those of the narrator and the historian, Naipaul reveals that Trinidad is, indeed, the bedrock of his emotional responses and the basis of all his perceptions about the world.

The book is also about Naipaul's changing relationship with Trinidad over the years, from the time that he was born in Chaguanas to the family shifting to Port of Spain for the first time to his leaving the island to study in England. On his return, things had changed, and he could not identify with the locals. He felt connected and unconnected to his surroundings. Trinidad was both familiar and unfamiliar because he knew so much more and could see so much more, yet he could not identify with the people or the politics. From independence to the 1970 Black Power Movement to the coup in 1990, Naipaul was a spectator, not a participant, in Trinidad. In a rare moment, Naipaul almost wishes that he could have felt these incidents first-hand. Naipaul, the detached narrator, becomes a curse to Naipaul, the writer, as he weighs in on the past and the future. While Columbus, Raleigh and Miranda were too disconnected from the locals to feel for them, many later politicians like Lebrun and Blair went away to participate in African politics because their work had finished locally with the establishment of a social welfare state in Trinidad. They were later unwelcome in the Caribbean and returned in coffins to be laid to rest. Judy Raymond reviewed the book and pronounced: 'For its verdicts on figures from local history *A Way in the World* might be subtitled "V. S. Naipaul's Book of Historic Failures"' (1994).

Though this has never received much attention, it is important to note that Naipaul's mother died in January 1991. She had outlived his father by 38 years. With the passing of 'Ma,' Naipaul lost the last of his moorings in Trinidad. Though Naipaul did not visit Trinidad to light her pyre, he must have been affected by it. If *A House for Mr Biswas* was an ode to his father, then *A Way in the World* may be read as an ode to his mother. While Naipaul had found it easier to talk about his relationship with his father, he never spoke about his mother from a public platform. Yet it was the mother who had kept the family together after his father's death. The book can also be read as an ode to his motherland—Trinidad—and to the vocation of his life—writing.

In *A House for Mr Biswas*, the foreword to *The Loss of El Dorado*, and 'Prologue to an Autobiography,' Naipaul had spoken about his ambition to be a writer. He had also spoken about Trinidad, from which he wanted to escape. In this book, Naipaul writes about the Trinidad he often came back to. The experience of coming back to Trinidad in 1956 was a defining moment in his life. He had graduated from Oxford, had married Patricia Hale (though he had not informed his family of the same), and was soon to be published. Yet, in the intervening six years, he had lost his father, had a bout of depression and faced innumerable rejections from potential employers and publishers. Though the coming back was neither momentous nor lasting, it had a profound effect on Naipaul because he felt immeasurably distant from his surroundings. It made him a different writer. *A Way in the World* documents this in hindsight.

Beyond Belief: Islamic Excursions among the Converted Peoples (1998: 1999)

Beyond Belief is part of Naipaul's return travels through countries he had previously travelled to in the non-Arab Muslim world. Naipaul is overly conscious that his earlier book, *Among the Believers*, had been read as part of an emerging Islamophobia in the West. In the prologue, he emphasises that 'Everyone not an Arab who is a Muslim is a convert. Islam is not simply a matter of conscience or private belief. It makes imperial demands [...] and in the Islam of converted countries there is an element of neurosis and nihilism' (1998: 1999, p. xi). As opposed to the first book, here he analyses not the faith but the reasons behind people's faith. In this adventure, he clarifies that he is particularly looking for the remnants of 'a kind of crossover from old beliefs, earth religions, the cults of rulers and local deities' (1998: 1999, p. xiii). One may well ask why he does not consider Christianity an imperial religion, but Naipaul steers away from the discussion by stating, 'The crossover from the classical world to Christianity is now history [...]' (1998: 1999, p. xiii). This is an idea that he carries forward from his essay, 'Our Universal Civilization' where he saw the present era as dominated by Western (a synthesis of classical and Christian) philosophy. In this, he hides his own history of being born into an Indian family in the West Indies, where Christian missionaries were often knocking on the doors to convert the 'heathen' Hindus. He was himself able to study at an Anglican school, go to England and become a writer without converting to Christianity. Naipaul found comfort in the thought that Christianity was never able to completely displace either the classical rational discourse or the Hindu discourse. Within the operative framework of his travel writing, he does not comment on the realities of religious conversion, where missionaries sought to convert not only through the promise of showing 'the right path' but also through promises of enlightenment, education, status, employment and travel. Naipaul attributed his own 'secular' attitude to his escape from Christianity rather than his Hindu background in Trinidad. He fashioned his narrator as a secular inquirer of the Islamic faith, but as we will see, references to his Hindu background slip into the narrative.

Naipaul's narrator now writes from a perspective where he is able to see beyond the immediate to a larger, wider civilisational history. Naipaul begins his journey in Indonesia, seeking to find the very people he met almost 15 years ago. It is a continuation of his quest to expose certain exponents of Islam since: 'For the new fundamentalists of Indonesia, the greatest war was to be made on their own past, and everything that linked them to their own earth' (1998: 1999, p. 48). Naipaul's narrator comments: 'The cruelty of Islamic fundamentalism is that it allows only to one people— the Arabs, the original people of the Prophet—a past, and sacred places, pilgrimages, and earth reverences [;...] of the converted peoples nothing is required but the purest faith (if such a thing can be arrived at), Islam, submission. It is the most uncompromising kind of imperialism' (1998: 1999, p. 64). Islam does not consider any other land sacred except Mecca. This triggers his own memories of his upbringing in Trinidad. He remembers that Trinidad had no sacred places, and 'it was nearly forty years after I had left the island that I identified the lack' (1998: 1999, p. 51). All Hindu ceremonies refer to the Ganga as the sacred river and Kashi (modern-day Varanasi) in India as the sacred city. But, in Trinidad, the lack of sacred places was never felt because the pundits amended and adapted the Hindu ceremonies to suit Trinidad realities. Gradually, the community became so well-settled that they never felt that they were lost. India was their past, Trinidad their present and for some, England, Canada or America were their future. Hence, he describes his inability to understand Islamic rage: 'So it is strange to someone of my background that in the converted Muslim countries—Iran, Pakistan, Indonesia—the fundamentalist rage is against the past, against history, and the impossible dream is of the true faith growing out of a spiritual vacancy' (1998: 1999, p. 52). He notes a fallacy since 'Religious or cultural purity is a fundamentalist fantasy' (1998: 1999, p. 59). One saw the seeds of this thought in the epilogue of *In a Free State* where he had contemplated that there was no true pristine state, and even in his acceptance of change as a natural phenomenon in *The Enigma of Arrival*. We see in this the basis of the narrator's inability to understand why the ancient exchange of cultures had been forgotten: 'All the Hindu and Buddhist past had been swallowed up […] And all that remained of two thousand years of great social organisation here, of a culture, were the taboos and earth rites […]' (1998: 1999, p. 63). And even these were under threat.

In Iran, Naipaul's narrator senses a general disillusionment with the revolution. For Naipaul's narrator, with his larger, more comprehensive vision of the world, the revolution was just a small churn in history: 'I know that for the emperor Jehangir (who ruled from 1605 to 1627), the India of his empire and the Persia of Shah Abbas (who ruled from 1587 to 1629) were the central powers of the globe […]' (1998: 1999, p. 233). A 100 years later India became a British colony. Such dramatic changes in power centres point back to Naipaul's thesis about the shifting power centres, once Islamic, now Christian or Western: 'The classical world had been overthrown and remade by Christianity and Islam. These were universal and not local religions; their religious and social ideas touched everyone and could seem familiar even to outsiders' (1998: 1999, p. 246). As opposed to *Among the Believers* where Naipaul's narrator travelled to Qom as the centre of revolution, he now travels to the shrine of Shah Cheragh. But the narrator tells us that upon his arrival at the shrine, he was accosted by a man begging for money because he had been robbed. The spirituality associated with the shrine is completely lost on the narrator.

Similarly, in his travels through Pakistan, Naipaul's narrator visits the Uch shrine, where he sees the Shiva lingam, emphasising the ancestral roots of the converted that are denied by institutionalised Islam. The narrator notes rather paradoxically that the British period 'was a time of Hindu regeneration,' the Muslims, 'wounded by their loss of power, and out of old religious scruples, stood aside' (1998: 1999, p. 247). Naipaul's narrator seems oblivious to the fact that the East India Company was a commercial enterprise that entered and conquered India through deception, firepower and subterfuge. There was no 'Hindu regeneration,' at least not due to any British encouragement. The British policy of divide and rule and the rivalry between Hindus and Muslims led to the formation of Pakistan in 1947. However, he finds it ridiculous that people who sacrificed so much in the name of Pakistan should hold on to ancient ways of life, proclaiming their caste and indulging in agriculture as a way of life. The presence of a *nai*, or barber, in Rahimullah's feudal estate leads him to think back on his own growing up in Trinidad, where the *nai* had performed his multifunctional role of being a barber, a messenger and a matchmaker. He had met a similar remnant of the past world as the village *coum* in Java, where the *coum* had taken on the duties of handling dead bodies and cooking. It surprises Naipaul to be reminded of his childhood in the things around him: the *nai*, the *chullah*, language, hospitality and honour—all these ideas connected him to his past. Recognising this familiarity, one may not be surprised with the choice of his second wife, Nadira Alvi, born in Kenya but with roots in Pakistan, because she is culturally closer to Naipaul's own upbringing in Trinidad.

Naipaul gets nostalgic once again when he reaches Malaysia because the vegetation reminds him of Trinidad. This nostalgia for a place that he did not call home is incredulous. Since Naipaul's narrator is not writing for an audience 'back home,' he preserves a sense of 'home' only to bond with his audience. Islam in Malaysia divides the dominant Malays from the minor Chinese ethnic groups. As opposed to his earlier travels when he focused solely on the Malays, the narrator now focuses on the minorities. The race riots of 1969 had made the Malay movement stronger with their conversion to an Islamic state. The Islamic erasure of history had led to a point where legends felt more real than history.

In this book, Naipaul's narrator is resolute in his conviction that Islam is a modern force of imperialism that erases local histories, traditions and cultures. In his view, there is no moderate Islam. And though this is problematic, it endorses the view that Naipaul is not a man of faith. Religions across the world respond to socio-economic-political challenges and provide solace by retaining faith in human abilities to adopt and adapt to the changing environments. Naipaul's narrator documents changes but chooses not to record faith in human adaptability. The book remains notable for his references to Trinidad as the basis of his assessment of the societies in Indonesia, Malaysia, Pakistan and Iran.

Letters Between a Father and Son (1999)

For Naipaul the writer, the century ended with the publication of *Letters Between a Father and Son*, a selective sequence of letter exchanges primarily between Seepersad Naipaul and his son V. S. Naipaul while he was at Oxford. The publication edited by his agent, Gillon Aitken, presents the relationship between the father and son as a *Guru* (teacher) and *chela* (student), where the father guides the son towards becoming a successful writer. The exchanges reveal several other aspects of their relationship as well: Seepersad was looking to be published in London and felt that his son could help him; he looked on V. S. Naipaul for monetary and physical support; he supported V. S. Naipaul through his studies in England and Kamla, then studying in India, by taking out loans in Trinidad; they together enjoyed the little successes of their stories being read on the BBC *Caribbean Voices* programme. This was Naipaul's attempt at another acknowledgement of his father's role in his success as a writer. Robert Winder, writing for the *New Statesman* reported: 'Naipaul knew he would immortalise his father through his work, even if it meant short-changing him in his life. It is not a pretty thing, but that's literature for you' (1999, p. 54). For Naipaul, his relationship with his father was an important aspect of his life, and he wished that relationship to be preserved as a relationship between an aspiring father and a successful son so that he could claim writing as a family profession in which V. S. Naipaul excelled. He kept up this thought as he entered the new millennium with the publication of a long essay, *Reading and Writing*.

An Assessment

Naipaul was accommodative and reconciliatory in his travels in the 1990s. Beginning with 'Our Universal Civilization,' he made peace with the Western world with its own set of prejudices because, in his view, it did not restrict its scientific and technological skills to only its Christian believers. However, this overlooked the fact that his universal civilisation was a world based on science and technology, not religion and faith. Nowhere does Naipaul criticise the underlying Christian viewpoint, whether it is in his use of the Christian calendar or conception of time or space. On the other hand, he does criticise other religions and faiths for their lack of openness and non-participation in the world of science and discovery. While Hinduism is founded upon the tenet of discussion and discursive knowing of the world with no absolutes, Naipaul criticises the fact that Hinduism is dead science. There is no rational approach, and its believers do not actively question or expand their base knowledge. The ancient texts are presented as achieved knowledge and, hence, are not to be copied, imitated or revised. Hinduism's passive approach makes the world uninteresting because the emphasis is on learning what is already known rather than setting and achieving new goals. Naipaul is unable to come to terms with the difficulties of reviving an ancient civilisation whose glorious days lie in the past. On a different plane, he analyses Islam and its teachings. The problems of everyday life are left unresolved as the emphasis shifts to achieving complete submission to God, often through the adoption of certain attires, foods and cultural practices. He also emphasises that the obliteration of local histories leads to a disassociation with land, and therefore, the believer is left with a sense of loss and victimisation rather than consolidation and gain. This causes disaffection between the local populations and their land. Naipaul cannot empathise with such an approach to land and its history because he advocates a connection to land as the primary way forward in life. According to Bridget Brereton, Naipaul invests in the history of Trinidad in *The Loss of El Dorado* because 'a historical sense allows for creativity, the full exercise of the imagination, and the capacity for change and growth' (2011, p. 211). This is emphasised and reemphasised in *A Way in the World* when dealing with the failures of Columbus, Raleigh and Miranda. It is also emphasised in his analyses of the failures of Blair and Lebrun. Paradoxically, he also recognises his failure to connect himself to a 'patch of the earth.' *The Enigma of Arrival* can be read as his attempt to forge this relationship with his chosen piece of earth. With the ostensible goal of removing himself from his books, Naipaul attempted to act as a filter for Indians, Indonesians, Pakistanis, Iranians and Malaysians as they told their stories. However, the narratives are not discursive and are pulled together by the personality and worldview of Naipaul. He tries to address the issue in his thesis about a 'citizen of the world' next who would not be locked down to a 'patch of the earth.'

Chapter 7

COMPOSING AGAIN
IN THE 2000s

This was a time when Naipaul felt rejuvenated by his travels. He won the Nobel Prize in 2001. Since the 1970s to the early 1990s, Naipaul remained a favourite to win the Nobel Prize for Literature. The rumours stopped only when Derek Walcott won the Nobel Prize in 1992. After this, nobody thought it was possible for another writer from the Caribbean to win this award until Naipaul actually won it in 2001. A long-cherished dream came true, and Naipaul was very gracious in accepting it. Earlier, he had come to believe that he would not be given the Nobel Prize because he didn't 'represent anything' (Blandford 1979, p. 51). But, true to himself, he sparked an immediate controversy by leaving out Trinidad in his initial response upon receiving the news of the award. There was a huge response from Trinidad and the Caribbean, with most people calling him an ungrateful son of the soil. Naipaul did little to make amends. In his Nobel Acceptance lecture, 'Two Worlds,' he did pay a lengthy tribute to Trinidad, though the lecture was more about his journey from Trinidad than about Trinidad. On his visit to Trinidad for a conference in his honour in 2007, his wife addressed a press conference upon his arrival at the airport, taking the blame for his initial reaction. It was a ploy to reduce resistance to his visit.

After a gap of nearly two decades, Naipaul got back to writing two novels. Having pronounced the novel dead quite early in the 1970s, Naipaul returned to the form. He wrote a story about the life of Willie Chandran, an Indian from India and his journeys across England, Africa, Germany and India. The story was narrated in two parts, *Half-a-Life* and *Magic Seeds*, each good as stand-alone novels by themselves. Naipaul's scope of writing was truly international. The protagonist studied the consequences of his actions, not the world at large. Naipaul had come to accept that the world is what it is and it is the actions that make or break an individual. The decade began with Naipaul paying another tribute to his father and Trinidad with a long essay, 'Reading and Writing' followed by the Nobel Acceptance lecture.

162   V. S. NAIPAUL OF TRINIDAD

Reading and Writing: A Personal Account (2000); rpt. in *Literary Occasions: Essays* (2003): 3–31

'Reading and Writing' is a long essay written in 1998 and originally published in *The New York Review of Books* in 1999. It was published as a stand-alone book in 2000. The essay had initially been written for the Charles Douglas-Home Memorial Trust. The long essay deals with Naipaul's ambition to be a writer, his reading of local material, his Indian inheritance and his position vis-à-vis other great writers. Rather than focusing on the richness of his heritage, he speaks about its limitations. On the one hand, Naipaul confesses that he invested heavily in his literary ambitions to become a writer; on the other hand, Naipaul refuses to take social responsibility for the fast disappearing cultural life of the Hindu households in Trinidad: 'It [his ambition] was a private idea, and a curiously ennobling one, separate from school and separate from the disordered and disintegrating life of our Hindu extended family' (2000: 2003, p. 5). Several Caribbean writers have spoken about Naipaul's lack of activism, nationalism and political will. Naipaul's concern is only with himself, projecting the gap between his upbringing and his ambition to become a writer: 'I wished to be a writer. But together with the wish there had come the knowledge that the literature that had given me the wish came from another world, far away from our own' (2000: 2003, p. 6). While Naipaul had never confessed to any other influences, in this long essay, he makes several concessions. He recognises that there were other writers who were writing and publishing in the region whom he admired intermittently. Naipaul recognised these writers in the Foreword to *The Adventures of Gurudeva and other Stories* and he does it again later in *A Writer's People*. He had known them and read them when he was a boy in Trinidad.

Besides his father's stories about the Indian way of life in Trinidad, Naipaul also confesses that the enactment of *Ramlila* based upon the *Ramayana* was 'a moral education for us all' (2000: 2003, p. 8). His father's stories anchored him in the world, for without them he 'would have known nothing of [his] ancestry' (2000: 2003, p. 11). He then catalogues what he did not know about novel writing as opposed to some of the greatest writers in English; for example, Conrad knew that 'the discovery of every tale was a moral one' (2000: 2003, p. 10); Evelyn Waugh knew that fiction was 'experience totally transformed' (2000: 2003, p. 13); Tolstoy knew how to move from being a descriptive writer to fiction, 'setting characters in motion, and bringing the reality closer' (2000: 2003, p. 13). Naipaul's training and readings, on the other hand, had not equipped him to write. He had to learn that himself. Similarly, when he decided to travel for writing, he realised that he couldn't travel like Huxley, Lawrence and Waugh whose

COMPOSING AGAIN IN THE 2000s 163

travel writings were semi-imperial, 'using the accidents of travel to define their metropolitan personalities against a foreign background' (2000: 2003, p. 16). Instead, he was a post-colonial traveller: 'To look, as a visitor, at other semi-derelict communities in despoiled land, in the great romantic setting of the New World, was to see, from a distance, what one's own community might have looked like' (2000: 2003, pp. 16–7). Naipaul's new location in England had lacked 'social depth' (2000: 2003, p. 16), while travel had allowed him to look 'through a multiplicity of impressions to a central human narrative' (2000: 2003, p. 20). He reiterates his own uniqueness: 'two worlds separated me from the books that were offered to me at school and in the libraries; the childhood world of our remembered India, and the more colonial world of our city' (2000: 2003, p. 20).

Naipaul analyses the gaps in his education as gaps between his reading and writing practices. While his reading told him that he must write about his society, a society that he knew and grew up in, it was the English language that prevented him from delving into the depths of his society and expressing it from within. Cultural markers within the English language prevented him from transitioning from reading to writing since Trinidad could never be in a position of power and its people could never be worthy of being written about. Yet his father had defied these restrictions and written about Trinidadian society. He had also introduced him to writings in and about the Indian subcontinent: the political writings of Nehru and Tagore; the colonial writings of Rudyard Kipling, E. M. Forster and Somerset Maugham; and the nostalgic writings of R. K. Narayan. And yet the India he went to was different: 'nothing had prepared me for the dereliction I saw' (2000: 2003, p. 21). Revisiting R. K. Narayan once again after his analyses in *An Area of Darkness* and *India: A Wounded Civilisation*, he writes how Narayan's world was complete and whole because his characters were 'oddly insulated from history' (2000: 2003, p. 26). He notes that Narayan's characters have no ancestry, only to refute this notion a few lines down, concluding: 'Narayan's world is not, after all, as rooted and complete as it appears when the history is known, there is less the life of a wise and eternal Hindu India than a celebration of the redeeming British peace' (2000: 2003, p. 27). This is contrary to his earlier view that Narayan wrote about a quintessential India. Naipaul realises that Indian writers were largely thankful to British rule because, after the devastation wrought on India by the Muslim invaders and rulers for more than 800 years, peace had prevailed. Naipaul had begun to re-read the writers who had influenced him, and these re-readings fed into his larger view of human civilisation.

Naipaul's rather inflated sense of himself and his craft was endorsed when he received the Nobel Prize for Literature in 2001. Naipaul was delighted, yet he claimed he was asleep when the academy called to announce their choice.

164 V. S. NAIPAUL OF TRINIDAD

In the initial response given to the media, he said, the Nobel was 'a great tribute to both England, my home, and India, the home of my ancestors.' When he was later asked about the absence of Trinidad from his response, he said he did not want to encumber the tribute (French 2008, Introduction, p. xii). Yet, when he went up to speak on the occasion, he spoke eloquently about Trinidad.

'Two Worlds' (2001e); later published in *Literary Occasions: Essays* (2003)

His lecture at the acceptance ceremony for the award, entitled 'Two Worlds,' is a treasure trove in which he recapitulates his early life in Trinidad, his sources of inspiration, and his own assessment of his writing. Naipaul makes a distinction between the writer and his social being. Quoting Proust at the beginning of the essay, Naipaul places the value of the writer as a writer above that of the writer as a social being. He conceptualises the writer's space as being away from society yet intricately connected to it. He identifies three elements that define his writing: his training in English literature, which gave him the ambition to be a writer; his father's writings on the Indo-Trinidadian community, which made him realise that his community could be written about; and his travels, that helped him develop a perspective on the world. Naipaul writes that he preferred to read the timeless, placeless and non-excluding worlds of Anderson and Aesop (classical writers) rather than Jawaharlal Nehru, Mahatma Gandhi (Indian political leaders), Rudyard Kipling, John Masters (British writers) or R. K. Narayan (an Indian writer in English), who did not provide him with any literary model to write about the Caribbean. He only acknowledged his father's writings as his inspiration, without which he would have remained ignorant about the 'general life of our Indian community' (2001e: 2003, p. 188).

Naipaul describes the life of his Hindu Indo-Trinidadian community as a minority culture transplanted from India, adapting the strange Amerindian name of Chaguanas to the Chauhan caste name. The 'silence of centuries' (2001e: 2003, p. 185) refers to the loss of verifiable and written history that could have provided the immigrants with a sense of the place they had arrived at. The libraries in England held some records that have little or no relevance to the people who safeguard them yet carry significance for those in the Caribbean islands who have little or no access to them. The Indians, arriving several centuries later than the Amerindians, have no relics or monuments of the earlier Amerindian tribes. Thus, Naipaul attacks the apathy of community elders who never made the effort to know the past or to make the younger generation understand the significance of the land

and its history. Naipaul contends that documented history is an integral part of knowing who one is, and a lack of such historical accounts both of the period of early discovery and later Indian migration made him view Trinidad as a country that lacked history and a strong identity. He had tried to rectify this situation by writing a laborious account of Trinidad's history from colonial records in *The Loss of El Dorado*.

He then goes on to speak about why he needed to travel to broaden his perspective, and the more he travelled, the more complicated and complex his own little world became. The simple life of *Miguel Street* made way for the colonial schizophrenia of *The Mimic Men*. Naipaul clarifies that *The Mimic Men* 'was not about mimics. It was about colonial men mimicking the condition of manhood, men who had grown to distrust everything about themselves' (2001e: 2003, p. 193). Even something as little as eating 'rice in the middle of the day, and wheat in the evenings' distinguished his family from their own people (2001e: 2003, p. 188). His personal sense of superiority (based on his Brahmanical caste, education and ambition) helped him maintain his balance in the immigrant society of London. Even so, Naipaul had tried to link himself with England in *The Enigma of Arrival*. His walks around Stonehenge were an essential element of his settling down in England. Further, he claimed that he was the sum of all his books—'the last book contained all the others' (2001e: 2003, pp. 182–3). He presented his own books as building blocks for his later works, claiming that he created a tradition for himself. The idea is an interesting one because he had yet to write his last novel, his last few analytical essays and his last piece of travel writing.

The *Trinidad Guardian* carried the lecture on five consecutive pages with subtitles: 'Two Worlds,' 'I am the sum of my books,' 'Naipaul—an intuitive writer,' 'Hard Path travelled' and 'Luck and Much Labour.' The feature also carried photographs of Naipaul, the St. James house; a photograph of Naipaul at the ceremony; a photograph of Naipaul with the former President of Trinidad and Tobago, Noor Hassanali receiving the Trinity Cross in August 1990; and the Lion's House in Chaguanas (December 14, 2001d, Features Supplement 2: pp. 1–5). While newspaper reports prior to Naipaul winning the Nobel Prize focused upon his criticism of Tony Blair and Islam (Clarke 2001; 'V. S. Naipaul Launches attack on Islam' 2001), the more immediate issue at hand was the controversy surrounding the proposed naming of the Central Library building in Port of Spain after V. S. Naipaul. The Government of Trinidad and Tobago finally decided to name the library the National Library of Trinidad and Tobago. Selwyn Cudjoe had advocated against the move because he felt that such a move would only serve the purpose of 'national ego-boosting' (1996). A similar controversy surrounded the government's decision to buy Naipaul's St. James house.

166 V. S. NAIPAUL OF TRINIDAD

This did not deter the Naipaul enthusiasts, who had formed a society, 'Friends of Mr Biswas' in 1996, asking the government to step in to buy the St. James house in 1998, and its subsequent transfer to them on a 99-year lease given to Professor Kenneth Ramchand in 2001. Yet in spite of his opposition to the naming of the library after V. S. Naipaul, Cudjoe's initial reaction to Naipaul's Nobel Prize was positive. He said:

> In honouring him as a Briton, they acted as though Trinidad was merely one of the literary locations about which Naipaul had written. Little did they understand that Trinidad is the place in which Naipaul was made and to which he returns, ever so often, for his spiritual sustenance and literary inspiration. (2001, p. 18)

The October 12, 2001 editions of the three leading newspapers (*Trinidad Guardian, Trinidad Express* and *Trinidad and Tobago Newsday*) in Trinidad and Tobago paid rich tributes to V. S. Naipaul on winning the Nobel Prize. The *Trinidad Guardian* Editorial (2001) wrote:

> [...] he has always delighted in perversity, and this lack of any acknowledgement of his birthplace is yet another example of his puckishness [...]. And although more than once he has written about Trinidad in words that have caused hurt and resentment, the more he writes, the more clearly can be seen the importance of his early years here, and the more explicitly he has acknowledged that debt. It is one that Naipaul has repaid handsomely, and the Nobel Prize is a richly deserved tribute to the lifetime achievement of a great Trinidadian writer (p. 16).

Various reports on the same day reported that his elder sister Kamla Tewari was 'just quietly pleased, not at all surprised, but in a way too surprised' (2001, p. 13). She also reminded everyone: 'There is no book, no magazine and no interview that does not mention his Trinidadian roots.' In a much later interview published in the United Kingdom, Naipaul said: "I always knew who I was and where I had come from" (Adams 2004). The *Trinidad Express* quoted George Lamming:

> Naipaul has gone around for a very long time expressing a certain scorn, and a certain contempt for the Caribbean, for Africa and to some extent for India.
>
> And this comes out of a very early insecurity—the insecurities inflicted on Naipaul being born Indian and Trinidadian in the 1930s growing up

COMPOSING AGAIN IN THE 2000s

in the 1940s. These insecurities were very, very deep and what he did was that he converted these insecurities into a form of snobbery. (2001, p. 3)

The *Trinidad and Tobago Newsday* reported Kenneth Ramchand as stating that Naipaul's Nobel was long overdue (Pickford-Gordon 2001). It also ran an article 'Naipaul—Wanderer of Endless Curiosities' by R. Z. Sheppard (courtesy of *Time* magazine, originally published July 10, 1989). In subsequent articles, Derek Walcott was quoted as saying, 'I'm very, very pleased. It's long overdue, even if he's written some very harsh things about the Caribbean' ('Naipaul's Sisters Delighted' 2001). Gordon Rohlehr observed that Naipaul had not found his centre but 'can't get the Caribbean out of his system' (Rambaran 2001, p. 14). Kevin Baldeosingh reported that Naipaul had made immediate amends by confessing that there had been a mix-up and that he had originally intended to recognise Trinidad in the press release: 'He said he had to thank England, the place that allowed him to be a writer, and India, which occupied his mind, and his agent, "and last but not the least, the place where I was born."' Baldeosingh also quoted him as saying that the Nobel Committee had been instructed to describe him as a Trinidad-born British writer, 'What more can one do?' he said (2001).

The newspapers also published several dissenting voices, with the *Trinidad and Tobago Newsday* editorial stating: 'He gives no recognition to the facts of his birth and early life in Trinidad. Still, our society has helped to produce him' (*Trinidad and Tobago Newsday*, October 12, 2001, p. 10). Raffique Shah, one of the original mutineers during the Black Power Movement in Trinidad and later a journalist, said: 'In *Guerrillas* he "took the mickey" out of revolutionaries (like myself)' (2001, p. 14). And *Trinidad Guardian*, quoting Merle Hodge, stated: 'That [his omission of Trinidad from the press release (2001)] makes him the ultimate *neemakharam*' (Springer 2001, p. 1). Ira Mathur, writing for the *Trinidad Guardian*, remembered the instance when she interviewed Naipaul at the airport in 1989: 'My favourite answer [...] to a question about our political situation was: "The politics of a country of one point one million people, does not interest me"' (2001). Strangely, the feeling of elation did not extend beyond Trinidad in the Caribbean. In a report in the *Trinidad Guardian*, it was reported that except for the *Guyana Chronicle*, there were no editorials and only a few first-page stories across the national dailies in the Caribbean (Naipaul—rising from 'nothing' 2001).

Half A Life (2001a)

The new millennium saw Naipaul return to fiction after more than two decades of travel and mixed-mode writing for nearly 22 years. His last novel,

A Bend in the River, was published in 1979. Since then, he had published a number of travel narratives and two books that were provocatively subtitled 'novel' and challenged the boundaries of the conventional novel. *Half a Life* marked this return. This is a more 'traditional' novel that begins in India but features London and Africa as well. If we go by Naipaul's dictum that 'the last book contained all the others,' we see a writer working out his own ghosts—his Indian ancestry, his African connection, and the place of England in this midst. The colonial power connects the two sub-continents of India and Africa but there is no direct link between the two. Naipaul's ancestors were sent to Trinidad, where they were met with the descendants of another migratory population, those that had been brought there as slaves from different parts of Africa. I suggest that the two novels, *Half a Life* and *Magic Seeds*, are another attempt at a veiled autobiography, though there is no reference to Trinidad.

This book spans the first 40 years of the life of its main protagonist, Willie Chandran—literally the first half of his life. It ends at a point when Willie is contemplating leaving Africa. Willie's father is the narrator-protagonist of his tale, which is told in the first person. Like Naipaul's *A House for Mr Biswas*, the point of view stays with Willie's father in the first part and shifts to Willie later. But, unlike *A House for Mr Biswas*, this book is definitely about the son and not the father. At any given moment in the novel, the narrator is aware of others watching him: 'They [the Principal and Somerset Maugham] talked about me and they looked at me while they talked, and I sat and looked through them like someone deaf and blind, and the crowd looked at all three of us' (2001a, p. 8). Naipaul is the master novelist who is using a technique that he developed in his early fiction, where the narrator-protagonist was always aware of how he presented himself and how the reader viewed him. The reference to Somerset Maugham is significant. Maugham had written a book about his India travels called *The Razor's Edge*, in which he met a sadhu in a temple. Naipaul uses the reference to write his own story from the other side of the encounter. But, more importantly, Naipaul's father had read Maugham to him, and he had won the Somerset Maugham Award for *Miguel Street* in 1961. Hence, Willie Chandran's name may also be suggestive of Naipaul's early beginnings.

Though Naipaul had portrayed many would-be writers as his protagonists in his early books, this is the first time that we see writing being used as a form of communication between a father and son. Willie writes three stories about a holiday on the beach, 'King Cophetua and the Beggar Maid' and 'A Life of Sacrifice;' the father interprets the stories as symbolising hate for the father, the mother and himself. Subsequently, he arranges for Willie's departure to

COMPOSING AGAIN IN THE 2000s

London on a scholarship. The three stories are interesting because they are sociological explorations that are interpreted psychologically by the father. It perhaps parodies the father-son relationship Naipaul shared with his father. While the real-life father-son relationship was a relationship of camaraderie, here it is distorted to emphasise the estranged relationship between the father and the son. The three tales loom under the shadow of the useless 'sacrifice' of Willie's father as a Brahmin in marrying a lower caste woman. The three tales also foreshadow Willie's future actions. As a young adult in England, Willie writes 'Indian' stories, which later serve to rescue him from a tricky situation in India. The reader is not told about these stories or how specifically they were 'Indian.' According to J. Dillon Brown:

> Naipaul's satirical portrayal of Willie as a writer who thoughtlessly imitates Hemingway and produces nonsensical, film-inspired prose stories finds precise parallel in Naipaul's own literary criticism on *Caribbean Voices*, in which he persistently censures writers (especially Garth St. Omer and John Hearne) for trying to sound like Hemingway and suggests that certain writers are too inspired by film and should concentrate more on structure and cohesion. (2013, p. 172)

This part of the book draws heavily on Naipaul's early experiences in England after his Oxford years. The fact that Naipaul portrays England as a land where races meet on an equal footing yet where there is little scope for immigrants without talent is interesting. Naipaul endorses his own survival and canonisation as a writer in England against Willie's poor talents and efforts to make it in England.

The story begins with Willie's father, a Brahmin, willingly marrying a lower-caste woman as an act of rebellion and commitment to the Gandhian anti-colonial movement. Unlike the heroes of his early books, he is not a victim but a revolutionary who chooses to rebel against set social norms. Yet Willie's father remains unrecognised, in spite of running an ashram later in the book, because the narrative is really about the success and failures of the son rather than the father. It is interesting that Willie's father can be read as another version of Seepersad's original figure of Gurudeva. London appears only briefly in the narrative as the place where Willie is most uncomfortable, even though he forges many friendships and manages to publish a book of stories. The Notting Hill race riots make Willie rethink his uncertain future in England, and he decides to go to Africa. This again reflects Naipaul's own sense of betrayal by the British in the late 1950s and early 1960s.

Told in the past tense, Africa in the narrative appears to be the background for Willie's adventures. Why does Naipaul leave Africa as an undifferentiated continent when it is composed of at least 55 nations? Even during colonial times, Africa was divided into territories controlled by no less than seven Western European countries. It is because the descendants in Trinidad suffered from forced amnesia due to their long enslavement and travel across the Atlantic. In their imagination, Africa was a unitary territory, with the West Coast being the most probable departure point. Naipaul deliberately adopts this attitude towards a nondescript Africa because it is reflective of both the colonialists and the ex-enslaved. The book is notable because it reflects Naipaul's unresolved relationship with Africa. It does not matter which country it is because Willie is unable to draw a connection with Africa despite living there for a significant portion of his adult life. He refuses to take responsibility for his actions because he can escape the racial binary by claiming to be an Indian who was 'colonised' elsewhere. His relationships with other women perhaps mirrors Naipaul's relationship with Pat and how distant he became from Pat while living together. He simply leaves behind his life in Africa, unable to strike a true connection, and returns to his sister in Germany.

Magic Seeds (2004)

While *Half a Life* traverses Willie's first 40 years of life, this book traverses only the next 15 or so years. Inspired by socialist ideals, Willie decides to join the underground movement among the backward tribes in India. This book expresses Naipaul's severest criticism of armed guerrilla warfare that creates unrest in the name of fighting for equality. Naipaul is convinced that the leftists train and brainwash many so-called educated young immigrants in British universities, who then begin their little wars in their own countries. He had seen them make war in India (Naxalites), Argentina ('The Return of Eva Perón'), Iran (Revolutionary Guards and the Communist Party), and Pakistan (the Baluch cause). He had been familiar with the tactics of Che Guevara and had named his novel *Guerrillas*, which was set against the background of the Black Power Movement in Trinidad. He had criticised the guerrillas in Argentina and Iran, but in Trinidad he had limited his criticism to the personality of Michael X. In *A Way in the World*, Naipaul presented Blair and Lebrun's interventions in Africa as men with missions but without morality. His persistent line of questioning was: Who gave them the guns? He was also unconvinced about their causes because the guerrillas were often unable to strike down the system. Their violent approach merely led to one set of elites being replaced by another set of elites.

The turning point in Willie's engagement with the Naxalite movement in India is stated at the beginning of the novel when Sarojini accuses Willie of always being a spectator to conflicts: 'It's the colonial psychosis, the caste

COMPOSING AGAIN IN THE 2000s

psychosis' (2004, p. 2). It is interesting that Naipaul looks upon the ultra-left movements as direct offshoots of colonial interferences in the time of decolonialisation. Willie takes the plunge into action, only to be disappointed soon. In India, the guerrillas are not 'Che Guevara and strong men in military fatigues' but helpless 'matchstick people' who are monuments to the cruelty of colonial history. He realises that these revolutionaries have little to replace the old systems: 'The fields of the liberated areas Willie knew had fallen into ruin; the old landlords and feudals had run away years before from the guerrilla chaos, and no secure new order had been established' (2004, p. 86). He meets a man who has been in the movement for 30 years living a life off the villagers to whom he preached freedom: 'I feel the life I am describing is similar to that of a high powered executive' (2004, p. 132). Naipaul's characterisation of the Naxalite movement is based on his own travels through India. In addition to meeting Dipanjan and Debu in *India: A Million Mutinies Now*, Naipaul had spoken to many individuals and had seen the disillusionment of the Naxalites with their revolution. Willie realises that in order to keep the movement going, these 'professional' Naxals 'tell people in the universities that the forest is a liberated area, and [they] tell people in the forest that the universities are a liberated area' (2004, p. 141). The confusion keeps the underground movement running like a well-oiled machine. Willie is arrested, and Sarojini organises Willie's release from jail through a left-wing firm in England, using Willie's first and only book of short stories to proclaim him 'a pioneer of modern Indian writing' (2004, p. 174). Thus ends Willie's India adventure after seven years and Naipaul's adventurism with the guerrillas.

Willie then joins Roger and his wife, Perdita, in London. He realises that the London he lived in 30 years ago was now full of 'black people everywhere, and Japanese; and people who looked like Arabs' (2004, p. 196). This is similar to Salim's impression of London in *A Bend in the River* but goes further to proclaim that the State had remained oblivious to their needs: 'I feel that these people [the British] don't know the other side of things [… they] don't understand nullity. The physical nullity of what I saw in the forest. The spiritual nullity that went with that, […]. Unless we understand people's other side, Indian, Japanese, African, we cannot truly understand them' (2004, p. 211). The book ends with Willie writing for a quality magazine about modern architecture and buildings (again, a reference to Naipaul's 'idle years' in London soon after graduation from Oxford); Sarojini coming back to Germany; Roger as an estate agent; and Marcus's success with having a white grandchild. But the success is a sham.

Hywel Dix reads *Magic Seeds* 'as a work produced late in a career and in the conscious presence of the earlier work [*A House for Mr Biswas*]' (2019,

p. 183): 'There, the idea of the house was an end in itself, whereas here it has become associated with a culture of economic greed and competitive individualism to the detriment of any notion of common good' (2019, p. 182). Clearly, Naipaul has moved on from his early writings. John Lanchester, in his *New York Review of Books* review of *Magic Seeds*, dubbed the India part of the story fantastical. He felt that the story really begins when Willie arrives in London 'where, for a British reader, the fun starts' (2005, p. 23). After all, if *The Enigma of Arrival* is taken as a marker of his settling down, then Willie's criticism of English life in *Magic Seeds* should be taken as Naipaul's final rejection of English society as a society of racial classist Englishmen and women. According to Lanchester, Naipaul 'is wonderfully, bracingly offensive about contemporary Britain' (2005, p. 24). Naipaul had always been critical of politics in Britain and elsewhere. With the revelation of Roger's rant against the 'servant' class and Perdita's copied ideas, Willie contemplates 'the darkness in which everybody walked'. The ending pays deference to the writer's task: 'It is wrong to have an ideal view of the world. That's where the mischief starts. That's where everything starts unravelling. But I can't write to Sarojini about that' (2004, p. 294). Judy Raymond saw the pessimism of the writer reflected in the book. She could not agree with Naipaul that the [Naxalite] movement justified the killings in the name of idealism, even though she limited her concerns to the unconvincing nature of the book rather than the real world (2004).

Of all the Naipaulian books, this book presents a resolution that is apt for writers: a realisation that change is inevitable, that authors write within a context, and that social churning produces changes that are more profound than short-lived revolutions. But it is not the job of the writer to tell the reader as much. Kenneth Ramchand finds the twin books disappointing because they are more formulaic, where the joy of discovery has been lost, while Naipaul's early fiction was vibrant and true to life. Besides Willie Chandran, all other characters are functional rather than fully developed. I would agree that the main character is fully developed, even at the expense of other characters. Willie's mother's story, his sister's story and Ana's story, are all side-lined while Willie is given prominence. This is true for Roger and Perdita as well. It seems that Naipaul concentrated all his energies on developing Willie's character. If we take Naipaul for his word that the last book contains all the rest, the focus on Willie implies that he is Naipaul's ultimate protagonist. Born in a world that is constantly changing, Willie is a migrant who spends the first 18 years of his life under his father's care, the next 18 years under his wife's care and finally takes the plunge into action, not that it makes much of a difference. He is a drifter, and Naipaul puts him in an amoral universe. Whether landowners are a problem or not, whether

COMPOSING AGAIN IN THE 2000s 173

the methods of the Naxalites are right or not, whether Willie's judgement is correct or not, the reader should not judge.

The two books are important markers in Naipaul's oeuvre as they retrace his interests in India, Africa and England. These novels have a global expanse and a protagonist who could be dubbed a 'citizen of the world' being comfortable everywhere with no ambitions. That his 'citizen of the world,' is not a metropolitan-born individual but a person born in an ex-colony goes to show his critics that they had misinterpreted his investment in England. There are two further differences from his earlier fiction: one, his protagonist is anchorless in a world that is itself amoral; and two, though the focus is still on the individual, it is the connection with his community that drives the individual forward. Naipaul had derived both of these notions in the early 1980s, when he revisited Trinidad after the death of his younger sister, Sati. The book can be read as Naipaul's fiercest criticism of the form of the novel. An individual without the anchors of community and society cannot be portrayed in a novel because the nineteenth-century novel places the central character in a specific time and place. 'The metropolitan novel [...] comes with metropolitan assumptions about society: the availability of a wider learning, an idea of history, a concern with self-knowledge' ('Reading and Writing' in *Literary Occasions* 2003, p. 24–5). These two novels lack supporting structures because the 'wider learning' is located in multiple locations and no one living in a single space has that wider knowledge; 'history' is violent and fragmentary—it allows men like Willie to fall through its cracks; and 'concern with self-knowledge' is a misplaced personal goal that reveals ugly truths. By totally obliterating Trinidad from his creative landscape, Naipaul moves forward. For Naipaul, his ultimate protagonist is a drifter rather than an achiever, a tribute to his post-colonial thinking rather than his colonial upbringing. And just when one thought that Naipaul had moved beyond Trinidad, he returns to write about Trinidad in the very next set of essays.

A Writer's People (2007)

A Writer's People: Ways of Looking and Feeling is a set of five essays on Naipaul's life as a writer. Naipaul, the writer, shows an extraordinary 'anxiety of influence,' reiterating his uniqueness. In this rather reconciliatory phase of his writing, he pays a tribute to his contemporaries from the Caribbean, England, Europe and India. Initially, he had been rather dismissive of the Caribbean, describing Trinidad as a 'dot on the map.' Now he writes: 'We were a small immigrant island, culturally and racially varied' (2007, p. 2). He remembers the time in 1949 when he first got to know Derek Walcott through the publication of his poems. Walcott's almost immediate popularity was related to the rise of a black middle-class and its investment in a local culture, the steel band and the dance. Naipaul appreciates Walcott's use of language, though not its sentimentality, his unpeopled landscapes, and his absorption into an Afro-Caribbean culture. Naipaul recognises that Walcott was received into a 'tradition of complaint in Negro poetry,' while his own father had no such tradition for support. He also analyses other writers, such as Edgar Mittelholzer and Samuel Selvon, from the region. Mittelholzer celebrated his white creole ancestry and Selvon his mixed East Indian urban background before moving on to the subject of the black West Indian immigrant in London. His father was the only writer who celebrated the East Indian country Indian. Naipaul felt that his father was truly a pioneer and perhaps 'the first writer of the Indian diaspora' (2007, p. 31). He expresses regret that his father could never gain widespread recognition for his writing. Naipaul reiterates how his father's stories, along with the enactment of *Ramlila*, gave him a strong sense of his community's background.

Naipaul then argues that he is the only writer who broke through the limitations of his Trinidadian background and surmounted any limitations that a British writer may have had. By contrast, the British/European/American writers like Anthony Powell, Graham Greene, Gustave Flaubert, Evelyn Waugh, Somerset Maugham and Henry James 'assumed too much.' Guy de Maupassant and Mark Twain were easier to handle because they provided many concrete details about time and place in their books. While these writers 'assumed too much,' the Indian writers refused to write about the most obvious of things, such as poverty and dirt in India. In most cases, people and writers did not record the concrete facts before them. The problem of 'not seeing' affected the first-generation migrants to Trinidad too, because they failed to record their first impressions either orally or in writing. Many of Naipaul's characters, such as Ralph Singh in *The Mimic Men* and Willie Chandran in *Half a Life* and *Magic Seeds*, display this trait of not seeing the obvious. He had given this more thematic consideration in *A Way in the World*, where he accused Columbus, Raleigh, Miranda, Blair, Lebrun, Foster Morris and himself of the same fault. Here, he plays with the same theme in analysing the writings of Rahman Khan, Mahatma Gandhi, Aldous Huxley, Jawahar Lal Nehru and himself.

Naipaul defines his own view as a cross between the English and Indian ways of looking. He defines it as a 'classical half-view' because artists must choose their material and keep up the joy of discovery in writing. In his opinion, Flaubert's *Salammbô* was too constructed and descriptive rather than precise and instinctive. *Madame Bovary* was written from personal experience,

COMPOSING AGAIN IN THE 2000s

while *Salammbô* was the fulfilment of an ambition and therefore less appealing. The same may be said of Naipaul's *A House for Mr Biswas* which was written from personal experience while *Half a Life* and *Magic Seeds* were ambitious attempts at surpassing his ancestry and inheritance. He struggled with his writing because neither the British nor the Europeans offered him a tradition to write within. The crowning glory of Naipaul's narrative is a passage taken from his mother's diary (now lost), where she mentions her own experience in India. In 1977, she was received by the extended family in India and served tea with one of the relatives bringing in sugar on the palm of her hand and another relative mixing it in with her finger. Naipaul's mother left her diary account in mid-sentence.

With this book, Naipaul re-ignited passions with his bleak assessment of Caribbean writers. It culminated in Derek Walcott reading a scathing poem, "The Mongoose", full of picong, at the Calabash Literary Festival in Jamaica in 2008. Walcott accused Naipaul of writing for the British, becoming their stooge and denigrating Trinidad. It also carried an honest criticism of Naipaul's last two novels:

Read his last novels. You'll see just what I mean:
A lethargy approaching the obscene.
The model is Maugham, more ho-hum than Dickens.
The essays have more bite. They scatter chickens,
Like critics. But each studied phrase is poison,
Since he has made that sneering style a prison.
Their plots are forced, the prose sedate and silly.
The anti-hero is a prick named Willy,
Who lacks the conflict of a Waugh or Lawrence
And whines with his creator's self-abhorrence [...]. (Lydon 2008)

The question that remains is why Naipaul continued to create an 'anti-hero' (not villainous) instead of creating a true hero. But is Willie Chandran any more of an anti-hero than Mohun Biswas? Most critics, in Trinidad and abroad, appreciated Walcott's sting while disassociating themselves from the more sedate assessment of Naipaul's writings. Naipaul's assessment of his fellow writers was pronounced 'Naipaul's gravest literary misjudgement' (de Caires 2008).

The 2007 Conference at UWI

Naipaul's glorious return to Trinidad in 2007, with The University of the West Indies holding a grand reception and symposium in his honour, was a huge event. Naipaul had been gracious enough to accept the invitation, as the university planned to celebrate three legendary Nobel Laureates from the Caribbean: Sir V. S. Naipaul, Sir Arthur Lewis and Sir Derek Walcott. Interestingly, Naipaul's citizenship to Trinidad and Tobago was 'restored' in March 2007, with Sir V. S. Naipaul visiting the High Commission of Trinidad and Tobago in England to receive his dual citizenship and passport ('Naipaul's citizenship restored,' 2007). In preparation for the honour, many pre-events were held to garner public interest. Among these was the serialisation of his most oft-quoted novel, *The Suffrage of Elvira*, in the *Trinidad Guardian* from February to August 2007, with illustrations by Louis Legendre. Bhoendradatt Tewarie, the then Pro-Vice Chancellor and Principal of the St. Augustine Campus of The University of the West Indies, is himself a Naipaul scholar. In an article published in *Sunday Guardian* on February 25, 2007, titled 'Naipaul's Political Drama: Novel shows corruption in pre-independent T&T,' Tewarie highlighted Naipaul's assessment of the colonial legacy in *The Suffrage of Elvira* which criticised the British for passing on 'the way of life of the plantation, with its support systems, slavery and indenture, with its legacy of human degradation, economic destitution, ethnic division and polarisation, not to mention a persistent obsession with the humiliation of others' (2007). Another article published highlighted that 'the land left to Vidia by his mother is tied up since the Town and Country Planning department does not allow the four acre plot to be further divided, as his mother left him half an acre' (Baboolal 2007). His Nobel winning lecture, 'Two Worlds' was re-published in *Sunday Guardian*, April 22, 2007 (2001c), with the introduction highlighting that Trinidad was mentioned no less than 13 times in the lecture. Tewarie recounts that a proposal had been passed by the university to rename The Institute of Critical Thinking as the V. S. Naipaul Institute of Critical Thinking. But Naipaul, though happy at the honour, asked the university to let it pass for the time being.

The event itself was well attended and, akin to his last public appearance at The University of the West Indies, was equally controversial. In an article, 'Mad Rush for Naipaul,' Sean Douglas reported that though Naipaul read eloquently from his books, *Half a Life*, 'His Chosen Calling' from *Miguel Street*, and *Among the Believers*, he struggled to 'pronounce in true Trinidadian dialect those very words that had brought him such plaudits. He read Trini slang in an Englishman's accent!' (2007). But this was not his only fault. When asked if he would write about Trinidad again, 'he said, "You write novels out of great knowledge." He was not familiar with Trinidad today and could not "pick up material" from the visit. Naipaul said he would have to live here for many years but he was an old man' (Pickford-Gordon 2007). Three articles in leading newspapers covered his interaction with

COMPOSING AGAIN IN THE 2000s

academics on stage: 'Sir V. S. Naipaul Loses his cool' by Carol Matroo, published in *Trinidad Guardian* (2007); 'Naipaul re-mystified' by Denzil Mohammed, published in *Sunday Guardian* (2007); and 'Sir Vidia's Week in Trinidad' by Kevin Baldeosingh, published in *Trinidad and Tobago Newsday* (2007). All the articles highlight Naipaul's sullenness in answering questions that he thought were too ordinary, mundane or too academic. Typically, he rebutted that he had ever agreed to his books being made into films either in Hollywood or Bollywood: 'Both ways would be damaging to my works. Bollywood is very operatic and in Hollywood everything becomes mantled to suit the stars or producers.' Asked if the Americanisation of the country could be reversed, Naipaul said: 'American culture is throughout the world [...]. There is nothing we can do about it. America has entered our pores. Why reverse it?' When asked by Dr Morgan Job, what about the perception 'Naipaul don't like black people?' Naipaul answered, 'The writer has no control over what happens to him. A writer in the end is not his works but his myth, and I have no control over myth.' In response to a question by Dr Evelyn O'Callaghan, Naipaul rejected the belief that the author had been the subject of his works, saying: 'Nonsense. I have not read any book that would give clues to the nature of my life.' Professor Gordon Rohlehr asked about his relations with C. L. R. James and how that informed the characterisation of Lebrun in *A Way in the World*. Naipaul told him that his relationship with James had left 'very little precipitate' in his mind and that Lebrun wasn't based on James. In another interactive session organised by the Sanatan Dharma Hindu Maha Sabha for schoolchildren, he refused to answer many of the questions, saying that it confirmed his belief that literature was not for children. So, the trip, which began with Naipaul's wife, Lady Nadira, taking the blame for the omission of Trinidad from his initial press release on winning the Nobel Prize, ended on a sour note, with people cherishing the opportunity to meet Naipaul but despising him for his sullenness.

This in no way affected the love–hate relationship between Trinidad and Naipaul. The TTFC (Trinidad and Tobago Film Festival) paid tribute to V. S. Naipaul by screening three films, Adam Low's *The Strange Luck of V. S. Naipaul*, Bhoe Tewarie's *V. S. Naipaul in Conversation* and Ismail Merchant's *The Mystic Masseur* (*Trinidad and Tobago Newsday*, September 19, 2008, p. 11) in 2008. Naipaul's 75th birth year celebrations in Trinidad lasted a whole year.

The Masque of Africa: Glimpses of African Belief (2010)

The Masque of Africa was the first full-length book about Naipaul's travels through the six nation-states of Uganda, Nigeria, Ghana, Ivory Coast, Gabon and South Africa. It was also the last published travel book by Naipaul.

178   V. S. NAIPAUL OF TRINIDAD

He had earlier set his novella 'In a Free State' and his novels *A Bend on the River*, and *Half A Life* in Africa. He had also written two non-fictional articles, 'A New King for the Congo: Mobutu and the Nihilism of Africa' and 'The Crocodiles of Yamoussoukro.' However, this is the most comprehensive book about his interests in Africa.

Naipaul's narrator announces his agenda on the very first page, stating that he was returning to Uganda after 42 years to look for material about 'the nature of African belief' (2010, p. 1). He repeatedly notes the proliferation of ecclesiastical churches and mosques across the landscape: 'Foreign religion, to go by the competing ecclesiastical buildings on the hilltops, was like an applied and contagious illness, curing nothing, giving no final answers, keeping everyone in a state of nerves, fighting wrong battles, narrowing the mind' (2010, p. 6). This was Naipaul's most scathing attack on European and Arab colonialism and attempts by English and Arabic educators to universalise their civilisations through religious conversions. He repeatedly recognises that African culture was destroyed and subordinated to colonial knowledge:

> But Mutesa's Baganda people, with their gift for social organisation, their military discipline, and their elaborate court ritual, evolved over some centuries, had a civilization of their own. They built the roads as straight as Roman roads; they had a high idea of sanitation; they had a fleet on Lake Victoria, with an admiral and naval techniques of their own, and they could launch invasions of Busogo across the Nile. They worked iron and made their own spears and knives; they knew how to make bark-cloth and were beautiful builders of grass houses [...]. (2010, pp. 5–6)

Yet, despite this stand, Naipaul casts his narrator as a nineteenth-century English traveller who relies on colonial records and colonial explorers such as H. M. Stanley and John Hanning Speke for guidance in travelling through Africa. He refuses to identify with the general public travelling on the airplane and after the fiasco of his taxi ride and the exchange of hotels and hotel rooms, Naipaul's narrator acknowledges his vulnerability: 'I had the luck of the innocent—it does exist: it has looked after me for all of my travelling life' (2010, p. 86). It is Naipaul's brief acknowledgement of luck (for most of his writing life, he claimed to be a victim).

The most distinguishing fact in this book is the ease with which Naipaul records his links with Trinidad. It is noteworthy that rather than referring to a nameless local government official for providing transportation (as in his travel to his native village in *An Area of Darkness*) or to nameless

COMPOSING AGAIN IN THE 2000s

benefactors in the government (as in his travels inside Indonesia in *Among the Believers*), Naipaul's narrator here acknowledges his use of Trinidadian contacts in his travels through Africa. In the last section on Uganda, Naipaul, the narrator, solicits help and accompanies Patrick Edwards, the Trinidadian ambassador, to Toro where the ambassador pays for Naipaul to look around the royal campus. He also solicits the help of John Mitchell, the Trinidad consul, to meet Jerry Rawlings, the past President of Ghana. When he visits the house of Binger, a former French colonial governor of the Ivory Coast, he notes: 'There are a score of grander public and private buildings in a small place like Trinidad, on the other side of the Atlantic' (2010, p. 211). Somehow, Trinidad's preservation of its colonial past is peddled as better than Africa's total disregard of its colonial past. It is a positive endorsement of his place of birth.

However, Naipaul's narrator continues to claim a European literary ancestry, naming the travellers who had previously visited Gabon, including Du Chaillu (1831–1903), Dr Schweitzer in 1915 and Mary Kingsley between 1889 and 1895:

> When I was a boy in Trinidad, on the other side of the Atlantic, I used to think that the light and heat had burned away the history of the place. You couldn't feel that bush or sea had a history. To have a sense of history you needed buildings, architecture; and history came to the place [...] in Marine square in the centre of the old Spanish town, and the few ambitious buildings of the British period. (2010, p. 275)

His notion that 'nothing was created in the West Indies' is now tempered to say that history was not dependent upon written texts or temporal creations. It existed in memories in oral cultures that have continuously adapted to change.

References to Trinidad form a comparative framework and are spluttered across the book: Naipaul's narrator remembers Trinidad in the 1940s, 'when the steel band was being perfected' (2010, p. 97), and the casual practice of letting horses loose once they had served their purpose on the racecourse (2010, p. 104). On the way to Kumasi in Ghana, he observes that the palace rails were similar to his 'school in Trinidad (built in 1904)' (2010, p. 171). He observes that 'For Black people in Trinidad a word that sounded like it [capital city of Accra] meant a kind of food' (2010, p. 182). However, in Nigeria, he makes an exception when he sees a mysterious sculpture of an African. He is unable to find anyone who could explain it until he comes across its reference in Mungo Park's *Travels in the Interior of Africa*. The African figure of a veiled man in a high hat, and a long coat, holding a thick stick was Mumbo Jumbo, who punished quarrelling women by beating them publicly in the village square. The figure was part of ancient customs, and the occasion of his arrival was a joyous event. Though there are clear parallels to be found between this figure and the Mumbo Jumbo of Trinidad Carnival, Naipaul's narrator chooses not to recognise this.

Further, his newfound sympathy and understanding of African beliefs find little support in his personal reactions to the physical world of Africa. While he is being given a tour of the place to see the oracles in Nigeria, he is not satisfied because he remembers the poverty, filth and squalor outside with the onset of his asthma. In Ghana, Naipaul's narrator lists the difficulties of travel: garbage, open clogged drains, noisy children, his awkwardness and narrowness of the places he visits. In Ivory Coast, he observes that since the death of Félix Houphouët-Boigny, the country has been in political decline: 'Hidden from the cathedral and its gardens were moraines of uncontrolled garbage that lay in all the streets of the town: Africa reclaiming its own' (2010, p. 206). In another instance, he informs us that the Abidjan sky was literally littered with four or five million bats in the late afternoon, darkening the whole atmosphere. Naipaul's narrator connects this to African cruelty towards animals, cats in particular, and encourages viewing the contagious Ebola virus as nature's revenge. It is with some finality that he puts down his boots in South Africa. He finds the racial divide separating the two Africas too disturbing and acknowledges his exasperation: 'The two Africas were separate; I could not bring them together' (2010, p. 284). Looking down at the merchandise available for the witch doctor's—things like herbs, animal parts, and even three horses' heads—he reasserts his Western rational identity: 'It was impossible for any rational person to feel that any virtue could come from the remains of these poor animals' (p. 284). How far he has come from the time when he had to accept that his own father, the reformist, had been bullied into sacrificing a goat in 1933.

In this narrative, we find Naipaul endorsing traditional 'arts and crafts,' local business models, family and community structures. In an interview with Patrick Marnham published in *Literary Review*, Naipaul blamed the progressives more than the colonials for having destroyed Africa: 'they've just taken their blueprint and applied […] this kind of nonsensical patronising tolerance' (2011). In a way, he rescues travel writing from one of the nineteenth-century travel writing traits where the metropolitan or colonial traveller went not only from civilised places to uncivilised places but also through a quasi-time structure that ensured that he saw the colonised caught in a static time frame with no organic growth. Naipaul records a changing Africa, even if it means one step forward and two steps back.

The 2000s saw Naipaul increasingly acknowledge that he had made peace with his Trinidadian self. He had received the Nobel Prize; he had exhumed the ghosts of his past in his fiction; he acknowledged his seniors and contemporaries in his writing; he recognised his Trinidadian connections in his non-fiction. But none of this prevented him from making himself the subject of his writing. He also acknowledged his limitations as a traveller. Naipaul's narrator finds himself incapable of entering the world of African beliefs: 'a whole vista of the relativity of perceptions, too much of a quicksand for the short–term traveller to go into' (2010, pp. 236–7). He is fascinated with the eating of eboga, a hallucinogenic plant, the initiation ceremony, and ancestral sites deep in the forests, but realises that he is inept at understanding the depth of the rituals. However, he is no longer dismissive of any beliefs. His message, in a slightly different context, is the same for everybody:

"You must not only think of other people victimising India, but also of what Indians can do for themselves," he said. "The idea of being a victim shouldn't be something we should dwell on too much." (Rampersad 2003, p. 3)

CONCLUSIONS

V. S. Naipaul and the Caribbean

I hope that through this analyses I have achieved the aims that I set out in my introduction. Naipaul began writing using his early childhood exposure to the East Indian culture in Trinidad as a basis for writing about the Caribbean. When he embarked on his travel writing, he explored 'areas of darkness' that were related to his limited knowledge about his own complex heritage: 'The land; the aborigines; the New World; the colony; the history; India; the Muslim world, to which I also felt myself related; Africa; and then England, where I was doing my writing. That was what I meant when I said that my books stand one on the other, and that I am the sum of my books' ('Two Worlds' 2001e: 2003, p. 190). As he expanded his horizons, so did he expand the history of Trinidad. No idea or event in Trinidad escaped his scrutiny—it included an exploration of Trinidad's pre-Columbian past, its 'discovery' and plantation history in *The Loss of El Dorado*, his childhood in post-indentureship Trinidad in 'Prologue to an Autobiography' and *Reading and Writing*, the 1946 Trinidad general election in *The Mystic Masseur*; the 1950 Trinidad general election in *The Suffrage of Elvira*; the preparations for Independence in *The Middle Passage*; the first elections in Trinidad post its independence in 1966 in *The Mimic Men*; the Black Power Movement in 'Michael X and the Black Power Killings in Trinidad' and *Guerrillas*; the installation of the first non-PNM government in 1987 and the 1990 coup in *A Way in the World*. He further explored various aspects of his East Indian heritage in the Forewords to *The Loss of El Dorado* and *The Adventures of Gurudeva and Other Stories*, and once again in *A Writer's People*. Perhaps Trinidadians could fault him for not commenting directly or obliquely on the first East Indian-dominated UNC government in 1995. However, this move away from Trinidadian politics was accompanied by a focus on what his own life had to offer the next generation. Eight out of 12 novels that Naipaul wrote, namely, *The Mystic Masseur, The Suffrage of Elvira, Miguel Street, A House for Mr Biswas, The Mimic Men, A Flag on the Island, In A Free State,* and *Guerrillas*, are based in Trinidad. The other novels have different settings: *Mr Stone and*

184 V. S. NAIPAUL OF TRINIDAD

the Knights Companion is set in England; *A Bend in the River* is set in a fictional African town; *Half A Life* is set in India, England and Africa; and *Magic Seeds* is set in Germany, India and England. In all other non-fictional/mixed-mode writings, Naipaul's narrator was always 'V. S. Naipaul from Trinidad'. This establishes the centrality of Trinidad in Naipaul's universe and to understanding his development as a writer.

The second aim was to prove that the Trinidadians had acknowledged, loved, hated and owned him through the years. Caryl Phillips recounts his experience at a conference: 'In the early [19]90s I gave a lecture at the University of the West Indies in Trinidad in which I spoke respectfully, but critically, about Naipaul's work and his hostility towards the Caribbean. As I looked up at the audience I could not help but notice the look of outrage and disbelief that marked the faces of those present. I quickly understood. Naipaul may be an ungenerous bastard, but he was their ungenerous bastard. Who the hell was I to talk about their son of the soil?' (Phillips 2001). Naipaul's reputation in Trinidad never waned. As early as 1973, a call arose for preserving the Lion house 'as a national relic' because of its portrayal in *A House for Mr Biswas* (Mills 1973). From the early 1980s, Naipaul's name was in the running for the Nobel Prize. This was reported in Trinidad almost annually, even when the rest of the world had stopped expecting it ('Naipaul in Running for the "Nobel"' 1980; 'Fans ask why Not Naipaul' 1981; 'Naipaul in Nobel running' 1988; Kanhai 1997). Michael Anthony (2000) and Satnarayan Maharaj (2000) wrote about him. Anthony Milne reported in the *Sunday Express* that Naipaul had been accorded a very warm welcome by the immigration and customs officials at the Piarco airport when he had arrived in Trinidad from Venezuela in 1982. He also reported that the taxi driver recognised Naipaul and told him, 'You is Naipaul?' When this was confirmed, the driver said, 'Well, I go take care of you eh. They ain't like you at all down here you know. But don't worry, I going to take care of you' (Milne 1982b). The anecdote tells us that Trinidadians always accorded a warm welcome to Naipaul, and Naipaul thought that he deserved it all.

In addition to the two aims, this assessment has revealed several other things that I think need to be taken note of. For instance, Naipaul felt displaced but not detached from Trinidad or the world. This displacement was not merely physical or geographical but ideological as well. His first displacement was from Chaguanas to Port of Spain because his father moved there to provide for better education of his children. In a much later interview with Andrew Robinson, Naipaul remembered: 'I was never beaten at school. The boys made room for me because I was always the youngest person around. And that encouraged my wit. It was nice that this could happen in a multicultural society' (1987, p. 108). A second point of displacement was when Naipaul

CONCLUSIONS

left Trinidad for England to study at Oxford. He knew that he had worked hard to 'escape' the fate of his father by winning the scholarship to study at Oxford. Yet he also knew that that was the beginning of the struggle to become a writer. When he did return to Trinidad in 1956, just before the publication of his first book, *The Mystic Masseur*, it became amply clear to him that Trinidad could not be a home for him. This was the more decisive displacement that was to inform all his writings. The trip confirmed his belief that he had to stay in England to maintain his success. Upon his return to England, he wrote *A House for Mr Biswas* as a tribute to his father, whom he dearly missed while he tasted his first success as a writer.

Naipaul was part of a movement of writers from the Caribbean to the London metropolitan centre, where they were all published during the period 1950–64. This was part of the trend that harboured the belief that unless a writer was published in England, the writer was not worth reading. Naipaul was to later analyse this movement as proof of the Caribbean lacking a publishing environment because there were no large printing houses, the populace was largely illiterate, and there was no critical milieu that supported writing. However, the Notting Hill Riots of 1958 were a definite wake-up call to all those writers who had imagined a peaceful integration into British colonial society. Though Naipaul never wrote about these riots directly, with the enactment of the Immigration Law in 1962, Naipaul felt betrayed. This was no doubt a fourth point of displacement. He also noted how his early novels had been received in British literary circles: 'Consider this comment on my first novel in a weekly paper, now justly defunct: "his whole purpose is to show how funny Trinidad Indians are." The *Daily Telegraph* says I look down a long Oxford nose at the land of my birth. The *Evening Standard*, however, thinks that I write of my native land with warm affection' ('London,' 1958b: 1972, p. 11). He emphasised that he could never have written about Trinidadians in that way. In an early review of *A House for Mr Biswas*, published in *The London Magazine* in 1961, Francis Wyndham wrote that Naipaul's work was distinctive because 'he avoids the turgid pomposity of one school of Caribbean literature, the sex–cum–race sensationalism of another, and the self–consciously whimsical charm of a third, that his sober respect for truth has been mistakenly interpreted as high-spirited caricature' (1961, p. 91). Naipaul found comfort in Francis Wyndham's views, and Naipaul and Wyndham became lifelong friends. Naipaul's sensitivity about his writing and how it was received by the British accentuated his lack of social engagement with British society. He sought travel as a way of knowing the world at large. I do not think he went to India looking to be integrated into Indian society, and his personal reaction to India was one of pathological revulsion. Naipaul, on his first India trip, distanced himself from his ancestry but embraced

186 V. S. NAIPAUL OF TRINIDAD

a Hindu philosophy: 'It [Hindu philosophy] had enabled me, through the stresses of a long residence in England, to withdraw completely from nationality and loyalties except to persons; it had made me content to be myself alone, my work, my name, [...]' (*An Area of Darkness* 1964a, p. 198). Post its publication, in an early interview with Derek Walcott in 1965, when Naipaul had already written seven books, Naipaul emphasised two things: one, that a writer could never 'abandon one's allegiance to one's community, or at any rate to the idea of one's community' and two, 'that people who write about a society ennoble that society' (1965, pp. 6–7). He also defended himself, saying that he did not do caricatures and did not laugh at people since 'irony and comedy come out of a sense of acceptance' (1965, p. 8). By his own definition, Naipaul was loyal to his community and country. However, that did not stop him from criticising the Trinidadians or protesting against being called a 'West Indian novelist' ('Naipaul is the Literary Curiosity,' 1968).

This assessment has also revealed that Naipaul's move from fiction to travel writing to writing hybrid texts that he could claim to be novels (such as *A Way in the World*) was not an accident but an ideological choice by which he questioned the very basis of colonial education. Though he never wrote a book in which he openly criticised English education, he made repeated attempts to convey how English literature excluded people of his background. He wrote that he had to demythologise the English language to make it his own, to speak about his background, a background which included things, people, worlds and worldviews that he did not understand as a child but to which he repeatedly reached out to in his travels. He also wrote that he had to invent a form of non-fiction that could accommodate his telling. His journalistic methods, derived from his ability to speak to people from varied backgrounds, helped him in his writing more than anything that he learnt in the university.

Through this assessment I also discovered that Naipaul's international interests were all borne out of his need to know his background in Trinidad, people he had seen, people he had met on the roads, people that reached out to him across the room and the globe to forge relationships, and people who became his helpers in gathering information because of their common connection to Trinidad. His writings have often sparked strong reactions from people in countries about which he has written. However, many a times, these international controversies failed to garner any strong reactions within Trinidad. His criticisms found mention but failed to either dent or rebuild his reputation in Trinidad. I also found that many Trinidadians had formed their opinion based not on his writing but his reputation. This is not something specific to Trinidadians because most people in any country are not scholars or academics but common people who get affected

CONCLUSIONS

187

by what is conveyed to them in the 'drawing room' discussions, or more appropriately for the Trinis, in their liming sessions.

Naipaul's thesis about the universal civilisation was rooted in his acceptance of historical forces that were once Hindu, then Christian, then Islamic, then Christian again. His travels were borne out of his concern for understanding that part of his island history that had remained hidden and unknown in his corner of the world. Said's high voltage criticism did not stop Naipaul from going to these countries *again* out of a will to know and document the remnants of traditional societies, societies that were on the verge of losing their distinctive identities because a large part of their populations had converted to Islam. In Africa, too, he saw large scale conversions to Islam and Christianity. This led to Naipaul being accused of talking about race and of being racial. He enjoyed the first but never agreed with the latter charge. Internationally, the Black Power Movement was a movement for the civil rights in America that transformed into a wave of pseudo-decolonisation in the rest of the world. Its failure to fully integrate minority groups within itself limited its success in England and Trinidad. Within Trinidad, it is now commemorated for a socio-cultural-political awakening to the rights of ethnic, social and cultural minorities. Naipaul saw in it the failure to incorporate change and adapt quickly to local conditions. Naipaul's criticism of the Black Power Movement fed his reputation as a hater of the Afro-creole culture in Trinidad. Derek Walcott called Naipaul 'V. S. Nightfall,' and compared him to 'scrofula,' a colonial disease, in his review of *The Enigma of Arrival* (1987, pp. 128–9). Naipaul took a long time to respond to this insult in his book, *A Writer's People*, circumscribing Walcott's success within the confines of the négritude movement. They were perhaps both indulging in picong.

In response to many Trinidadians accusing Naipaul about his inability to write about the Afro-Trinidadians, and by extension, Africans, with sympathy, almost as a rebuttal, Naipaul wrote *A Bend in the River*. Even though Naipaul wrote about Africa through the eyes of an Indian descendant and the portrayal of Africans was relegated to the background, his descriptive passages about Africa won him some critical approval. Writing the story from the point of view of an Indian Muslim in Africa, he was able to sift through his material and present a plausible Africa. When many critics find fault with him on his writings about the Islamic countries, they forget his earlier investment in a Muslim narrator. Equally, some critics express total surprise at his later sudden marriage to Nadira Alvi in 1996, pointing out that he bashed Muslims and then married one of them. They forget that Nadira's cultural background was similar to Salim's in Africa. To quote from the book, though the Indian traders in Africa were Muslims, they 'were closer to the Hindus of north–western India' (1979, p. 12) than African Muslims, and 'from the way they behaved you would have thought that the river just down the road was the Ganges, with temples and holy men and bathing steps' (1979, p. 31). The book is also relevant for the development of Naipaul's thoughts on the universal civilisation. He recorded how the Africans looked upon the Western scientists and innovators as 'impartial gods up in the clouds' since their discoveries were made available without effort. This thought was carried forward in *Among the Believers* and in the essay, 'Our Universal Civilization.'

This assessment would not be complete without attaching value and relevance to Naipaul's travels across the world, especially to India, Africa and the Islamic world. Naipaul decided early that neither Africa nor India could provide any vision for recovery or development of Trinidad. Both locations were part of the same decolonised space and were struggling to decolonise themselves. And no amount of trips "back home" could provide Trinidadians with any solutions to *their* problems. His travels broadened his vision to realise the pervasiveness of the colonial empire and ideology. He saw the deep-rooted impact of colonial education (that continued to be offered in schools across the previously colonised states) on individuals who lacked motivation, entrepreneurship and innovation. While recording responses from individuals (some very idiotic remarks as well) Naipaul highlighted his impatience (even in his last published book) with society fooled by rituals and an inability to invest in real knowledge. The real thrust has to be to recover civilisational knowledge of survival, and its dissemination to all of humanity.

It is recognised that Naipaul's unique contribution to Caribbean literature is the presentation of the middle-class Indo-Trinidadian sensibility. Within the politics of the Caribbean critical scene, an emphasis on creolisation has the possibility of marginalising specific ethnic, racial and religious interests. This assessment has shown me how Africa's and Trinidad's histories of slavery were important elements of Naipaul's negotiation with the contemporary world. At least four fictional tales, *The Mimic Men, A Flag on the Island*, 'Tell me who to kill' in *In a Free State*, and *Guerrillas*; and four non-fictional books, *The Middle Passage, The Loss of El Dorado*, 'Michael X and the Black Power Killings in Trinidad' and *A Way in the World* focus upon racial relations in Trinidad; and another three fictional and three non-fictional works, 'In a Free State,' *A Bend in the River, Half a Life*; 'A Congo Diary,' 'The Crocodiles of Yamoussoukro,' and *The Masque of Africa* are set in Africa. Naipaul's engagement with Africa was an attempt to understand if there was a basis for any underlying racial hostilities. He discovered that the hostilities were purely political. Race relations in Trinidad were occasionally hostile but never on a personal level. Naipaul never invested in the Carnival because its promise was temporary. He disassociated

CONCLUSIONS

himself from advocating an Indo-Caribbean discourse because its politics was confrontational. By investing heavily in his own individuality, Naipaul was able to avoid the pitfalls of an Afro-centric or Indo-centric discourse. There is no other Caribbean writer who has so heavily invested in exploring the culture of *another* majority community. His investment in his own survival skills helped him visualise the writer as a trickster, a confidence man, who was able to juggle the roles of creator and disruptor to sell his wares to the world. The writer was no different from the common man in the tropics, who had to invent, create and define himself constantly to survive. On the one hand, Naipaul created a myth about the writer as a creative person escaping the shackles of a poor country. On the other hand, he demystified his writing by constantly speaking about the latent and real difficulties of being a writer from the Caribbean. As opposed to most writers in the Caribbean, who foresaw the importance of their participation in the change that they desired to see in their society, Naipaul felt fulfilled by merely showing a mirror to his society.

Gordon Rohlehr defined Naipaul's antipathy towards Trinidad as derived from the fact that 'Trinidad had not supplied him, could not supply him, with the backing or recognition he needed to find "a way into another world"' (2011, p. 95). We heard another version of this same thought when Savi Naipaul Akal said that Trinidad was a 'quagmire that stultified, a land of quicksand that swallowed him' (2018, p. 165). Not taking their verdict literally, I encourage you to look upon Naipaul's connection to Trinidad as an organic one, where he saw the world reflected in a microcosm, where his conflicting emotions could be grafted, where his raw nerves were irritated, and where he could allow his emotions to run free. It is true that Naipaul never wrote a book while in Trinidad, but the trips energised him enough to sit back and write about the world when he reached England. Moreover, this analyses has also revealed to me how Naipaul tried to synthesise the separate worlds of his childhood. He knew of their existence but had never thought about them from the point of view of a writer. As an adult, he tried to explore these other worlds of his childhood through travel. He wrote about Trinidad's history (*The Loss of El Dorado*) as a way to come to terms with the violence that it hid: 'Ever since I had begun to identify my subjects I had hoped to arrive, in a book, at a synthesis of the worlds and cultures that had made me. The other way of writing, the separation of one world from the other, was easier, but I felt it false to the nature of my experience. I felt in this history I had made such a synthesis' (*The Enigma of Arrival* 1987, pp. 171–2).

Kenneth Ramchand is convinced that of Naipaul's 29 books, at least seven are likely to endure and he lists them as: *Miguel Street, A House for Mr Biswas, The Mimic Men, A Bend in the River, The Loss of El Dorado, In a Free State* and

The Enigma of Arrival (2018b, p. 30). In a critical review of the pertinent question, 'Did Naipaul hate Trinidad?' Ramchand carefully analyses *The Middle Passage* that set the tone for most of such criticism. Through a careful textual reading, Ramchand shows that Naipaul criticised the British for their cruelty; the Africans for their disregard of their African past; and the East Indians for preserving their culture and making no effort to communicate with the Afro-Trinidadians. By comparing Naipaul to James Joyce, who had a love–hate relationship with Ireland, Ramchand is convinced that no hate exists without love. In fact, he attaches a positive note to Naipaul's visits to Trinidad in that his 1956 visit led to the writing of *A House for Mr Biswas*, the second in 1960 to *The Middle Passage* and the third in 1968–69 to *The Loss of El Dorado*: 'It was Trinidad that finally broke the hold that England had over him' (2018b, p. 77).

Naipaul's later disengagement with Trinidad was on a more personal level since he failed to find a 'patch of the earth' to call home. In spite of having written about Trinidad from an exclusively Indo-Trinidadian perspective in the first four novels and later portraying Trinidad's multi-racial society in his novels of the 1960s and the 1970s, Naipaul increasingly disengaged himself from contemporary Trinidad. He consistently refused to give permissions for interviews to Caribbean commentators and critics. He also refused to engage in any criticism about Selvon, Lamming, Harris and Brathwaite with non-Caribbean readers. He rarely engaged in discussions regarding the limitations of the label 'Caribbean Literature.' He did acknowledge that he named minor characters in *A House for Mr Biswas* after the Caribbean writers: George, Edgar and Sam. But these small gestures did not endear him to the Caribbean people. The biggest of his betrayals was the non-acknowledgement of Trinidad in his initial reaction on winning the Nobel Prize ('Naipaul wins the Nobel' 2001b). Scholars working on Naipaul and the Caribbean have highlighted how Naipaul dodged his relationship with Trinidad. Naipaul could not have cared less about being branded a lost son of the soil because notoriety brought its own pleasures to a Trinidadian. He preferred talking with the 'Doubles' guy than with so-called intellectuals. His sullenness at public events was in sharp contrast to his enjoyment of Trinidad's outdoors—its breeze, its mountains, the rivers, the seas and the beaches. Being made a subject for a calypso would, without a doubt, have been his crowning glory.

Appendix A

A NOTE ON TRINIDAD

The Caribbean is geographically situated between the Americas, almost like a bridge connecting the continents of North and South America. The population in Trinidad identifies itself as being of African, Indian, mixed-race, European, Middle Eastern and Chinese descent.

Trinidad was part of the Spanish empire from the time of its 'discovery' by Columbus in 1498 until 1797, when its political control was transferred to the British. Trinidad remained a plantation economy during the whole period of its colonial occupation. While there are no official estimates about the number of slaves brought into Trinidad until the abolition of slavery in 1834, it is estimated that 3.1 million Africans were shipped to the Americas across the Atlantic between 1662 and 1807.

Between 1838 and 1917, a total of 147,592 Indians had been imported to the sugar plantations in Trinidad and 239,000 in neighbouring Guyana (Deen 1998, p. 6). Of those indentured, 85% were Hindus and close to 14% were Muslims. Though indentureship was outlawed in 1917, the actual indenture period for those last indentured continued until 1920, when all the existing contracts were annulled.

According to the 2011 census, the so-called 'East Indians,' or the more politically correct term Indo-Trinidadians, constitute 35.43%, with 18.2% Hindus and 5% Muslims. The others are 34.22% Afro-Trinidadians, 7.66% mixed of African and East Indian and 15.16% mixed-other.

Culturally, East Indians are a strong community, maintaining their Hindu culture. Only 17% of Indians had converted to Christianity by the 1960s in Trinidad. The two main political parties, the People's National Movement and the United National Congress, advocate an inclusive creole culture. Creole culture has a strong slant towards the steel band, the calypso and the carnival, which have traditionally been dominated by the Afro-Trinidadians. However, the Sanatan Dharma Hindu Mahasabha, the Swaha Satsang, the Chinmaya Mission and the International Society for Krishna Consciousness (Iskcon), among many other Hindu bodies, have a strong presence on the island of Trinidad. The Sanatan Dharma Hindu Mahasabha is the central body that operates over 150 temples, 50 schools, a radio station and a television station in Trinidad. They bring out their own almanac based on the coordinates in the western and southern hemispheres. The strong presence of a central body has led to the consolidation of the Hindus in Trinidad.

Appendix B

A NOTE ON V. S. NAIPAUL'S TERMINOLOGY AND USE OF SPELLINGS

V. S. Naipaul was a man of his times. Historical references to Guyana before independence appear as Guiana or British Guiana. Surinam, which was also known as Dutch Guiana until 1948, appears as Surinam and not Suriname.

V. S. Naipaul constantly uses the terms Negro, Indians, and East Indians in his books to refer to the Afro-Trinidadians, Amerindians (People of the First Nation) and Indo-Trinidadians, respectively. Frequently, these are simplifications because a large population is mixed, and the culture is definitely mixed. In the 1930s, when Seepersad Naipaul wrote, and in the 1950s and 1960s, when V.S. Naipaul wrote about Trinidad, the Indo-Trinidadians constituted one third of the Trinidadian population. During the late 1960s and early 1970s, the Afro-Trinidadians identified themselves as Blacks.

V. S. Naipaul uses the spelling Ralegh for Sir Walter Raleigh in *The Loss of El Dorado* but reverts to the more commonly used spelling of Raleigh in *A Way in the World*. I have used Raleigh throughout the book except when in actual quotes.

V. S. Naipaul uses the spelling of Anantamurti for the Indian writer U.R. Ananthamurthy in *India: A Wounded Civilization*. I have used the spelling Ananthamurthy except when quoting Naipaul directly.

Naipaul uses the term 'Mohemmedans' for Muslims in *A Way in the World*. I have used Muslims to refer to the followers of Prophet Mohammed.

WORKS CITED

Primary Texts

Naipaul, V. S. 1957. *The Mystic Masseur*. London: André Deutsch. rpt. Fifth impression, 1978. All references are to the 1978 edition and appear parenthetically in the text.

Naipaul, V. S. 1958a. *The Suffrage of Elvira*. London: André Deutsch.

Naipaul, V. S. 1958b. "London." *The Times Literary Supplement*, August 15. Rpt. in *The Overcrowded Barracoon and other Articles*, 9–16, and rpt. in *Critical Perspectives on V. S. Naipaul*, 5–15. All references are to its publication in *The Overcrowded Barracoon and other Articles* (1972), 9–16.

Naipaul, V. S. 1959. *Miguel Street*. London: André Deutsch.

Naipaul, V. S. 1961. *A House for Mr. Biswas*. London: André Deutsch.

Naipaul, V. S. 1962. *The Middle Passage: Impressions of Five Societies--British, French, and Dutch – in the West Indies and South America*. Rpt. New York: Vintage Books, 1981. All references are to the 1981 edition and appear parenthetically in the text.

Naipaul, V. S. 1963. *Mr. Stone and the Knights Companion*. London: André Deutsch.

Naipaul, V. S. 1964a. *An Area of Darkness*. London: André Deutsch. rpt. New York: Vintage Books, 1981. All references are to the 1981 edition and appear parenthetically in the text.

Naipaul, V. S. 1964b. "Jasmine." *The Times Literary Supplement* on June 4. Rpt. in *The Overcrowded Barracoon and other Articles*, 23–29, and rpt. in *Critical Perspectives on V. S. Naipaul*, 16–22. All references are to its publication in *The Overcrowded Barracoon and other* Articles (1972), 23–9.

Naipaul, V. S. 1967a. *A Flag on the Island*. London: André Deutsch.

Naipaul, V. S. 1967b. *The Mimic Men*. London: André Deutsch. rpt. Harmondsworth: Penguin, 1973. All references are to the 1973 edition and appear parenthetically in the text.

Naipaul, V. S. 1969. *The Loss of El Dorado: A History*. London: André Deutsch. rpt. London: Picador 2001. All references are to the 2001 edition and appear parenthetically in the text.

Naipaul, V. S. 1971. *In a Free State*. London: André Deutsch. rpt. Harmondsworth: Penguin, 1973. All references are to the 1973 edition and appear parenthetically in the text.

Naipaul, V. S. 1972. *The Overcrowded Barracoon and Other Articles*. London: André Deutsch.

Naipaul, V. S. 1973. Foreword to *The Loss of El Dorado: A History*, London: Penguin: 13–4.

Naipaul, V. S. 1975a. *Guerrillas*. London: André Deutsch. rpt. London: Picador 2011. All references are to the 2011 edition and appear parenthetically in the text.

Naipaul, V. S. 1975b. "A Plea for Rationality: Address to 1975 Conference." *East Indians in the Caribbean*: 1–8. Conference Papers, The University of the West Indies, St. Augustine, Trinidad and Tobago.

196   V. S. NAIPAUL OF TRINIDAD

Naipaul, V. S. 1976. Foreword. *The Adventures of Gurudeva and Other Stories*, by Seepersad Naipaul. London: André Deutsch, pp. 7–23.

Naipaul, V. S. 1977. *India: A Wounded Civilization*. London: André Deutsch. rpt. New York: Vintage Books, 1978. All references are to the 1978 edition and appear parenthetically in the text.

Naipaul, V. S. 1979. *A Bend in the River*. New York: Alfred A. Knopf. rpt. London: Picador 2011. All references are to the 2011 edition and appear parenthetically in the text.

Naipaul, V. S. 1980a. "Michael X and the Black Power Killings in Trinidad." In *The Return of Eva Perón with The Killings in Trinidad*. New York: Alfred A. Knopf. rpt. New York: Vintage 1981. All references are to the 1981 edition and appear parenthetically in the text.

Naipaul, V. S. 1980b. *The Return of Eva Perón, with The Killings in Trinidad*. New York: Alfred A. Knopf. rpt. New York: Vintage, 1981. All references are to the 1981 edition and appear parenthetically in the text.

Naipaul, V. S. 1981. *Among the Believers: An Islamic Journey*. New York: Alfred A. Knopf. rpt. New York: Vintage, 1982. All references are to the 1982 edition and appear parenthetically in the text.

Naipaul, V. S. 1984. *Finding the Centre: Two Narratives*. London: André Deutsch.

Naipaul, V. S. 1987. *The Enigma of Arrival*. Harmondsworth: Viking.

Naipaul, V. S. 1989. *A Turn in the South*. Harmondsworth: Viking.

Naipaul, V. S. 1990a. *India: A Million Mutinies Now*. London: Heinemann.

Naipaul, V. S. 1990b. "Our Universal Civilization." *The New York Times*, 5 November, 1990. rpt. In *The Writer and the World: Essays*, edited by Pankaj Mishra, Picador, 2002, pp. 503–17. Rpt. London: Picador, 2011. All references are to the 2011 edition and appear parenthetically in the text.

Naipaul, V. S. 1991a. 'Argentina and the Ghost of Eva Perón, 1972–1991'; rpt. In *The Writer and the World: Essays*, edited by Pankaj Mishra, Picador, 2002, pp. 346–437. Rpt. London: Picador, 2011. All references are to the 2011 edition and appear parenthetically in the text.

Naipaul, V. S. 1991b. 'A Handful of Dust: Cheddi Jagan and the Revolution in Guyana'; rpt. In *The Writer and the World: Essays*, edited by Pankaj Mishra, Picador, 2002, pp. 485–502. Rpt. London: Picador, 2011. All references are to the 2011 edition and appear parenthetically in the text.

Naipaul, V. S. 1994. *A Way in the World*. New York: Alfred A. Knopf.

Naipaul, V. S. 1998. *Beyond Belief: Islamic Excursions among the Converted People*. London: Little Brown and Company. rpt. New York: Vintage 1999. All references are to the 1999 edition and appear parenthetically in the text.

Naipaul, V. S. 1999. *Letters Between a Father and Son*. With an Introduction and Notes by Gillon Aitken. London: Little, Brown and Company.

Naipaul, V. S. 2000. *Reading and Writing: A Personal Account*. New York: New York Review of Books.

Naipaul, V. S. 2001a. *Half a Life*. London: Picador.

Naipaul, V. S. 2001b. Press Release by V. S. Naipaul. "Naipaul wins Nobel Prize." *Taipeitimes.com*, October 12, 2001. http://www.taipeitimes.com/News/front/print/2001/10/12/0000106743. Accessed July 26, 2013.

Naipaul, V. S. 2001c. "Two Worlds." *Sunday Guardian*, April 22, 2007.

Naipaul, V. S. 2001d. "Two Worlds." *Trinidad Guardian*, December 14, 2001, Features Supplement 2: 1–5.

Naipaul, V. S. 2001e. "V.S. Naipaul – Nobel Lecture: Two Worlds". rpt. In *Literary Occasions: Essays*, introduced and edited by Pankaj Mishra, 181–95. London: Picador, 2003.

WORKS CITED 197

Naipaul, V. S. 2002a. *The Nightwatchman's Occurrence Book and Other Comic Inventions.* London: Picador.

Naipaul, V. S. 2002b. *The Writer and the World: Essays,* edited by Pankaj Mishra. Rpt. London: Picador, 2011. All references are to the 2011 edition and appear parenthetically in the text.

Naipaul, V. S. 2003. *Literary Occasions: Essays,* introduced and edited by Pankaj Mishra. London: Picador.

Naipaul, V. S. 2004. *Magic Seeds.* London: Picador.

Naipaul, V. S. 2007. *A Writer's People: Ways of Looking and Feeling.* London: Picador.

Naipaul, V. S. 2010. *The Masque of Africa: Glimpses of African Belief.* London: Picador.

Naipaul, S. 1943. *Gurudeva and Other Indian Tales.* Port of Spain: Trinidad Publications.

Secondary Sources

Book-Length Studies

Akal, Savi Naipaul. 2018. *The Naipauls of Nepaul Street: A Memoir of Life in Trinidad and Beyond.* Leeds: Peepal Tree.

Bahadur, Gaiutra. 2013. *Coolie Woman: The Odyssey of Indenture.* Gurgaon: Hachette India.

Bala, Suman. 2003. *V. S. Naipaul: A Literary Response to the Nobel Laureate.* New Delhi: Khosla Publication House.

Ball, John Clement. 2003. *Satire and the Postcolonial Novel: V. S. Naipaul, China Achebe, Salman Rushdie.* New York: Routledge.

Barrow, Dagmar. 2003. *Naipaul's Strangers.* Bloomington: Indiana University Press.

Bhat, Yashoda. 2000. *V. S. Naipaul: An Introduction.* Delhi: B. R. Publications.

Blanton, Casey. 2002. *Travel Writing: The Self and the World.* New York: Routledge.

Boxill, Anthony. 1983. *V. S. Naipaul's Fiction in Quest of the Enemy.* Fredericton, N.B: York Press.

Brathwaite, Edward Kamau. 1986. *Roots.* Havana, Cuba: Casa de Las Americas.

Brereton, Bridget. 1979. *Race Relations in Colonial Trinidad: 1870–1900.* Cambridge: Cambridge University Press.

Coovadia, Imran. 2009. *Authority and Authorship in V. S. Naipaul.* London: Palgrave Macmillan.

Cudjoe, Selwyn R. 1988. *V. S. Naipaul: A Materialist Reading.* Amherst, MA: University of Massachusetts Press.

Dabydeen, David, Jonathan Morley, Brinsley Samaroo, Amar Wahab and Brigid Wells, eds. 2007. *The First Crossing: Being the Diary of Theophilus Richmond, Ship's Surgeon Aboard the Hesperus, 1837–8.* The Coventry: Derek Walcott Press.

Dissanayake, Wimal and Carmen Wickramagamage. 1993. *Self and Colonial Desire: Travel Writings of V. S. Naipaul.* New York: Peter Lang.

Dooley, Gillian. 2006. *V. S. Naipaul: Man and Writer.* Columbia, SC: University of South Carolina Press.

Döring, Tobias. 2002. *Caribbean-English Passages: Intertextuality in a Postcolonial Tradition.* New York: Routledge.

Edmondson, Belinda. 2009. *Caribbean Middlebrow: Leisure Culture and the Middle Class.* New York: Cornell University Press.

Feder, Lilian. 2001. *Naipaul's Truth: The Making of a Writer.* Lanham, MD: Rowman and Littlefield.

198   V. S. NAIPAUL OF TRINIDAD

French, Patrick. 2008. *The World is What it is: The Authorised Biography of V. S. Naipaul.* London: Picador.

Froude, James Anthony. 1888. *The English in the West Indies or the Bow of Ulysses.* London: Longmans, Green & Co.

Ghosh, William. 2021. *V. S. Naipaul, Caribbean Writing and Caribbean Thought.* Oxford: Oxford English Monographs.

Gorra, Michael. 1997. *After Empire: Scott, Naipaul, Rushdie.* Chicago: University of Chicago Press.

Government of Trinidad and Tobago. 1990. "Dear Prime Minister: Letters to the Prime Minister of Trinidad and Tobago, August 1990." Booklet.

Griffith, Glyne. 2016. *The BBC and the Development of the Anglophone Caribbean Literature, 1943–1958.* London: Palgrave Macmillan.

Gupta, Suman. 1999. *V. S. Naipaul.* Devon: Northcote House.

Hamner, Robert D. 1973. *V. S. Naipaul.* New York: Twayne Publications.

Hamner, Robert D, ed. 1977. *Critical Perspectives on V. S. Naipaul.* Washington, DC: Three Continents Press.

Harris, Wilson. 1967. *Tradition, the Writer and Society.* London: New Beacon.

Hassan, Dolly, Z. 1986. *West Indian Response to V. S. Naipaul's West Indian Works.* PhD Dissertation, George Washington University, Washington D. C.: UMI Dissertation Services, 1987.

Hayward, Helen. 2002. *The Enigma of V. S. Naipaul: Sources and Context.* London: Palgrave Macmillan.

Holland, Patrick and Graham Huggan. 1998. *Tourists with Typewriters: Critical Reflections on Contemporary Travel Writing.* Ann Arbor: University of Michigan Press.

Hughes, Peter. 1988. *V. S. Naipaul.* London: Routledge.

Joshi, Chandra B. 1994. *V. S. Naipaul: The Voice of Exile.* New Delhi: Sterling.

Jussawalla, Feroza, ed. 1997. *Conversations with V. S. Naipaul.* Jackson: University of Mississippi.

Kamra, Shashi. 1990. *The Novels of V. S. Naipaul: A Study in Theme and Form.* New Delhi: Prestige.

Kaplan, Caren. 1996. *Questions of Travel: Postmodern Discourses of Displacement.* Durham, NC: Duke University Press.

Kelly, Richard. 1989. *V. S. Naipaul.* New York: Continuum.

King, Bruce. 1993. *V. S. Naipaul.* Second ed. Basingstoke: Macmillan, 2003.

Kingsley, Charles. 1871. *At Last: A Christmas in the West Indies.* London: Macmillan.

Koningsbruggen, Peter. 1997. *Trinidad Carnival: A Quest for National Identity.* London: Macmillan.

Lamming, George. 1960. *The Pleasures of Exile.* London: Michael Joseph.

Levy, Judith. 1995. *V. S. Naipaul: Displacement and Autobiography.* New York: Garland.

Lisle, Debbie. 2006. *The Global Politics of Contemporary Travel Writing.* Cambridge: Cambridge University Press.

Mahabir, Winston. 1975. *In and Out of Politics: Tales of the Government of Dr Eric Williams from the notebooks of a Former minister.* Trinidad: Imprint Caribbean Ltd.

Maharaj, J. Vijay, ed. 2019. *Seepersad and Sons: Naipaulian Synergies.* Leeds: Peepal Tree.

Mair, John, Richard Lance Keeble and Farrukh Dhondy, eds. 2018. *V. S. Naipaul 1932–2018: The Legacy.* Goring, England: Bite-Sized Books.

Mann, Harveen S. 1986. *Among the Mimic Men: The Fictional Works of V. S. Naipaul.* PhD Dissertation, Purdue University: UMI Dissertation Services, 1995.

WORKS CITED

Mawby, Spencer. 2012. "Uncle Sam, We Want Back We Land": Eric Williams and the Anglo-American Controversy over the Chaguaramas Base, 1957–1961." Pub. January 19, 2012. https://doi.org/10.1111/j.1467-7709.2011.01012.x.

Mishra, Vijay. 2007. *The Literature of Indian Diaspora: Theorising the Diaspora Imaginary.* New York: Routledge.

Morris, Robert K. 1975. *Paradoxes of Order: Some Perspectives on the Fiction of V. S. Naipaul.* Columbia: University of Missouri Press.

Mustafa, Fawzia. 1995. *V. S. Naipaul.* Cambridge: Cambridge University Press.

Nightingale, Peggy. 1987. *Journey Through Darkness: The Writing of V. S. Naipaul.* St. Lucia: University of Queensland Press.

Nixon, Rob. 1992. *London Calling: V. S. Naipaul, Postcolonial Mandarin.* New York: Oxford University Press.

Pantin, Raoul. 1990. *Black Power Day: The 1970 February Revolution. A Reporter's Story.* Santa Cruz, Trinidad: Hatuey Productions.

Panwar, Purabi. 2000. *India in the Works of Kipling, Forster and Naipaul: Postcolonial Revaluations.* Delhi: Pencraft.

Panwar, Purabi, ed. 2003. *V. S. Naipaul: An Anthology of Recent Criticism.* Delhi: Pencraft.

Poynting, Robert Jeremy. 1985. *Literature and Cultural Pluralism: East Indians in the Caribbean.* Three Volumes. Ph.D Thesis. University of Leeds. http://etheses.whiterose. ac.uk/821/3/uk_bl_ethos_355497.

Quinn, Kate, ed. 2014. *Black Power in the Caribbean.* Gainesville, FL.: University of Florida.

Rahim, Jennifer, and Barbara Lalla, eds. 2011. *Created in the West Indies: Caribbean Perspectives on V. S. Naipaul.* Kingston: Ian Randall.

Rai, Sudha. 1992. *Homeless by Choice: Naipaul, Jhabvala, Rushdie and India.* Jaipur: Printwell.

Ramchand, Kenneth. 1970. *The West Indian Novel and its Background.* Rev. ed., with a new Introduction, Kingston: Ian Randle, 2004.

Seecharan, Clem. 2015. *Finding Myself: Essays on Race, Politics and Culture.* Leeds: Peepal Tree.

Shah, Raffrique. 1988. *Race Relations in Trinidad: Some Aspects.* Trinidad: Committee for Labour Solidarity.

Suleri, Sara. 1992. *The Rhetoric of English India.* Chicago: University of Chicago Press.

Theroux, Paul. 1972. *V. S. Naipaul: An Introduction to his Works.* London: André Deutsch.

Theroux, Paul. 1998. *Sir Vidia's Shadow: A Friendship Across Five Continents.* London: Penguin, 1999. All references are to the 1999edition and appear parenthetically in the text.

Thieme, John. 1987. *The Web of Tradition: Uses of Allusion in V. S. Naipaul's Fiction.* Hertford: Hansib/ Dangaroo.

Thompson, Carl. 2011. *Travel Writing.* London: Routledge.

Trollope, Anthony. 1859. *The West Indies and the Spanish Main.* London: Chapman and Hall.

Walcott, Derek. 1998. *What the Twilight Says: Essays.* London: Faber and Faber.

Walsh, William. 1973. *V. S. Naipaul.* Edinburgh: Oliver and Boyd.

Weiss, Timothy. 1992. *On the Margins: The Art of Exile in V. S. Naipaul.* Amherst: University of Massachusetts Press.

White, Landeg. 1975. *V. S. Naipaul: A Critical Introduction.* London: Macmillan.

Williams, Eric E. 1964. *History of the People of Trinidad and Tobago.* London: André Deutsch.

Williams, Eric E. 1966. *British Historians and the West Indies.* London: André Deutsch.

Williams, Eric E. 2022. *The Blackest Thing in Slavery was not the Black Man: The Last Testament of Eric Williams,* edited by Brinsley Samaroo. Kingston: University of the West Indies Press.

Winer, L. 2009. *Dictionary of the English/ Creole of Trinidad and Tobago: On Historical Principles.* Montreal: McGill-Queen's University Press.

200 V. S. NAIPAUL OF TRINIDAD

Individual Essays and Newspaper Reports

Adams, Tim. 2004. "A home for Mr Naipaul." *Sunday Express UK*, September 26, 2004: 33.

Akbar, Ahsan. 2018. "His Gentle Side." In *V. S. Naipaul 1932–2018: The Legacy*, 126–8.

Ali, Azard. 2018. "Naipaul cremated after private funeral." *Trinidad and Tobago Newsday*. August 28, 2018. https://newsday.co.tt/2018/08/28/naipaul-cremated-after-private-funeral/.

Ali, Tariq. 2018. "Mr Ford's Hacienda." In *V. S. Naipaul 1932–2018: The Legacy*, 57–8.

Alam, Fakrul. 2003. "The Enigma of V. S. Naipaul." In *V. S. Naipaul: An Anthology of Recent Criticism*, 187–95.

"An Area of Brilliance." 1971. [rpt. from London *The Observer*]. *Trinidad Guardian*. December 5, 1971: 5.

Anthony, Michael. 2000. "The Name for Literary Excellence." *Trinidad Express*, December 20 and December 27, 2000: 12, 13, 28, 29.

Appiah, Anthony. 1984. "Strictures on Structures: the prospects for a Structuralist poetics of African Fiction." In *Black Literature and Literary Theory*, edited by Henry Louis Gates, Jr., 127–50. New York: Methuen.

Athill, Diana. 2018. "He was Easily the Most Difficult Writer I've ever Worked With." In *V. S. Naipaul 1932–2018: The Legacy*, 102–3.

Atlas, James. 1987. "V. S. vs the Rest: The Fierce and Enigmatic V. S. Naipaul Grants a Rare Interview in London." Rpt. in *Conversations with V. S. Naipaul*, 99–105.

Baboolal, Yvonne. 2007. "Red Tape Ties up Sir Vidia's lands." *Trinidad Guardian*, February 24, 2007.

Baldeosingh, Kevin. "2001. So many loyalties, says Naipaul." *Trinidad Express*. October 30, 2001: 1.

Baldeosingh, Kevin. 2007. "Sir Vidia's Week in Trinidad." *Trinidad and Tobago Newsday*, Section B, April 28, 2007: 9.

Barratt, Harold. 1983. "In Defence of Naipaul's Guerrillas: A Reply." *Caribbean Quarterly* 29, no.2 (June): 63–71.

Baugh, Edward. 2011. "'The History That had Made Me': The Making and Self-Making of V. S. Naipaul." In *Created in the West Indies: Caribbean Perspectives on V. S. Naipaul*, 3–19.

Beckles, Hilary. 2018. "He was the All-seeing, Inner Eye that Witnessed Inconvenient Truths." In *V. S. Naipaul 1932–2018: The Legacy*, 54–6.

Behr, Edward. 1980. "People are Proud of Being Stupid, The Master of the Novel: V. S. Naipaul." *Newsweek*, August 18, 1980: 38.

Best, Lloyd. 2018. "Scientist as well as Artist." In *V. S. Naipaul 1932–2018: The Legacy*, 86–9.

Blandford, Linda. 1979. "Man in a Glass Box." Rpt. in *Conversations with V. S. Naipaul*, 50–6.

Boxill, Anthony. 1974. "The Concept of Spring in V. S. Naipaul's *Mr Stone and the Knights Companion*." *Ariel: A Review of International English Literature* 5, no. 4: 21–8.

Brereton, Bridget. 2010. "'All ah we is not one:' Historical and Ethnic Narratives in Pluralist Trinidad." *The Global South* 4, no. 2 (Fall): 218–38.

Brereton, Bridget. 2011. "Naipaul's Sense of History." In *Created in the West Indies: Caribbean Perspectives on V. S. Naipaul*, 204–13.

Brereton, Bridget. 2018. "The Sense of Historical Wonder Never Left him." In *V. S. Naipaul 1932–2018: The Legacy*, 90–1.

WORKS CITED

"The Brothers Naipaul." 1987. *Sunday Express*, February, 22, 1987: 31.

Brown, J. Dillon. 2013. Coda to *Migrant Modernism: Postwar London and the West Indian Novel*, 169–83. Charlottesville: University of Virginia Press.

Brown, Wayne. 1984a. "The Descent and Ascent of Naipaul." *Trinidad Guardian*, July 18, 1984: 22.

Brown, Wayne. 1984b. "Naipaul will go on Ascending." *Trinidad Guardian*, August 22, 1984: 6.

Brown, Wayne. 1984c. "Naipaul's judgments are no less acid." *Trinidad Guardian*, September 6, 1984: 26.

Cadogan, Garnette. 2007. "To Make You See." *The Caribbean Review of Books* (August). http://caribbeanreviewofbooks.com/crb-archive/13-august-2007/to-make-you-see/.

Caulfield, Holden. 1981. "Around the Town: Answer to V. S. Biswas." *Trinidad Express*. December 14, 1981: 11.

Chee Moone, Robert A. 1982. "The Middle Passage of Naipaul – a Passage to nowhere: Vidia Naipaul [...].detest all you may, steelband marches on." *Sunday Express*, Section 2, May 16, 1982: 41.

Chitre, Dilip. 1978. "Naipaul and India 2." *New Quest* 9 (May-June): 174–86.

Clarke, Robert. 2001. "Sir Vidia's Venom." *Trinidad Express*, August 9, 2001: 23.

Cobham-Sander, Rhonda. 2011. "Consuming the Self: V. S. Naipaul, C. L. R. James and *A Way in the World*." In *Created in the West Indies: Caribbean Perspectives on V. S. Naipaul*, 51–76.

Cowie, D.W. (Petit Valley). 1982. "In defence of Naipaul." *Trinidad Express*, January 18, 1982: 8.

Cudjoe, Selwyn. 1979. "Revolutionary Struggle and the Novel." *Caribbean Quarterly* 25, no.4, (December): 1–30.

Cudjoe, Selwyn. 1996. "Recognising National Literature." *Trinidad Guardian*, August 21, 1996: 10.

Cudjoe, Selwyn. 1998. "Living in Naipaul's Shadow." *Trinidad Guardian*, October 5, 1998: 9.

Cudjoe, Selwyn. 2001. "From the Other World." *Trinidad Guardian*, October 24, 2001: 18.

Cuffie, Maxie. 1990. "Naipaul: Indian Alienation due to Petty Politics." *Trinidad Guardian*, April 9, 1990: 1.

de Caires, Brendan. 2008. "What Vidia Saw." *The Caribbean Review of Books* (February). http://caribbeanreviewofbooks.com/crb-archive/15-february-2008/what-vidia-saw/.

de Villegas, Consuelo Lopez. 1977–78. "Matriarchs and Man-eaters: Naipaul's Fictional Women" *Revista/ Review Interamericana*, 7, no. 4; (Winter) 1977–78: 605–14.

Dabydeen, David. 2018. "When a University Audience asked the Great Writer to read a Happy Passage." In *V. S. Naipaul 1932–2018: The Legacy*, 48–53.

Deen, Shamsu. 1998. *Lineages and Linkages, Solving Trinidad Roots in India*. Princes Town, Trinidad: Shamsu Deen.

Derrick, A. C. 1977. "Naipaul's Technique as a Novelist." In *Critical Perspectives on V. S. Naipaul*, 194–206.

Dev, Ravi. 2002. "A Reply" to Stabroek News Editorial "Sir Vidia's Shadows." October 25, 2001. *Caribbean Quarterly* 48, no. 2/3 (June-September): 7–11.

Dhondy, Farrukh. 2018. "Farrukh, Farrukh, You've Heard of my Little Spot of Good Luck." In *V. S. Naipaul 1932–2018: The Legacy*, 17–28.

Dix, Hywel. 2019. "From Tonka Beans to Magic Seeds: V. S. Naipaul's Late Career Fiction of Self-Retrospect." In *Seepersad and Sons: Naipaulian Synergies*, edited by J. Vijay Maharaj, 175–86. Leeds: Peepal Tree.

202   V. S. NAIPAUL OF TRINIDAD

Dooley, Gillian. 2008. "'What Trouble I Have with Jane Austen!' V.S. Naipaul's Blind Spot." *Idiom* 44, no. 1: 32–8.

Douglas, Sean. 2007. "Mad Rush for Naipaul." *Trinidad and Tobago Newsday*, April 22, 2007: 3.

Driscoll, Beth. 2016. "The Middlebrow Family Resemblance: Features of the Historical and Contemporary Middlebrow." *Post 45*. July 1, 2016. http://post45.research.yale.edu/2016/07/the-middlebrow-family-resemblance-features-of-the-historical-and-contemporary-middlebrow/.

Eastley, Aaron. 2009. "V. S. Naipaul and the 1946 Trinidad General Election." *Twentieth Century Literature* 55 (1): 1–35.

Editorial. 2001. *Trinidad Guardian*, October 12, 2001: 16.

Editorial. 2001. "Tribute to Naipaul." *Trinidad and Tobago Newsday*, October 12, 2001: 10.

Engdahl, Horace. 2001. Award Ceremony Speech: The 2001 Nobel Prize for Literature, Official Website of the Nobel Foundation. <https://www.nobelprize.org/prizes/literature/2001/ceremony-speech/>.

Erapu, Laban. 1972. "V. S. Naipaul's In a Free State." *Bulletin of the Association for Commonwealth Literature and Language Studies* 9 (March): 66–84.

Ezekiel, Nissim. 1976. "Naipaul's India and Mine." *Journal of South Asian Literature* 11, no. 3/4: 193–205.

"Fans ask why Not Naipaul." 1981. *Trinidad Express*, November 16, 1981: 12.

Fraser, Fitzroy. 1960. "A Talk with Vidia Naipaul." Rpt. in *Conversations with V. S. Naipaul*, 3–4.

Ghosh, William. 2019. "Caribbean Travel and the 'Realistic Shock': Lamming, Naipaul, Condé." *Research in African Literatures* 50, no. 2 (Summer): 177–97.

Gosine, V. Ramsamooj. 1985. "Naipaul making it hold together" [Report on Naipaul's interview with Mel Gussow]. *The New York Times*, January 10, 1985: T8.

Greig, Geordie. 2018 "A Final Valediction." In *V. S. Naipaul 1932–2018: The Legacy*, 9–10.

Hamilton, Ian. 1971. "Without a Place: V. S. Naipaul in Conversation with Ian Hamilton." Rpt. in *Conversations with V. S. Naipaul*, 14–21.

Hamner, Robert. 1977. "Introduction." In *Critical Perspectives on V. S. Naipaul*, xv–xxxi.

Hamner, Robert. 1977. "Character and Setting." In *Critical Perspectives on V. S. Naipaul*, 208–40.

Hardwick, Elizabeth. 1979. "Meeting V. S. Naipaul." *New York Times Book Reviews*, May 13, 1979: 36. Rpt. in *Conversations with V. S. Naipaul*, 45–9.

"Heckling at UWI as Naipaul ignores 'frivolous' questions." 1975. *Trinidad Guardian*. June 27, 1975.

Henry, Jim Douglas. 1971. "Unfurnished Entrails – The Novelist V. S. Naipaul in Conversation with Jim Douglas Henry." Rpt. in *Conversations with V. S. Naipaul*, 22–3.

Hope, Fred. 1970. "What else is new, Mr Naipaul?" *Trinidad Express*, November 4, 1970.

Hosein, Clyde. 1969. "Naipaul's latest called a novel about history." *Sunday Guardian*, December 14, 1969: 20.

"A House for Mr Naipaul by V. S. Biswas." 1981. *Trinidad Express*, October 11, 1981: 11.

Huntington, Samuel. 1993. "The Clash of Civilisations?," *Foreign Affairs*, 72, no. 3 (Summer): 22–49.

Hussein, Aamer. 1994. "Delivering the truth: An interview with V. S. Naipaul." Rpt. in *Conversations with V. S. Naipaul*, 154–61.

WORKS CITED

Jackson, Elizabeth. 2022. "Problematizing National/Cultural Affiliations in Postcolonial Literature: Inclusions and Exclusions in the Reception of Doris Lessing and V. S. Naipaul." *The Journal of Commonwealth Literature* 57, no. 1(April): 32–46. DOI: 10.1177/0021989418771112

Jaikarran, J. P. (County Caroni). 1982. Letter to Editor. "We should be grateful to Naipaul, not condemn him." *Trinidad Express*, August 25 and August 26, 1982: 35, 36.

Johnson, Andrew. 1982. "Gunga Din of Caribbean Literature." *Trinidad Express*, March 7, 1982: 16.

Kalliney, Peter. 2007. "Metropolitan Modernism and its West Indian Interlocutors: 1950s London and the Emergence of Postcolonial Literature", *PMLA* 122, no. 1: 89–104.

Kanhai, Viki. 1997. "Once again Naipaul gets the Snub." *Trinidad and Tobago Newsday*, October 19, 1997: 13.

Kaseram, Romeo. 1987. "Fleeing from decay into desolation." *Sunday Guardian*, September 13, 1987: 20.

"Keeping faith with the Naipaul Legacy." 1986. *Trinidad Express*, November 2, 1986: 21.

Khan, Nisa. 1984. "A Bit of Biography from Mr Naipaul." *Trinidad Guardian*, October 7, 1984: T3.

Khan, Riza. 1982. "Was Naipaul's visit to Islam a waste of time and Money?" *Trinidad Express*, Sunday, April 4, 1982: 13.

Lalla, Barbara. 2011. "Signifying Nothing: Writing about Not Writing in *The Mystic Masseur*." In *Created in the West Indies: Caribbean Perspectives on V. S. Naipaul*, 99–110.

Lanchester, John. 2005. "Where the fun starts." *The New York Review* LII, no 7 (April 28, 2005): 22–3.

Laughlin, Nicholas. 2016. "Naipaul's Letters Between a Father and Son (and Mother and Sister)." First published in *Caribbean Quarterly* 62, no. 3/4 (September–December): 406–21. http://nicholaslaughlin.net/LAUGHLIN-CQ-naipaul-letters.pdf.

Laughlin, Nicholas. 2018. "His World was What It was: The Enigma of V. S. Naipaul." In *V. S. Naipaul 1932–2018: The Legacy*, 95–8.

Lee, R.H. 1967. "The Novels of V. S. Naipaul." *Theoria: A Journal of Social and Political Theory* 27 (October): 31–46.

Levin, Bernard. 1983. "V. S. Naipaul: A Perpetual Voyager." Rpt.in *Conversations with V. S. Naipaul*, 93–8.

Lovelace, Earl. 1970. "Poor Naipaul! He has become his biggest Joke." *Trinidad Express*, October 26, 1970: 10.

Lydon, Christopher. 2008. "Derek Walcott: Calabash '08." *Radio Open Source: Arts, Ideas, and Politics with Christopher Lydon.* May 28, 2008. https://radioopensource.org/calabash-08-first-the-fireworks/.

Lynch, Hugh. 1983. "V. S. Naipaul: The Barbarity of V. S. Naipaul." *Trinidad Express*, July 24, 1983: 31.

Lynch, Hugh. 1985. "Should he be without Honour in his country?: Naipaul's name dragged into citizenship wrangle." *Sunday Express*, May 12, 1985: 43.

Lynch, Hugh. 1987. "Naipaul is still a prisoner of his past." *Sunday Express*, August 16, 1987: 3.

McClure, John A. 1978. "V. S. Naipaul and the Politics of Despair." *Marxist Perspectives* 1, no.3 (Fall): 1–19.

McSweeney, Kerry. 1976. "V. S. Naipaul: Sensibility and Schemata." *Critical Quarterly* 18, no. 3: 73–9.

Marnham, Patrick. "Lines from the Laureate: An Interview with V. S. Naipaul." *Literary Review* 386 (April 2011). https://literaryreview.co.uk/interview-vsnaipaul.

Maes-Jelinek, Hena. 1968. "V. S. Naipaul: A Commonwealth Writer?" *Revue Des Langues Vivantes*. 499–512. https://orbi.uliege.be/bitstream/2268/192402/1/Maes_VS-Naipaul-Commonwealth-Writer_1967.pdf.

Maharaj, Parsuram (An executive member of the Sanatan Dharma MahaSabha). 2001. "Naipaul: Hindu Hero." *Trinidad and Tobago Newsday*, October 16, 2001: 10.

Maharaj, Satnarayan. 2000. "Naipaul may have been Misinterpreted." *Sunday Guardian*, June 25, 2000: 15.

Maharaj, J. Vijay. 2011. "A Mala in Obeisance: Hinduism in Selected Texts by V. S. Naipaul." In *Created in the West Indies: Caribbean Perspectives on V. S. Naipaul*, 121–34.

Maharaj, J. Vijay. 2013. "Mr Biswas: Paragon of Creole Virtues." In *A House for Mr Biswas: Critical Perspectives*, edited by Meenakshi Bharat, 73–92. Delhi: Pencraft International.

Maharajh, Mahabir (Maracas, St Joseph).1982. "The deeper meaning of Naipaul's 'bush'." *Trinidad Guardian*. January 18, 1982: 8.

Mair, Christian. 1989. "Naipaul's *Miguel Street* and Silvan's *Lonely Londoners* – Two approaches to the Use of Caribbean Creole in Fiction." *Journal of Commonwealth Literature*, 24 (1): 138–54.

Mathur, Ira. 2001. "An Identity we can Claim." *Trinidad Guardian*, October 14, 2001: 10.

Matroo, Carol. 2007. "Sir V. S. Naipaul Loses his cool." *Trinidad Guardian*, April 21, 2007: 13.

Maxwell, John. 2002. "War is at My Black Skin." *Caribbean Quarterly* 48, no. 2/3 (June-September): 13.

Medwick, Cathleen. 1981. "Life, Literature, and Politics: An Interview with V. S. Naipaul." Rpt. in *Conversations with V. S. Naipaul*, 57–62.

Meighoo, Kirk. 2018. "The Great, Frustrating, Hilarious Trinidadian showed what we can be in the World." In *V. S. Naipaul 1932–2018: The Legacy*, 81–5.

Michener, Charles. 1981. Naipaul in *Newsweek*. [reproduction of photograph of the infant Vidya with his parents, pictures of Michael X]. *Trinidad Express*, November 29, 1981: 23. Also rpt. as "The Dark Visions of V. S. Naipaul." Rpt. in *Conversations with V. S. Naipaul*, 63–74.

Mills, Therese. 1973. "The House of Mr Biswas." *Sunday Guardian*, January 28, 1973: 11.

Milne, Anthony. 1982a. "In Defence of V. S. Naipaul." *Trinidad Express*, January 4, 1982.

Milne, Anthony. 1982b. "The Day I met V. S. Naipaul." *Sunday Express*. Sunday, July 11, 1982: 29.

Misra, Nivedita. 2015. "Naipaul and Hinduism: Negotiating Caste in India." *South Asian Review* 36, no. 2: 215–31.

Misra, Nivedita. 2017. "From Tramp to Traveller: V. S. Naipaul Mirrors Immigrant Experiences in *In a Free State*." *Transnational Literature* 9, no. 2: 1–10. Rpt. in *Seepersad and Sons: Naipaulian Synergies* (2019), edited by J. Vijay Maharaj, 240–50. Leeds: Peepal Tree.

Misra, Nivedita. 2023. "Finding a home for Ram in Trinidad: V. S. Naipaul's *A House for Mr Biswas* and the traditions of *Ramleela* and *Krishnaleela* in Trinidad." In *Journey Round Myself: Crossing Borders, Strengthening Connections, Breaking Boundaries in the Caribbean Cultural Ecology*, edited by Suzanne Burke, 322–336. Kingston: Ian Randle.

Mohammed, Denzil. 2007. "Naipaul re-mystified." *Sunday Guardian*, April 22, 2007: 3.

Mohan, Dinesh. 1982. "'Naipaul – the Flawed Mirror' A Review of *Among the Believers*." *Trinidad Guardian*, July 8, 1982: 12–13.

WORKS CITED

Morgan, Paula. 2005. "With a Tassa Blending: Calypso and Cultural Identity in Indo-Caribbean Fiction." *Anthurium* 3, no. 2, p. 10. DOI: http://doi.org/10.33596/anth.54.

Mukherjee, Bharati and Robert Boyers. 1981. "A Conversation with V. S. Naipaul." *Salmagundi* 54 (Fall): 4–22. Rpt. in *Conversations with V. S. Naipaul*, 75–92.

"Naipaul is the Literary Curiosity." 1968. *Trinidad Guardian*. November 10, 1968.

"Naipaul comes for doctorate." 1975. *Trinidad Guardian*, 26 November, 1975.

"Naipaul Failed his audience." 1975. Sunday Express Reporter. *Trinidad Express*, June 29, 1975: 31.

"Naipaul in Running for the 'Nobel'." 1980. *Trinidad Express*, October 1, 1980.

"Naipaul – Snob provocative artist, or what?" 1981. Letter to Editor. December 28, 1981: 5.

"Naipaul in Nobel running." 1988. *Trinidad Guardian*, October 13, 1988, 1.

"Naipaul – rising from 'nothing': A Caribbean Perspective." 2001. *Trinidad Guardian*, October 15, 2001: 13. Rpt. "Naipaul – Out of Nothing: Praise, Criticism for Caribbean Icon, by Rickey Singh, *Caribbean Quarterly* 48, 2/3 (June-September 2002): 3–5.

"Naipaul's Sisters Delighted." 2001. *Trinidad and Tobago Newsday*, November 12, 2001: 6.

"Naipaul's citizenship restored." 2007. *Trinidad Guardian*, March 27, 2007.

Noel, Jesse. 1967. "The Trinidadian Novelist: Together the Voices of Anthony and Naipaul form a harmonious duet." *Trinidad Guardian*, September 17, 1967.

Paravisini-Gebert, Lizabeth. 2008. "V. S. Naipaul's *The Mystic Masseur*." In *Literature of the Caribbean*, 159–174. London: Greenwood Press.

Parekh, Bhikhu. "From India with Hope." *New Statesman and Society* 5 (October 1990): 33-34.

Patterson, Orlando. 2018. "How he out-Trumped Trump on Africans and West Indians." In *V. S. Naipaul 1932–2018: The Legacy*, 111–2.

Phillips, Caryl. "Reluctant Hero." *The Guardian*. 12 Oct 2001. https://www.theguardian.com/books/2001/oct/12/fiction.vsnaipaul.

Pickford-Gordon, Lara. 2001. "Ramchand: Naipaul's Nobel prize Long Overdue." *Trinidad and Tobago Newsday*, October 12, 2001: 6.

Pickford-Gordon, Lara. 2007. "Naipaul: No More Trinidad Novels." *Trinidad and Tobago Newsday*, April 21, 2007: 22.

Press Release of the Swedish Academy. 2001. NobelPrize.org. October 11, 2001. https://www.nobelprize.org/prizes/literature/2001/press-release/.

Pyne-Timothy, Helen. 1984. "Women and Sexuality in the Later. Novels of V. S. Naipaul." Mary Ingraham Bunting Institute of Radcliffe College (Working Paper): 1–14.

Rahim, Jennifer. 2011a. "Introduction." In *Created in the West Indies: Caribbean Perspectives on V. S. Naipaul*, ix–xxvi.

Rahim, Jennifer. 2011b. "The Shadow of Hanuman: V. S. Naipaul and the 'Unhomely' House of Fiction." In *Created in the West Indies: Caribbean Perspectives on V. S. Naipaul*, 135–50.

Rambaran, Irma. 2001. "In search of Naipaulian depths of satisfaction." *Trinidad Guardian*, October 28, 2001: 14.

Rampersad, Arnold. 1990. "V. S. Naipaul: Turning in the South." *Raritan* 10, no. 1: 24–39.

Rampersad, Kris. 2003. "Naipaul Chides Indians." *Trinidad Guardian*, January 12, 2003: 3.

Ramchand, Kenneth. 1965. "Decolonisation in West Indian Literature." *Transition*, no. 22: 48–9.

206   V. S. NAIPAUL OF TRINIDAD

Ramchand, Kenneth. 1988. "Need for Self-searching: Naipaul's Message in *The Mimic Men*." *Trinidad Guardian*, May 4, 1988: 9.

Ramchand, Kenneth. 1993. "To Sir Vidia, with Respect." *Trinidad Express*, March 29, 1993: 40.

Ramchand, Kenneth. 2018a. "The Futility of Human Effort – the Key Naipaulian Preoccupation." In *V. S. Naipaul 1932–2018: The Legacy*, 29–35.

Ramchand, Kenneth. 2018b. "Did Naipaul Hate Trinidad?" In *V. S. Naipaul 1932–2018: The Legacy*, 64–80.

Ravi-Ji, Hindu Prachar Kendra. 1990. *Trinidad Guardian*, April 15, 1990: 14.

Raymond, Judy. 1993. "Well, Can you imagine Naipaul playing Mas?" *Trinidad Guardian*, April 4, 1993: 16.

Raymond, Judy. 1994. "Finding a Way to feel at home" *Sunday Express* 2, July 17, 1994: 3.

Raymond, Judy. 2004. "Stuck on the Beanstalk." *The Caribbean Review of Books* (November). http://caribbeanreviewofbooks.com/crb-archive/2-november-2004/stuck-on-the-beanstalk/.

Regis, L. 1998. "Calypso: The Anatomy of Controversy." *Caribbean Dialogue: A Journal of Contemporary Caribbean Policy Issues*, 3 (4): 31–8.

Richmond, Angus. 1982. "Naipaul: the Mimic Man." *Race and Class* 24.2: 125–36.

Roach, Eric. 1972. "Fame, A Short-lived Cycle, Says Vidia." Rpt. in *Conversations with V. S. Naipaul*, 37–8.

Robinson, Andrew. 1987. "An Elusive Master: V. S. Naipaul is Still Searching." Rpt. in *Conversations with V. S. Naipaul*, 106–9.

Robinson, Andrew. 1990. "Going Back for a Turn in the East." Rpt. in *Conversations with V. S. Naipaul*, 110–3.

Robinson, Andrew. 1992. "Stranger in Fiction." Rpt. in *Conversations with V. S. Naipaul*, 130–4.

Rohlehr, Gordon. 1977a. "Character and Rebellion in A House for Mr Biswas." In *Critical Perspectives on V. S. Naipaul*, 84–93.

Rohlehr, Gordon. 1977b. "The Ironic Approach: The novels of V. S. Naipaul." In *Critical Perspectives on V. S. Naipaul*, 178–93.

Rohlehr, Gordon. 1992a. "Articulating a Caribbean Aesthetic: The Revolution of Self-perceptions." In *My Strangled City and Other Essays*, 1–16. Port of Spain, Trinidad: Longman.

Rohlehr, Gordon. 1992b. "The Problem of the Problem of Form." In *The Shape of that Hurt and Other Essays*, 1–65. Port of Spain: Longman.

Rohlehr, Gordon. 2007. "Intersecting QRC Lives." *Transgression, Transition, Transformation*, 199–221. Trinidad: Trinidad Lexicon.

Rohlehr, Gordon. 2011. "The Confessional Element in Naipaul's Fiction." In *Created in the West Indies: Caribbean Perspectives on V. S. Naipaul*, 79–98.

Rouse, Ewart. 1968. "Naipaul: An Interview with Ewart Rouse." *Trinidad Guardian*, November 28, 1968. Rpt. in *Conversations with V. S. Naipaul*, 10–3.

Rowe-Evans, Adrian. 1971. "V. S. Naipaul: A *Transition* Interview." Rpt. in *Conversations with V. S. Naipaul*, 24–36.

Roy, Amit. 2018. "Naipaul's invitation-only funeral held." *The Telegraph* (online edition), August 24, 2018. https://www.telegraphindia.com/world/naipaul-s-invitation-only-funeral-held/cid/1531903.

Said, Edward. 2018. "An Intellectual Catastrophe." 1998. In *V. S. Naipaul 1932–2018: The Legacy*, 117–20.

WORKS CITED

Samaroo, Brinsley. 2008. "The World of Seepersad Naipaul." *The Arts Journal: Critical Perspectives on Contemporary Literature, History, Art and Culture of Guyana and the Caribbean* 4, no. 1/2: 11–9.

Samaroo, Brinsley. 2012. "The Caribbean Consequences of the Indian Revolt of 1857." In *Indian Diaspora in the Caribbean: History, Culture and Identity*, edited by R. L. Hangloo, 71–93. New Delhi: Primus Books.

Samaroo, Brinsley. 2016. "Recharging the Ancestral Battery: Physical and Spiritual Return to Bharat Mata". In *The Legacy of Indian Indenture: Historical and Contemporary Aspects of Migration and Diaspora*, edited by M. S. Hassankhan, Lomarch Roopnarine and Hans Ramsoedh, 127–37. New Delhi: Manohar.

Samaroo, Brinsley. 2019. " 'In But Not of the Society': The Crusading and Critical Eye of Seepersad Naipaul (1906–1953)." In *Seepersad and Sons: Naipaulian Synergies* (2019), edited by J. Vijay Maharaj, 60–9. Leeds: Peepal Tree.

Scott, Lawrence. 2011. "The Novelist and History – Pleasures and Problems: V. S. Naipaul's *The Loss of El Dorado – A History, The Enigma of Arrival – A Novel*, and *A Way in the World – A Sequence*." In *Created in the West Indies: Caribbean Perspectives on V. S. Naipaul*, 165–82.

Seecharan, Clem. 2018. "In Sir Vidia's Shadow: Out of Historical Darkness." In *V. S. Naipaul 1932–2018: The Legacy*, 39–47.

Shah, Raffique. 2001. "Naipaul's mastery." *Sunday Express*. October 14, 2001: 14.

Sheppard, R. Z. 2001. "Naipaul – Wanderer of Endless Curiosity." (courtesy *Time*) *Trinidad and Tobago Newsday*, October 12, 2001: 10, 11, 43.

Siboney, Iere (Port of Spain). 1982. Letter to Editor, "Naipaul warned us but we did not listen." *Trinidad Express*. August 18, 1982: 7.

Smith, Keith. 1999. "Out of Africa." *Trinidad Express*, August 3, 1999: 13.

Springer, Attillah. 2001. "Nobel for Naipaul." *Trinidad Guardian*, October 12, 2001: 1.

Sudama, Trevor. 1967. "Walcott-Naipaul." *Trinidad Guardian*, August 20, 1967.

Taylor, Jeremy. 1981. "V. S. Naipaul: *Among the Believers: An Islamic Journey*." *Trinidad Express*, November 28, 1981: 25.

Taylor, Jeremy. 2002. "Guerilla." *Caribbean Quarterly* 48, no. 2/3 (June-September): 45–56.

Taylor, Macdonald Celestin (Arima). 1982. "Don Taylor takes Naipaul to Task." *Trinidad Express*, January 18, 1982.

Tejpal, Tarun. 1999. Interview with V. S. Naipaul. "Christianity didn't damage India like Islam." November 15, 1999. https://www.outlookindia.com/magazine/story/christianity-didnt-damage-india-like-islam/208406.

Tewarie, Bhoendradatt. 1992. "V. S. Naipaul – 21 Books later." *Sunday Guardian*, February 23, 1992: 9.

Tewarie, Bhoendradatt. 2007. "Naipaul's Political Drama: Novel shows corruption in pre-independent T&T." *Sunday Guardian*, February 25, 2007, 21/23.

Tewarie, Bhoendradatt. 2011. "V. S. Naipaul as Critical Thinker." In *Created in the West Indies: Caribbean Perspectives on V. S. Naipaul*, 183–203.

Thieme, John. 1981. "Calypso Allusions in Naipaul's *Miguel Street*." *Kunapipi* 3, no. 2, Article 5: 18-32. https://ro.uow.edu.au/kunapipi/vol3/iss2/5.

Thieme, John. 1982. "Authorial Voice in V. S. Naipaul's *The Middle Passage*." *Prose Studies: History, Theory, Criticism* 5, no. 1: 139–50.

Thieme, John. 1983. "Rama in Exile: The Indian Writer Overseas." In *The Eye of the Beholder*, edited by Maggie Butcher, 65–74. London: Commonwealth Institute.

Thieme, John. 1984. Naipaul's English Fable: *Mr Stone and the Knights Companion*." *Modern Fiction Studies* 30, no. 3: 497–503.

Thieme, John. 2002. "Naipaul's Nobel." In *V. S. Naipaul: Fiction and Travel Writing*, edited by Rajeshwari Mittapalli and Michael Hensen, 1–10. Delhi: Atlantic 2002.

Trinidad Guardian October 12, 2001: 13.

Trinidad Guardian, October 28, 2001: 14

Trinidad Express, October 12, 2001: 3.

Trinidad and Tobago Newsday, October 12, 2001: 10.

"Trinidad and Tobago Film Festival." 2008. *Trinidad and Tobago Newsday*, September 19, 2008: 11.

"Vidia Naipaul looks back in Blackness." 1970. [Summary of his article in September 3 issue of *The New York Review*, titled Power] *Sunday Express*, October 11, 1970.

"V. S. Naipaul Launches attack on Islam." 2001. *Trinidad and Tobago Newsday*, October 6, 2001: 12.

Walcott, D. 1962. "History and Picong [...] in the Middle Passage." In *Critical Perspectives on Derek Walcott*, (1993) edited by R. D. Hamner, 18–9. London: Three Continents Book/ Lynne Rienner.

Walcott, D. 1965. "Interview with V. S. Naipaul." Rpt. in *Conversations with V. S. Naipaul*, 5–9.

Walcott, D. 1967. "Is V. S. Naipaul an angry Young Man?" *Trinidad Guardian*. August 6, 1967.

Walcott, D. 1987. "The Garden Path: V. S. Naipaul." In *What the Twilight Says: Essays*, 121–33.

Westall, Claire. 2005. "Men in the Yard and On the Street: Cricket and Calypso in *Moon on a Rainbow Shawl* and *Miguel Street*." *Anthurium* 3, no. 2, Article 14. http:// scholarlyrepository.miami.edu/anthurium/vol3/iss2/14.

Wheeler, Charles. 1977. "'It's Everman for Himself' – V. S. Naipaul on India." Rpt. in *Conversations with V. S. Naipaul*, 39–44.

Wilson-Tagoe, Nana. 1998. "History as Loss: Determinism as Vision and Form in V. S. Naipaul." In *Historical Thought and Literary Representation in West Indian Literature*, 54–76. Gainesville: University Press of Florida.

Winder, Robert. 1999. "Voices from the Past." *New Statesman*, November 1, 1999: 53–4.

Winokur, Scott. 1991. "The Unsparing Vision of V. S. Naipaul." Rpt. in *Conversations with V. S. Naipaul*, 114–29.

"Writer shows disdain for Land of his birth – Ince." 1982. *Trinidad Express* August 15, 1982: 1.

Wyndham, Francis. 1961. "Review of V. S. Naipaul's *A House for Mr Biswas*." *London Magazine* 1, no. 7 (October): 90–3.

INDEX

Achebe, Chinua 62
Adams, Tim 166
Aitken, Gillon 16, 83, 159
Akal, Savi Naipaul 3, 15, 26, 42, 50, 84,
    151, 183
    The Naipauls of Nepaul Street 15
Akbar, Ali 12
Alam, Fakrul 62
Ali, Azard 3
Ali, Tariq 14
Among the Believers 9, 23, 119, 121, 126, 130,
    135, 136, 140, 147, 149, 150, 155,
    157, 176, 179, 188
Appiah, Anthony 110
An Area of Brilliance 89
Area of Darkness, An 8, 41, 57, 58, 60–64,
    73, 106, 109, 132, 135, 146, 148,
    163, 178
Athill, Diana 85, 100
Atlas, James 79
Austen, Jane 38, 67, 71

Baboolal, Yvonne 176
Bahadur, Gaiutra 15
Bala, Suman 12
Baldeosingh, Kevin 167, 177
Ball, John Clement 145
Barratt, Harold 100
Barrow, Dagmar 12
Baugh, Edward 5, 18
Beckles, Sir Hilary 5
Behr, Edward 9, 150
Bend in the River, A 11, 22, 83, 85, 110,
    111, 114–16, 119, 121, 125, 130, 132,
    151, 168, 171, 184, 187–89

Best, Lloyd 4, 7
Beyond Belief 23, 126, 144, 155
Bhabha, Homi 145
Bhagvad Gita 3, 41, 140
Bharati Mukherjee and Richard Boyle
    8, 126
Bhat, Yashoda 12
Bissoondath, Neil 131
Black Power Movement 11, 22,
    83, 85, 89–97, 100–3, 108,
    129, 137, 151, 154, 167, 170,
    183, 187
Blandford, Linda 111, 116, 161
Blanton, Casey 144
Boxill, Anthony 12, 68
Brathwaite, Kamau 17, 18, 75
Brereton, Bridget 61, 78, 108, 160
Brown, J. Dillon 169
Brown, Wayne 130
Bushnell, Cameron Fae 45

Cadogan, Garnette 130
Capildeo, Rudranath 26, 36, 37, 50
Capildeo, Simbhoonath 28, 29, 36,
    143, 184
Caribbean Voices 10, 31, 39, 81, 159
Chitre, Dilip 109
Clarke, Robert 165
Cobham-Sander, Rhonda 35, 72
Columbus, Christopher 79, 85, 134, 154,
    160, 174
Conrad, Joseph 122
Coovadia, Imran 12
Cudjoe, Selwyn 10, 12, 18, 45, 101, 114,
    144, 145, 165

210 V. S. NAIPAUL OF TRINIDAD

Dabydeen, David 4
de Boissiere, Ralph
  Crown Jewel 31
  Rum and Coca Cola 31
de Caires, Brendan 175
de Villegas, Consuelo Lopez 38
Defoe, Daniel *Robinson Crusoe* 31
Derrick, A. C. 44, 68
Dhondy, Farrukh 13, 62
Dissanayake and Wickramagamage 136
Dix, Hywel 171
Dooley, Gillian 12, 38, 50, 57, 131, 145
Döring, Tobias 52
Douglas, Sean 176
Driscoll, Beth 6n1
Durgasingh, Ryan 100

Eastley, Aaron 26, 30
Edmondson, Belinda 6n1
Engdadl, Horace 9
Enigma of Arrival, The 23, 59, 131, 133–36,
  140, 141, 144, 153, 157, 160, 165,
  187, 190
Erapu, Laban 110
Ezekiel, Nissim 8, 62

Feder, Lilian 12, 52, 114, 147
Finding the Centre 23, 34, 127, 130,
  140, 188
Flag on the Island, A 11, 22, 34, 35, 65, 69,
  71, 73, 81, 183, 188
Forster, E. M. 59, 163
Fraser, Fitzroy 63
French, Patrick 4, 5, 7–9, 11, 26, 28,
  29, 37, 38, 42, 47, 51, 55, 79, 81,
  82, 84, 98, 100, 111, 117, 138, 145,
  151, 164
  *The World is what it is: The Authorised
  Biography of V. S. Naipaul* 9
Froude, James Anthony 49, 52–54, 63

Ghosh, William 12, 50, 129
Gomes, Albert
  All Papa's Children 31
Gooding, Margaret 9, 84
Gorra, Michael 144
Greig, Geordie 3
Guerrillas 11, 22, 37, 83, 97, 98, 100, 102,
  111, 114, 115, 119, 130, 148, 167,
  170, 183, 188

Gupta, Suman 12, 144
Gussow, Mel 116

Half a Life 23, 168, 170, 174, 176, 188
Hamilton, Ian 94
Hamner, Rober 41, 44, 45, 83, 117
Hardwick, Elizabeth 8, 104, 116, 120
Harris, Wilson 17
Hassan, Dolly 91
Hayward, Helen 12, 78, 114
Henry, Jim Douglas 89
Holland and Huggan 144
Hosein, Clyde 79
House for Mr Biswas, A 7, 20, 21, 25, 27, 33,
  36–38, 40, 42–45, 62, 68, 69, 73,
  81, 119, 132, 155, 168, 171, 183–85,
  189, 190
Hughes, Peter 144
Huntington, Samuel 125, 151
Hussein, Aamer 70, 127, 139, 147
Huxley, Aldous 52, 60, 162, 174

Illustrated Weekly of India 10, 141
In a Free State 2, 11, 22, 37, 83, 85–87, 110,
  114, 115, 119, 130, 133, 157, 178,
  188, 189
Ince, Basil 120, 121
India: A Million Mutinies Now 23, 139, 144,
  146, 147, 153, 171
India: A Wounded Civilization 125
Isis 10

Jackson, Elizabeth 57
Jagan, Cheddi 64, 73, 152
James, C. L. R. 31, 62, 63, 73, 75–77,
  154, 177
  Minty Alley 31
Jasmine 19, 66, 132
Johnson, Andrew 119
Joshi, Chandra 144
Jussawalla, Feroza 120

Kalliney, Peter 81
Kamra, Shashi 12
Kanhai, Viki 184
Kaplan, Caren 144
Kaseram, Romeo 134
Kelly, Richard 144
Khan, Nisa 130
Khan, Riza 126

INDEX

Killings in Trinidad, The 11, 20, 95, 102, 129, 188
Kincaid, Jamaica 126
King, Bruce 144, 147
Kingsley, Charles 52–54, 63
Kipling, Rudyard 59, 163, 164

Lalla, Barbara 30
Lamming, George 5, 17, 44, 75, 129, 131, 166
Lanchester, John 172
Laughlin, Nicholas 16
Lawrence, D. H. 52, 162
Lee, R. H. 68
Letters Between a Father and Son 16, 37–39, 43, 60, 158
Levin, Bernard 125, 130, 134
Levy, Judith 144
Lion House 25, 36, 42, 184
Lisle, Debbie 145
Literary Occasions 162, 173
London 18, 66, 132, 185
Loss of El Dorado, The 11, 22, 23, 77, 78, 85, 126, 129, 155, 165, 183, 188–90
Lovelace, Earl 6, 92, 93
Lydon, Christopher 175
Lynch, Hugh 119, 130, 140, 141

Maes-Jelinek, Hena 68
Magic Seeds 23, 132, 153, 161, 170, 171, 174, 184
Maharaj, Bhadse Sagan 50
Maharaj, J. Vijay 45
Maharaj, Parsuram 126
Maharajh, Mahabir 120
Mair, Christian 41
Mann, Harveen 12, 68, 144
Marnham, Patrick 180
Masque of Africa, The 2, 23, 129, 177, 188
Mathur, Ira 167
Matroo, Carl 177
Maugham, Somerset 2, 163, 168, 174
Maxwell, John 5
McClure, John 100
McSweeney, Kerry 114
Medwick, Cathleen 104, 116
Meighoo, Kirk 5, 100

Mendes, Alfred
  Black Fauns 31
  Pitch Lake 31
Michener, Charles 83, 116, 118–20, 125
Middle Passage, The 5, 6, 49–52, 55–58, 60, 62–64, 73, 78, 101, 126, 132, 135, 183, 188, 190
Miguel Street 2, 6, 21, 27, 34, 35, 38, 40, 41, 44, 46, 69, 71, 73, 81, 130, 132, 165, 176, 183, 185, 189
Milne, Anthony 119, 184
Mimic Men, The 2, 22, 65, 73–75, 77, 80, 81, 85, 87, 112, 115, 130, 132, 138, 165, 174, 183, 188, 189
Miranda, Francisco 79, 80, 154, 160, 174
Mishra, Vijay 131
Misra, Nivedita 45, 86
Mittelholzer, Edgar 72, 174
Mohammed, Denzil 177
Mohan, Dinesh 126
Moone, Robert Chee 52
Morgan, Paula 35
Morris, R. K. 83
Mr Stone and the Knights Companion 2, 22, 66–69, 112, 132, 138, 184
Mustafa, Fawzia 12, 47, 50, 144, 145, 147
Mystic Masseur, The 2, 7, 11, 21, 27–30, 32, 34, 37, 40, 44, 63, 73, 119, 126, 132, 177, 183, 185

Naipaul, Droapatie 15, 16, 25, 26, 37
Naipaul, Lady Nadira 2, 9, 158, 177, 187
Naipaul, Patricia 9, 46, 64, 82, 84, 86, 95, 118, 124, 155
Naipaul, Seepersad 10, 21, 25–28, 31, 32, 37, 40, 42, 43, 59, 81, 128, 159, 190
  The Adventures of Gurudeva 26, 27, 31, 38, 40
Naipaul, Shiva 15, 23, 84, 131, 153
Narayan, R. K. 59, 109, 163, 164
New Statesman 10, 63
New York Review of Books 10, 22, 84, 110, 115, 117, 162, 172
Nightingale, Peggy 12
The Nightwatchman's Occurrence Book 65, 70, 71

Nixon, Rob 12, 30, 47, 52, 54, 136, 137, 144, 145
Noel, Jesse 76

Overcrowded Barracoon, The 22, 66, 79, 85, 88, 91, 93, 107, 109
Oxford Tory 10

Pantin, Raoul 90, 96
Panwar, Purabi 144
Paravisini-Gerbert, Lizabeth 29
Parekh, Bhikhu 147
Patterson, Orlando 4
Phillips, Caryl 11
Pickford-Gordon, Lara 176
Poynting, Jeremy 41, 45, 66, 74
Press Release of the Swedish Academy 2
Prologue to an Autobiography 114
Pyne-Timothy, Helen 115

Quinn, Kate 90

Rahim, Jennifer 45, 187
Rai, Sudha 144
Raleigh, Walter 78–80, 143, 154, 160, 174
Ramayana 27, 41, 45, 162
Rambaran, Irma 167
Ramchand, Kenneth 34, 41, 69, 82, 113, 131, 138, 148, 166, 167, 172, 189
Rampersad, Arnold 137
Rampersad, Kris 181
Ravi-Ji 146
Raymond, Judy 148, 155
Return of Eva Perón, with The Killings in Trinidad, The 11, 20, 22, 83, 115, 170
Richmond, Angus 51, 101
Roach, Eric 94
Robinson, A. N. R. 138, 144
Robinson, Andrew 109, 134, 141, 144, 184
Rohlehr, Gordon 6, 44, 62, 75, 80, 167, 177, 189
Rouse, Ewart 77
Rowe-Evans, Adrian 86, 88, 94
Roy, Amit 3

Said, Edward 9, 62, 119, 125, 145
Samaroo, Brinsley 29, 34, 42, 57, 58, 90
Scott, Lawrence 101
Seecharan, Clem 4, 16, 17
Selvon, Sam 6, 41, 81, 174, 190
Shah, Raffrique 91, 167
Suffrage of Elvira, The 7, 21, 27, 32, 33, 37, 43, 44, 71, 119, 122, 126, 176, 183, 185
Suleri, Sara 144
Swanzy, Henry 46

Taylor, Jeremy 101, 120, 126
Tennyson, Alfred
    "Crossing the Bar" 3
Tewarie, Bhoe 105, 151, 176, 177
Theroux, Paul 8, 83
    Sir Vidia's Shadow: A Friendship Across Five Continents 4, 8
Thieme, John 6, 7, 12, 35, 45, 56, 57, 68, 131, 144, 145
Thompson, Carl 145
Times Literary Supplement, The 10
Trinidad and Tobago Newsday 126, 167, 177
Trinidad Express 96, 118, 119, 130, 166
Trinidad Guardian 25, 28, 42, 59, 63, 79, 128, 135, 138, 165–67
Trinity Cross 3, 143, 146, 165
Trollope, Anthony 52, 53, 63
Turn in the South, A 23, 88, 135, 136, 138–40

Walcott, Derek 5, 17, 36, 62, 75–77, 126, 145, 161, 167, 173–76, 186, 187
1965 25
Walsh, William 12, 83
Waugh, Evelyn 52, 152, 162, 174
Way in the World, A 23, 28, 62, 73, 102, 151, 153–55, 160, 170, 174, 177, 183, 188
Weiss, Timothy 12, 50, 68, 114, 144, 145
Westall, Claire 35
Wheeler, Charles 62, 108
White, Landeg 83

INDEX

Williams, Eric 47, 49, 50, 62, 64, 73, 74, 77, 90, 91, 94, 102, 108, 113, 118
  British Historians and the West Indies 63
  History of the People of Trinidad and Tobago 63
Wilson-Tagoe, Nana 78
Winer, Lise 5, 6
  Dictionary of the English/ Creole of Trinidad and Tobago: On Historical Principles 5
Winokur, Scott 126, 127
Writer and the World, The 148
Writer's People, A 23, 162, 173, 183, 187
Wyndham, Francis 185

Milton Keynes UK
Ingram Content Group UK Ltd.
UKHW012211191223
434677UK00003B/59